PLUTOCRACY in AMERICA

PLUTOCRACY in AMERICA

★

How Increasing Inequality Destroys
the Middle Class and Exploits the Poor

RONALD P. FORMISANO

Johns Hopkins University Press
Baltimore

© 2015 Johns Hopkins University Press
All rights reserved. Published 2015
Printed in the United States of America on acid-free paper
9 8 7 6 5 4 3 2 1

Johns Hopkins University Press
2715 North Charles Street
Baltimore, Maryland 21218-4363
www.press.jhu.edu

Library of Congress Cataloging-in-Publication Data

Formisano, Ronald P., 1939–
   Plutocracy in America : how increasing inequality destroys the middle
class and exploits the poor / Ronald P. Formisano.
      pages cm
   Includes index.
   ISBN 978-1-4214-1740-0 (hardcover : alk. paper) — ISBN 978-1-4214-1741-7
(electronic) — ISBN 1-4214-1740-5 (hardcover : alk. paper) — ISBN
1-4214-1741-3 (electronic) 1. Equality—United States. 2. Poverty—United
States. 3. Income distribution—United States. 4. Democracy—United States.
5. United States—Economic conditions—2009– 6. United States—Social
conditions—1980– I. Title.
   HN90.S6F67 2015
   305.50973—dc23   2014043206

A catalog record for this book is available from the British Library.

*Special discounts are available for bulk purchases of this book. For more informa-
tion, please contact Special Sales at 410-516-6936 or specialsales@press.jhu.edu.*

Johns Hopkins University Press uses environmentally friendly book materials,
including recycled text paper that is composed of at least 30 percent post-
consumer waste, whenever possible.

CONTENTS

ACKNOWLEDGMENTS

With this book, I have been fortunate to work with Robert J. Brugger, editor, historian, Vietnam vet, and friend, a second time. Others at Johns Hopkins University Press who have also guided it and me through the process and deserve thanks are Andre Barnett, Becky Clark, Julie McCarthy, and Kathy Alexander. I was lucky to have Kathleen M. Capels as my copyeditor. The copyeditors for my previous books with Hopkins and other presses had all done competent, even excellent work, but none was so engaged, so well informed, or helpful. She and her husband, Terence Yorks, also took on the difficult task of compiling an index for a complex book.

The press's anonymous reader of the manuscript provided criticism that improved the final result.

The research fund associated with my William T. Bryan Chair of American History at the University of Kentucky, from which I recently retired, provided resources that helped to make this book possible. My superb research assistant, Dana Caldemeyer, a doctoral student and promising historian, could not have carried out her duties any better than she did. She did everything she was asked to do, quickly, responsibly, and usually ahead of schedule.

Several colleagues and graduate students in the University of Kentucky History Department came to a discussion of an earlier version of chapter 2 and made valuable suggestions.

Dean Baker of the Economic Policy Institute kindly read chapter 3 and corrected some errors; other errors, mine, may yet have crept in there and elsewhere.

As usual, my historian friends Joseph A. Conforti and John Zeugner, whose own writing I admire, read parts of the manuscript, improved the prose, and gave steady encouragement. Last, but most important, Erica, Laura, and Matthew provide the kind of support that no one else on the planet can give.

PLUTOCRACY in AMERICA

INTRODUCTION

In the state the good aimed at is justice; and that means what is for the good of the whole community. Now it is pretty clear that justice in a community means equality for all.

—ARISTOTLE, *Politics*

In 2008–2009 the Great Recession devastated the economy, and millions of Americans lost jobs, homes, health insurance, retirement funds, and more, sinking into a netherworld of struggling to get by. Even before then, the startling increase of inequality in income and wealth in the United States had attracted the attention of scholars and pundits. Inequality's arrival as a topic at the forefront of public consciousness was ratified when it entered popular culture as a source of jokes for late-night talk show hosts. The revelations regarding unethical and fraudulent practices by financial firms, which triggered the economic debacle, intensified the public's awareness of inequality. So too did the Bush and Obama administrations' bailouts of reckless firms with taxpayer money, while borrowers with risky mortgages lost their homes. The federal government's tender concern for Wall Street at the expense of Main Street came into sharp relief.

This recession also cast a harsh light on the persistence of poverty, re-igniting politicians' debates about the effectiveness of the nation's safety net. Not since the launch of the War on Poverty in the 1960s have the political and media establishments devoted so much rhetoric and conflicting diagnoses as to the best methods of helping fellow citizens damaged by the plunging economy.

When Occupy Wall Street erupted in the fall of 2011 with the slogan "We Are the 99 Percent," it succeeded in casting a spotlight on the excessive gains of the inordinately wealthy, on overpaid and undertaxed executives, on corporations that pay no taxes at all, and on all those enriched by financially friendly laws and deregulation. Protesters in the OWS camps, both young and old, asked the nation: where are the jobs, and what had happened to equal opportunity? Corporate America and Wall Street suddenly became targets of populist anger on the Left and Right, and high-flying CEOs and hedge-fund managers morphed from celebrities into villains. The backlash against concentrated capital recalled the excoriation of robber barons during the First Gilded Age of the late nineteenth century and the pointed criticism of "malefactors of great wealth" during the Progressive Era in the early twentieth century, and was last experienced when President Franklin Roosevelt denounced "economic royalists" in the throes of the 1930s Great Depression.

A momentary hiccup in the reputations of the superrich, however, did nothing to stop the flow of income to the top, which continued to accelerate. The land of opportunity now is rightly taunted as the "United States of Inequality for All."[1] Social mobility *has* diminished. That fact has not really penetrated the consciousness of most Americans, who do not realize that almost all other economically advanced countries enjoy greater socioeconomic mobility than the United States. Instead, the platitudes of politicians and the Horatio Alger mythology of rags to riches still hold wobbly sway in the popular imagination.

Middle-class and low-income families putting in long hours at work, often holding two jobs, as well as workers' increased productivity, were not delivering America's promise. As 2014 ended, the wealth gap between upper-income and middle-income families reached "record high levels," the widest in thirty years, according to a report from the Pew Research Center. In 2013, the median income of the most affluent had surged to $639,400, nearly seven times that of middle-income households ($96,000). The dollar needle for middle-class people did not move since the Great Recession, reinforcing "the larger story of America's middle-class household wealth stagnation over the past three decades." The upper tier's wealth rose to nearly 70 times that of the lowest-income families. From the middle to the bottom rungs of the socioeconomic ladder, most of America was not recovering from the recession.[2]

Inequality has undermined democracy. The United States was never a pure democracy, but not too long ago Americans could confidently describe its political culture or its character as democratic; no longer. Now Congress and a reactionary Supreme Court majority cater to a hydra-headed plutocracy that enjoys a government of the rich, by the rich, and for the rich. Is that last sentence too blunt, or an oversimplification? I argue that it is not. Economic inequality, together with the overwhelming power of big money in politics, has made the U.S. government responsive primarily to powerful elites and no longer representative of the vast majority of Americans. In an exhaustive survey examining which income groups' policy preferences are listened to by the national government, Princeton political scientist Martin Gilens found that "responsiveness is strongly tilted toward the most affluent citizens [the ninetieth percentile]." Of course, political equality is an ideal and "equal influence over policy making" is unattainable, given the many inequalities among citizens in their economic and other resources. Yet Gilens observed that "when inequalities become too large, democracy shades into oligarchy (rule by the few) or plutocracy (rule by the wealthy)."[3] The steady growth of economic inequality over the past three to four decades has heightened political inequality and cast a dark shadow of plutocracy over the United States.

Income inequality has "significantly" retarded economic growth, according to a December 2014 report from the Organisation for Economic Co-operation and Development, often called "the west's leading economic think tank." (In 1961, fourteen western nations formed the OECD "to promote policies that will improve the economic and social well-being of people round the world.") Not only is the gap between rich and poor the highest in thirty years in thirty-two of the organization's thirty-four member countries, but growing inequality between 1990 and 2010 has cost the United Kingdom's economy almost nine percentage points of GDP growth, and the United States, almost seven points. Yet the OECD researchers found that, on balance, redistribution via taxes and benefits does not impede economic growth.[4]

"Economic inequality," quipped two prominent political scientists, "has moved from chats in faculty lounges and academic conferences to headline news."[5] The growing disparities of income and wealth and their effects on equality of opportunity now command frequent attention on television news programs, in documentaries, in the nation's major newspapers, in progressive journals, on the websites of research centers and think tanks, and even in political campaigns. A steady flow of books has addressed how inequality has come about, notably by describing the shift in government policies since the 1970s that contributed to the dramatic flow of income and wealth to the top income strata. This volume incorporates their findings, as well as a wide array of studies exploring the consequences of inequality for the starkly unequal ways Americans live their lives, pursue health and happiness, and participate in the polity as citizens—*or too often are prevented from doing so.*

Plutocracy in America differs from most other studies by bringing together the multiple effects of inequality on Americans' lives. Admittedly, surveying the entire landscape of these consequences is impossible, but in what can be called a tsunami of printed and electronic material on the subject, discussions of many dimensions of inequality are often compartmentalized. I connect the often unconnected and, by addressing the ever-widening impacts of inequality, describe the many ways in which they comingle to afflict people's lives.

Inequality in the United States resembles a spider web in that all the concentric circles and crosshatches are inescapably linked to one another. The diminished opportunity and lessened social mobility that Americans experience has many causes. They range from the concentration of poverty in distressed neighborhoods to an educational system skewed to the wealthy and filled with broken promises. It also results from the rise of for-profit colleges and technical schools promising jobs but often delivering debt; administrative bloat in higher education; and the parallel emergence of a new academic proletariat in the form of "contingent," or adjunct, faculty. It results from stark disparities in access to health care, and obstructions to the exercise of political voice. The connections go on and on; read on.

To illuminate the *consequences* of inequality leads inevitably to *causes*, because consequences in turn deepen the degree of inequality and create new drivers of disadvantages—as well as additional gains for the top. To expose the many facets of inequality in American life is to point to what needs to be done to reverse what seems an inexorable march toward greater economic and social inequality.[6] I show what has to change through diagnoses of the manifold circumstances that perpetuate inequality. Diagnoses point to remedies, and these are forthcoming. The federal minimum wage, for example, is worth less in purchasing power today than it was in 1968. The discussion in chapter 4 shows that the benefits of a substantial increase in the minimum wage will accrue not only to the working poor but also to the entire economy. Already several states and cities are moving in this direction; other remedies will require large shifts in federal policy.

If the amount of attention devoted to inequality in the past two decades could be translated into actions to reduce it, then the widening gap between the 1 percent and everybody else might be stalled and even narrowed. The brutal truth is that inequality of income and wealth continues to grow, with damaging effects that ripple throughout economic, social, cultural, and political life—even in such a mundane matter as the ability to shop for healthy food. The chapters that follow explore "social ills" engendered by inequality—a phrase used by Pope Francis in his remarkable encyclical, *Evangelii Gaudium*, that rejected an "economy of exclusion [of the poor]," "the new idolatry of money," "trickle-down economics," and "the inequality which spawns violence."[7]

After an introductory discussion of inequality in chapter 1, chapter 2 addresses the dual decline of opportunity and education. These are often invoked as the great equalizers, but even a cursory examination reveals that they no longer promote social mobility. As a consequence, the middle class in the United States, examined in chapter 3, is also declining. The disappearance of good jobs, decreases in wages, and the war against unions is shrinking the American middle class, which was once the envy of the world and hailed by political scientists as the foundation of a civil and democratic political culture. Now the socioeconomic ladder is trending into a distorted hourglass. Chapter 4 describes the rich getting along swimmingly by thriving at the expense of the middle class, and the poor struggling to stay afloat. An infrastructure (*not* that of the safety net) created by federal and state policies keeps the poor in place while increasing their numbers and bestows a Midas touch on corporate executives.

Chapter 5 examines how a very different quality of life results across an increasingly demarcated socioeconomic scale. The most basic expectations of a free society—the quality of life and life expectancy itself—fail to be met for the least-advantaged sector of the population. In health and mortality the United States ranks far from "Number 1" when measured against other advanced nations. These conditions result in large part from plutocracy trumping democracy, or, as chapter 6 recounts, from representative institutions no longer functioning in the public interest, while concerted efforts to limit the nation's political voice to the moneyed and powerful are advancing. A hegemonic "dollarocracy," to use a term from John Nichols and Robert W. McChesney, has tilted these institutions toward the benefit of elites and influential interest groups who employ legions of lobbyists, consultants, lawyers, and publicists to shape policy at state and federal levels. The owners of media corporations, Nichols and McChesney charge, are part of "the new order. . . . They do not challenge it, as the crusading editors and publishers of another age did. Rather, advertising departments position media outlets to reap windfall profits through the broadcasting of invariably inane and crudely negative political campaign advertising, which is the lingua franca of American electioneering in the twenty-first century."[8] The combination of a complicit corporate media, political polarization in the nation's government, a dysfunctional Congress, and a plutocratic political economy has pushed the United States far off the course set by its founders.

Chapter 7, "The Fracturing of America," picks up themes from earlier chapters and—for readers with open minds who have come this far—aims to educate and persuade. So too does the concluding chapter, which takes the bold step of discussing the "undeserving poor" and the "undeserving rich" in relation to one another. My intention is to prompt readers to think differently about the poor—all of the poor—and about some of the rich, and to think with more awareness about inequality in American society. Trying to change minds is perhaps a quixotic ambition, but one that is needed—along with changes in governance and policy—to restore fairness and justice for the whole community.

Inequality of income and wealth damages society as a whole, with only the top 10 or 20 percent immune to its material effects but perhaps not entirely removed from its spiritual and psychic harm. Americans, like college students watching their team winning a football game, love to chant "We're Number 1." But in reality the United States is not at the top in terms of social progress, defined by the Social Progress Index as "the capacity of a society to meet the basic human needs of its citizens, establish the building blocks that allow citizens and communities to enhance and sustain the quality of their lives, and create the conditions for all individuals to reach their full potential." The small countries of New Zealand, Switzerland, and Iceland are ranked highest on this index in terms of social progress, followed by a second group of thirteen nations that is headed by Austria and Germany, with the United States mired in sixteenth place.[9]

The early republic of George Washington and his successors was not a democratic republic, and the Declaration of Independence's glittering phrase that "all men are created equal" contained unspoken limits on its application. In time its boundaries expanded as a democratic republic evolved, although in some cases, such as with people of color, only in a distant future. Nonetheless, the framers of the Constitution believed that if extreme inequality was allowed to flourish within the body politic, it would undermine their experiment in representative government.

The vast majority of Americans today, Democrats, Republicans, and independents, believe that excessive inequality—not as a theoretical condition but as a present reality—undermines democracy and maintains unfairness throughout society. Quite simply, most citizens recognize that the country's economic system benefits the few at the expense of the many, Wall Street at the expense of Main Street. In 1983, historian Benedict Anderson brilliantly defined a nation as "an imagined political community. . . . It is imagined because the members of the smallest nation will never know most of their fellow-members, meet them, or even hear of them, yet in the minds of each lives the image of their communion."[10] In 2015, what image of their nation resides inside the minds of Americans? Do they imagine communion with their fellow citizens? There could be many answers to these questions.

Much has been written about citizens of the United States "sorting" themselves into groups with different lifestyles, conflicting political allegiances, and other societal subcultures. These analyses bring to mind a nation increasingly lacking cohesion or common goals. I suggest that another image increasingly occupying space in Americans' minds, at the expense of the imagined community, is that of a hierarchical society, with increasingly explicit and visible class lines. Many members of this nation now envision it as something other than a community, nor do they feel a sense of communion across class or (the long-standing) racial lines. What sense of national community exists between an employee working two minimum-wage jobs and a hedge-fund manager? Across most of the bottom half or more of the socioeconomic spectrum, images of separation and distance are replacing a sense of unity. Hence the ties that bind a nation together, the imagined community, dissolve.

So long as extreme disparity of income and wealth perpetuates hardship and undermines representative government, it needs to be discussed. So long as inequality harms the life chances for tens of millions of one's fellow citizens, it must be shown the light of day. While a distended plutocracy reigns and tramples a democratic political culture underfoot, then its arrogance must be confronted. So long as millions of the disadvantaged are denied access to the vote and even to effective citizenship, those un-American circumstances must be illuminated. As a nation, the United States once aspired to be better, as, in Lincoln's words during the "fiery trial" of the Civil War, "the last best hope on earth." While a gap has always existed, too often as a broad chasm, between our ideals and our practice, this is one of those times—a New Gilded Age—when the gulf between them has grown to undermine our very sense of who we are.

Before the United States existed as a political entity, Americans thought of themselves as "exceptional." Whatever the notion of exceptionalism signified across more than two centuries, it did not rest on a bedrock of inequality.

THE WEB OF INEQUALITY

*Today we also have to say "thou shalt not" to an economy of
exclusion and inequality. Such an economy kills. How can it be
that it is not a news item when an elderly homeless person dies of
exposure, but it is news when the stock market loses two points.
This is a case of exclusion. Can we continue to stand by when
food is thrown away while people are starving? This is a case of
inequality. . . .*

*As long as the problems of the poor are not radically resolved
by rejecting the absolute autonomy of markets and financial
speculation and by attacking the structural causes of inequality,
no solution will be found for the world's problems or, for that
matter, to any problems. Inequality is the root of social ills.*

POPE FRANCIS, *Evangelii Gaudium*

Of course, Pope Francis knows that social ills arise from causes other
than inequality. They often follow on the heels of natural disasters.
Cultural, religious, and racial differences contribute to the world's
problems. The personalities of individuals play a role. Mental illness
afflicts both the poor and the rich. But in the second decade of the
twenty-first century, inequality must command the attention of citizens and governments throughout the world. And the United States,
once an egalitarian society, a "city on a hill" offering opportunity,
hope, and the "untrammeled pursuit of happiness," has become instead an exemplar of the scourge of inequality.

THE FOUNDERS' VISION

This was not the vision of America's founders. Although the framers of the Constitution of the United States launched a new republican government that was well insulated from popular majorities and possessed aristocratic elements, in another generation the nation would become a democratic republic with an egalitarian political culture. Even before then, during the early years of rule by the gentry, political rivals often accused one another of being "aristocrats." This pejorative tarred opponents with the stigma of un-republican attitudes and actions, of posturing as privileged elite set apart from ordinary citizens. Aristocrats, in the mind of a democratic republican like Thomas Jefferson, wanted to lord it over the great majority—their "inferiors"—by flaunting their wealth with displays of luxury. But the American Revolution ingrained a conviction in men and women who shared Jefferson's mentality that "republican simplicity" should prevail among the citizenry.

Some of the gentlemen who formed the governing class in the early republic privately modeled themselves (at least to a certain degree) on the European grandees they publically scorned. Jefferson treasured books and learning and enjoyed fine French wine, as well as the comforts dozens of African American slaves provided on his Virginia plantation. Other founders, northerners as well as southerners, also benefited from slave labor. But many of those who framed the Constitution believed that the survival of a republican form of government depended on a very general "equality of condition" that prevailed in society among white males. Enfranchising women and people of color did not cross their minds, and they had reservations about "the lower orders" of white males participating in the body politick. They envisioned no measures to redistribute property, much less a classless utopia, but they did see America as a land of opportunity absent the extremes of wealth and privilege of Old Europe.

That ideal of the founders has been forgotten—if not discarded—by contemporary plutocrats and their enablers, forming a political class that has turned government and society into entities very much resembling an aristocracy. A republic of opportunity has been submerged by a government of the extremely wealthy who now isolate and remove themselves from contact with ordinary citizens by a withdrawal into gated neighborhoods, private jets, chauffeured limousines, and helicopters and by disdain for mingling in common, public spaces. This plutocracy continues to enjoy the fruits of years of government policy directed toward maintaining their inordinate political influence that, in turn, enables the upper caste's continued accumulation of wealth at the expense of everyone else.

This development is hardly a well-kept secret. A huge outpouring of information addressing inequality and its consequences for democracy has appeared in print and on the Internet in the past few years. Many voices warn that the United States *is losing* its character as a democratic republic. Former secretary of labor Robert B. Reich, who has tried as much as anyone to alert Americans to the destructive force of inequality, echoes many commentators in asserting that the country "is perilously close to losing an economy and a democracy that are meant to work for everyone and replacing them with an economy and a government that will exist mainly for a few wealthy and powerful people." I assert that such a government already exists. Several decades of legislation, along with rulings by the current bloc of five reactionary Supreme Court justices, have created an economic and political infrastructure "rigged," as Reich himself acknowledges, in favor of plutocratic elites, even as public opinion has come to favor measures to increase opportunity and, hence, redistribute wealth. While the Obama administration has taken steps to reduce inequality, powerful reactionary forces inside and outside government press ever harder to defend and initiate policies that transfer income and wealth from the bottom and middle to the top.[1]

"An economy and a democracy that are meant to work for everyone" has been lost. The United States is more plutocracy than democracy and is developing aristocratic features scorned by many of the Revolutionary and Constitution-framing generation of founders. Representative government and an equitable society have been undermined by extreme inequality. In addition, the upper classes, and particularly the political class, unabashedly practice a degree of nepotism perhaps unparalleled in the past, which is a corruption of the meritocratic society that Jefferson and even the aristocratic

Alexander Hamilton hoped for. It is a development that has not received the scrutiny it deserves. Whether some of these few have climbed to the top through merit or have eased up by wealth, family connections, or political patronage, the policies of plutocratic government are enabling them to pull the ladder up behind them.

AMERICANS THINK
THEY LIVE IN SWEDEN

Since the 1970s, economic inequality in the United States has increased to a degree not experienced since either the 1920s or the First Gilded Age of the late nineteenth century. Whether measured by income or wealth, the gap in the United States between the wealthiest 1 percent, and in particular the wealthiest 0.01 percent, and everyone else outdistances the disparities that exist in other nations with comparable economic development and similar political systems. To be sure, inequality of income and wealth has become a global phenomenon, perhaps most notable in China, a rising economic power where, according to the politically conservative magazine the *Economist*, "in little more than a generation Mao's egalitarian dystopia has become a country with an income distribution more skewed than America's." Inequality is also surging in Russia, India, Indonesia, and Brazil, "though less dramatically than China." But inequality in America clashes with an egalitarian self-portrait of democracy that boasts of opportunity for all.[2]

Inequality's ascent has been more rapid and extreme in the United States in the last three to four decades than in its peer countries. Given the yawning chasm between rich and poor, in an ironic twist from the colossus of the north looking down on its neighbors to the south, the United States could well be called a "banana republic," even though bananas are not grown here. In fact, income distribution in the United States is now more unequal than in Latin American countries such as Uruguay, Nicaragua, Guyana, and Venezuela. Indeed, inequality is declining in South America as it steadily rises in what many Latinos still think of as a land of opportunity.

Americans should draw little comfort from the fact that inequality is more pronounced in China (or anywhere else for that matter) especially when their country compares unfavorably on multiple measures of social well-being with almost every other economically developed and relatively democratic nation. Since the 1970s, inequality in the United States has raced ahead of other rich nations, with a doubling of the income share of the top 1 percent. The United Kingdom has experienced a dramatic growth in inequality as well, but at about half the rate of the United States, which has far outdistanced Sweden, Belgium, Germany, Spain, Canada, Italy, Ireland, France, the Netherlands, and Denmark.[3]

For most of the history of the United States, income distribution was not as dramatically disproportionate as it is at present, according to economists Emmanuel Saez at the University of California, Berkeley, and Thomas Piketty at the Paris School of Economics. Their studies of income distribution over time have been the starting point for most of the recent commentary on rising inequality. From World War II to the late 1960s, the benefits of a growing U.S. economy percolated from the bottom through the middle to the top of society. For three decades after 1945, a relatively equally distributed prosperity built a strong middle class that was the envy of the world. As John F. Kennedy put it, "a rising tide lifts all boats." Those in the lower classes gained as much or more than those in the higher ones.

The current state of disequilibrium in the United States began in the 1970s, when the top 1 percent earned about 10 percent of the national income. Since then the income of the richest soared to 15–19 percent of the total in the late 1990s; in 2007, the richest 1 percent took home 23.5 percent of all income. In the upper precincts of the 0.1 percent, 13,000 households took in more than 11 percent of the nation's income.

The economic collapse in 2008 momentarily slowed these trends, but then exacerbated them. During a limited recovery from 2009 to 2011, the income of the top 1 percent grew by 11.2 percent while that of the bottom 99 percent declined by 0.4 percent. The 0.01 percent superrich, amounting to about 15,000 households with an average income of $23.8 million, did even better in 2010, raking in 37 percent of that growth. By 2012, the top 10 percent had recovered very nicely, according to Saez and Piketty, taking home over half of all income,

FIGURE 1.1. The top 0.01% tax income share, 1913–2012

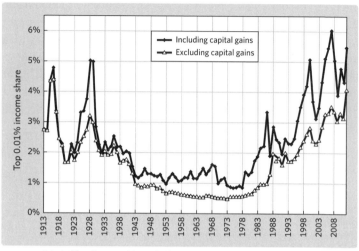

Adapted from Emmanuel Saez, "Striking It Richer: The Evolution of Top Incomes
in the United States," University of California, Berkeley, September 3, 2013.

the highest proportion since 1913. In early 2014, the top 1 percent had
garnered 95 percent of all income growth since the Great Recession.
But median family income (adjusted for inflation) has gone into a
free-fall at a pace not experienced since the Great Depression of the
1930s, and wage-earning families remain stuck in a rut.[4]

If this income gap is severe, the wealth gap—measured by net
worth—is even more extreme. During early 2013, a video went viral
on YouTube in the United States and around the world. A Harvard
University business professor and a Duke University behavioral
economist first asked 5,000 Americans how they thought wealth
was distributed in the United States, and then what these individuals imagined would be the ideal distribution for it. Ninety-two percent of them (Republicans and Democrats alike) pictured the ideal
as being much more equitable than the actuality, because they were
(as many are) disposed to think wealth is rather unfairly distributed.
Little did they know.

Next, the narrator put what that 92 percent considered the ideal
distribution ought to be on a curve and compared it with a curve
of what they thought the actual distribution was. The divergence

was "not that great" between the respondents' ideal and what they believed to be the more disproportionate reality, commented the video's narrator. Nonetheless, in the respondents' reality curve the location of the poorest 20–30 percent was quite distant from their proposed position on the ideal curve, the middle class was "struggling," and both the wealthy and the rich were roughly 100 times ahead of the poorest and ten times ahead of the middle class.

But neither of those two distribution curves approached the true picture. In the actual distribution of wealth, the poorest do not even register, and the middle class is barely distinguishable from those below it. Only the top 10 percent are better off, and the top 2–5 percent, stated the narrator, "are actually off the chart at this scale, and the top 1%, this guy, well his stack of money stretches to ten times higher than we can show." The top 1 percent own 40 percent of all the wealth in America, and the bottom 40 percent own 1 percent of the wealth. *The top 5 percent own 72 percent of all the wealth in the United States, and the top 1 percent have a greater collective net worth than the bottom 90 percent.* As the narrator noted, "the reality in this country is not even close to what we think it is." The researchers also gave their respondents two unidentified wealth distributions— that of the United States and a slightly modified version of Sweden's ("Equalden")—and asked them where they would prefer to live. More than 90 percent, coming from across the political and income spectrum, chose the distribution close to that of Sweden's.[5]

Americans also do not come "close to the reality" in guessing what CEOs of major national corporations earn. In one survey in 2007, ordinary citizens guessed that CEOs made $500,000 per year, and a surprising majority—given Americans' broad acceptance of inequality and rewards for hard work—believed this was too much and that a compensation of around $200,000 was fairer! The reality was that CEOs of the S&P 500 companies garnered about $14,000,000 per year, with eight CEOs at the stratospheric level of $100,000,000 or more each. In a 2014 survey, Americans "drastically" underestimated how much less ordinary workers earn compared with S&P 500 company CEOs. In the past three decades, CEO pay "has exploded" to a ratio of 354 to 1, but their fellow citizens thought it to be about 30 to 1. As Nobel prize–winning economist and *New York Times* columnist

Paul Krugman has suggested, the perception gap may result mostly because "we don't see private equity managers commuting by helicopter to their immense mansions in the Hamptons. The commanding heights of our economy are invisible because they're lost in the clouds."[6]

While the superrich own many of the big-ticket luxuries—yachts, private jets, helicopters, jewelry, art treasures, and multiple McMansions, all of which are nonfinancial assets—what really counts is their disproportionate accumulation of the nation's financial assets. Federal Reserve policy has led to a stock market boom and an increased inequality of income, and corporate profits are at an all-time high, while "76 percent of people in this country live paycheck to paycheck." The rich not only "hoard all the toys," but the wealthiest Americans almost unanimously reported enjoying better health than everyone else, with 90 percent describing themselves as being in excellent or good health, compared with similar claims from only 75 percent of the remaining population.[7]

THE MIDDLE CLASS AND POVERTY

As politicians declared so often during the 2012 U.S. election campaigns, the middle class was not doing very well. Federal Reserve data from 2010 showed that at least half of American families had a lower net worth (in inflation-adjusted terms) than they did two decades earlier. Although wage-earning workers received less attention from campaigning candidates, a male laborer paid the median wage in 2007 earned less than the adjusted median wage from thirty years before. Ironically, as American workers became more productive, their real hourly compensation since the late 1970s lagged well behind. The disparity in the decades after 1970 arose in part because of changes in price indexes, but, according to the *Monthly Labor Review*, from 2000 to 2009 "an unprecedented decline" in workers' wages, salaries, and benefits "accounted for most of the gap." Similarly, a detailed report by the Organisation for Economic Co-operation and Development pointed to a continuing increase in wage disparity between high-salaried earners and lower-income workers as the main driver of rising inequality.[8]

During the 2000s, as workers and the middle class fared badly, the poverty rate in the United States increased, to over 15 percent of the population. In 2012, by various measures, roughly 47–50 million Americans were living in poverty. Among the twenty-one member nations in the Organisation for Economic Co-operation and Development, the United States had the most children living in poverty (23.1%), almost five times as many as Iceland, with the lowest rate (4.7%). A UNICEF report in 2013 gave the same percentage for the United States and ranked it thirty-fourth out of thirty-five rich countries, just ahead of Romania. UNICEF also looks at what it calls the "child poverty gap," measuring how many children fall below the average poverty line, and the United States again ranks next to last. Poverty in the United States can be found anywhere; it does not simply exist in pockets of poverty in urban ghettos or rural Appalachia or the Mississippi Delta. After the housing collapse of 2008 wiped out the assets of many middle-class families, suburban poverty reached new highs. Even before this recession, for three decades the poor population had grown faster in the suburbs than in urban or rural areas. Poverty is "as diverse as the United States itself."[9]

Diverse, yes, but growing more concentrated. The Brookings Institution found that between 2000 and 2008–2012, the number of people living in distressed neighborhoods grew by over 5 million. More lived in big cities, but the suburban poor concentrated at an alarming pace of 138 percent, almost three times the rate of cities. Distressed neighborhoods pull poor people down with their multiple challenges, imposing "the 'double burden' of not only their own poverty, but also the disadvantages of those around them."[10]

A minority of Americans believe that "government welfare" perpetuates poverty. The truth is very different, and complex (more on this in chapters 4 and 5). While the poverty rate has not changed much over several decades, government programs (e.g., food stamps, unemployment insurance, the Earned Income Tax Credit) have kept millions out of poverty. Yet many of those millions, particularly the "working poor," experience lives of insecurity and stress. Indeed, the people living in poverty and those struggling to get by with incomes just above that level very likely exceed the Census Bureau's measurement, and strong evidence exists that the number of those in "extreme poverty," especially children, are undercounted. The poverty and un-measured near-poverty of the past four decades has been exacerbated by the growth of inequality and a dearth of economic opportunity.[11]

RISING PUBLIC AWARENESS

Those are simple brute facts, a glimpse at some dimensions of pov-erty and the inequality of income and wealth in the United States. Since 2008, a depressed economy has moved inequality to the fore-front of public consciousness, well before the eruption of Occupy Wall Street in the fall of 2011, with its slogan "We Are the 99 Percent," and before President Barack Obama made inequality and fairness prominent themes in his 2012 presidential campaign. While hedge-fund managers looking down on the OWS encampments dismissed the protesters as hoi polloi needing a shower or a job, these execu-tives perhaps are finding it more difficult to ignore the International Monetary Fund's new emphasis on inequality as a destabilizing fi-nancial force. After the OWS encampments disappeared from Wall Street and most other cities, a Pew Research Center survey released in early 2012 found that "class conflict has captured a growing share of the national consciousness," with about two thirds of the public believing there are "strong" or "very strong" conflicts between the rich and the poor. While latent opinion may or may not have trans-lated into votes for President Obama, the existence of negative pub-lic opinion about inequality has scarcely mattered. And despite its awareness of the problem, the Obama administration has had limited success in checking inequality's seemingly inexorable growth.[12]

Since the economic collapse of 2008–2009, what Paul Krugman called the "Great Divergence"—alluding to the departure from the relatively equitable distribution of wealth and income in the United States up to the 1970s—has garnered unprecedented attention, though this has not prompted extensive remedial policies from the federal or state governments. Indeed, Congress and several states have acted to make inequality worse. Although the role of the gam-blers and financial predators of Wall Street who precipitated the eco-nomic collapse of 2008 with their unethical and very likely criminal behavior has been well documented, not one of them has gone to jail; no Wall Street "Master of the Universe" has taken a "perp walk."[13]

Some economists dispute both the severity of economic inequality as well as the degree to which it has been caused by government policy. But many more, including the distinguished economist Joseph Stiglitz, have echoed political scientists and pointedly argued that the concentration of wealth is unhealthy for democracy and, in fact, undermines republican government—raising a plutocracy in its stead. The words of the great Progressive Era Supreme Court justice Louis D. Brandeis have never been more relevant: "We can have democracy in this country, or we can have great wealth concentrated in the hands of a few; we can't have both."

That inequality has undermined democracy should no longer be in question. Some excellent books have addressed how government policies over several decades have fostered inequality, describing the shift in U.S. governmental policies since the 1970s that have contributed to its dramatic increase. To mention just a few: Lawrence R. Jacobs and Theda Skocpol, eds., *Inequality and American Democracy: What We Know and What We Need to Learn* (2005); Larry M. Bartels, *Unequal Democracy: The Political Economy of the New Gilded Age* (2008); Jacob S. Hacker and Paul Pierson, *Winner-Take-All Politics: How Washington Made the Rich Richer—and Turned Its Back on the Middle Class* (2010); Robert B. Reich, *Aftershock: The Next Economy and America's Future* (2010); Judith Stein, *Pivotal Decade: How the United States Traded Factories for Finance in the Seventies* (2010); Molly C. Michelmore, *Tax and Spend: The Welfare State, Tax Politics, and the Limits of American Liberalism* (2012); and Hedrick Smith, *Who Stole the American Dream?* (2012). These and other studies have thoroughly examined how policy choices, as well as Congressional inaction, has created and deepened inequality. My book differs; it attempts to bring together the many ways inequality feeds on itself, interacts, and multiplies. While not ignoring politics, I focus on the economic, social, and cultural consequences of inequality.

Chrystia Freeland's *Plutocrats: The Rise of the New Global Super-Rich and the Fall of Everyone Else* synthesized studies of the impact of globalization on the creation of inequality, paying particular attention to the United States. Freeland focused on "winner-take-all markets" that have proliferated as technology and virtually global media have led to rapid gains at the very top for "superstars" in business and elsewhere. Celebrities such as musicians, athletes, and movie stars now can reach millions of people worldwide and thus command enormous paychecks compared with others in the same fields.

Different writers explaining inequality have emphasized an increase in the labor supply due to legal and illegal immigration, free trade agreements, and the "offshoring" (factories being relocated outside of their country of origin) of millions of manufacturing jobs from the United States during the last decades of the twentieth century, particularly to China. It has been estimated that trade with low-wage nations, negligible until recent years, "is responsible for 12 to 13 percent of the Great Divergence, and perhaps more."[14]

Economists have also studied "job polarization," namely, the impact of technology in bifurcating occupations into either low-skilled or high-skilled, professional, high-paying jobs. Erik Bynjolfsson and Andrew McKee have argued in *Race against the Machine* that technological change is eliminating high-skilled as well as low-skilled jobs.[15] For decades, corporate consolidation has caused workers to lose jobs or be displaced, and mergers often have served to weaken unions or workers' rights and benefits. These developments are frequently classed as nonpolitical, which is misleading, since decisions by governments are usually inextricably connected to politics.

Another kind of "Great Divergence" has also contributed to inequality, according to Enrico Moretti: "America's new economic map shows growing differences, not just between people but also communities. A handful of cities with the 'right' industries and a solid base of human capital keep attracting good employers and offering high wages, while those at the other extreme, cities with the 'wrong' industries and a limited human capital base, are stuck with dead-end jobs and low average wages." Moretti's "brain-hub cities" possess "a well-educated labor force and a strong innovation sector"; at the opposite pole are "cities once dominated by traditional manufacturing, which are declining rapidly, losing jobs and residents." Moretti usefully points out that for each manufacturing job lost, 1.6 additional jobs disappear, mostly service workers such as barbers, waiters, carpenters, doctors, cleaners, retailers, and construction laborers.[16]

Moretti admires the "brain-hub cities" but does not discuss the growing inequality of income, wealth, and quality of life *within* such cities. Talented, brainy people from all over the world flock to New York City, and its glittering financial elite enjoy lavish executive salaries and millions of dollars in bonuses. But according to new data, New York has "solidified [its] standing as the most unequal major city in the world's most unequal developed country." In November 2013, the city—with a poverty rate of over 20 percent and unemployment at just over 9 percent—had a landslide vote for a mayor (Bill de Blasio) whose campaign theme was a "tale of two cities" and a promise to address inequality. The same theme lifted a Socialist (Kshama Sawant) to the Seattle City Council. In that city, the top fifth of households earn about eighteen times more than the bottom fifth, not as extreme as the forty-times factor in Manhattan, but even with the nation's highest minimum wage ($9.32), the bottom fifth of 58,000 households in Seattle earn about $13,000 a year. In San Francisco an influx of millionaire "technocrati" are driving up housing prices, pushing out artists and the city's trademark bohemians as well as middle-class families and workers. A Brookings Institution study released in early 2014 confirmed that large, economically dynamic cities have become the most unequal, in part because of the rich getting richer and low-income and poor people being hard hit by the Great Recession and its aftermath.[17]

Yet Moretti's analysis affirms that the causes *and* consequences of inequality are multiple and interrelated. Some are unintended results of social progress, such as the phenomenon known as "assortative mating." As more women have acquired higher education, broken glass ceilings, and entered better-paying professions, they have tended to marry other higher-income professionals, contributing to income inequality. With multiple drivers of inequality, many economists conclude, as Stiglitz has observed, that "it is hard to parse out cleanly and precisely the role of different forces." But Stiglitz and many others entertain little doubt that political decisions rather than impersonal forces count the most, and they have argued persuasively that inequality played a major role in causing the Great Recession of 2008–2009 and slowing recovery.[18]

THE GREAT RECESSION

Dean Baker, codirector of the Center for Economic and Policy Research, pinpoints the shift from a consumption- and high-wage-driven economy to one driven by asset bubbles. Underlying this directional change were policies promoted by Reagan's and subsequent administrations that allowed money to "flow upward" by implementing tax cuts benefiting high-income earners; weakening unions by eviscerating their right to organize or strike; pursuing a tight-money policy to fight inflation at the cost of rising unemployment; deregulating major sectors such as airlines and trucking, which also weakened unions; and enacting so-called "free trade agreements" that do not undermine highly educated professionals but put middle-level American workers "in direct competition with low-paid workers in the developing world."

Meanwhile, the pay of top corporate management soared to heights hundreds of times greater than that of the average worker. Thus even though workers' productivity increased over the last four decades, their share of the income generated by it diminished. Money flowed upward, but "ordinary workers stopped sharing in the gains of productivity growth"; they had less money to spend, and "inadequate demand" hogtied an economy that nonetheless still worked for those at the top. The surge of what is now enormous compensation to the highest-level executives—a case of top managers setting their own pay, as it turns out—is, according to economist Thomas Piketty, the main driver of inequality of income and wealth.[19] (Sky-high CEO compensation and Piketty's *Capital in the Twenty-First Century* will be discussed in chapter 4).

The recession preoccupied President Obama during his first term, though his administration made some attempts to lessen the degree of inequality and struggled with Republican opponents to maintain the "safety net" that helps sustain the poor and the unemployed. The Affordable Care and Patient Protection Act (commonly called "Obamacare"), the signal legislation of Obama's first term, is allowing millions of uninsured Americans to gain health insurance. Obamacare alleviates inequality with a redistributive component and also aims to prevent a major cause of bankruptcy for families and individuals by protecting them from encountering massive health-care costs while uninsured. But inequalities in the health care that Americans receive extend beyond the factor of too many uninsured.

Unequal access to health care is but one example of how income inequality creates a proliferating range of consequences not often discussed in relation to one another. None of these subjects has been ignored or unreported somewhere, either in print or on the Internet. But by drawing many of these topics together and showing interconnections, I highlight the widespread consequences of inequality as it washes through society like a noxious flood. This approach rejects arguments that downplay the effects of governmental or corporate policies and instead invoke the role of impersonal forces, such as globalization, as mainly being responsible for inequality in income and wealth. The OECD finds that "the evidence as to the role of globalization in growing inequality is mixed." Whatever globalization has contributed to inequality as an independent cause, corporations have set the rules in global markets that virtually eliminate workers' bargaining power, while environmental and other standards have been ignored.[20]

It is too easy to blame impersonal forces like globalization. Moretti's assertion that Wall Street is not "guilty" of killing blue-collar America—rather, "history did it"—sets aside decisions by governments, financial institutions, and corporations. Wall Street alone did not displace workers from manufacturing jobs, but Moretti's claim neglects the process by which, beginning in the 1970s, the United States "traded manufacturing for finance," as well as the campaigns of business-interest groups, their think tanks, and conservative Republicans to do everything in their power to weaken and discredit unions.[21]

During his second term, President Obama finally focused on economic inequality, beginning with a wide-ranging interview in July 2013 in which he stated that long-standing and growing inequality, along with the lingering effects of the financial crisis, were eroding the nation's social fabric and undermining equality of opportunity. Upward mobility, he said, was what defined Americans, "and that's what's been eroding over the last 20, 30 years, well before the financial crisis."[22]

Near the end of that forty-minute interview, Obama briefly addressed race in relation to inequality, predicting that if inequality continued, "racial tensions won't get better; they may get worse, because people will feel as if they've got to compete with some other group to get scraps from a shrinking pot." Obama couched his brief remarks in race-neutral terms, rhetoric that, as the nation's first African American president, he has (perhaps understandably) employed often. He did not dwell on poverty or the greater degree of inequality experienced by African Americans and Hispanics, especially since the Great Recession. Nor did he address (again perhaps understandably) the nation's staggering rate of incarceration, particularly of black males. With 5 percent of the world's population, the United States has imprisoned almost a quarter of all of the globe's inmates—around 2.2 million in 2012—and spends over $80 billion a year on jails and prisons. While African Americans compose approximately 12–13 percent of the nation's population, they make up just over 40 percent of the prison population.[23]

Yet the scandal of the United States as a "prison nation" encapsulates the many ways that inequality, combined with discrimination against blacks and poor whites, "frays the social fabric." Although incarceration rates for blacks, especially black women, fell between the years 2000 and 2009 (with rates for white men and women *increasing*), the effects of imprisoning African Americans in hugely disproportionate numbers after the 1970s is still reflected in the population of the nation's almost 4,600 prisons (Russia has 1,029).

Several results flow from this long-standing unequal application of criminal laws, reaching back to the post-Emancipation South and Jim Crow laws that allowed sheriffs to seize black men for "vagrancy" and then force them to work in privately owned mines, factories, and labor camps. Currently, imprisoned black men are not figured into data regarding the progress of African Americans, which thus overstates the advances of blacks; black incarceration distorts unemployment numbers, a phenomenon the *New York Times* labeled "How Prisoners Make Us Look Good"; and imprisoned black men not only cannot vote, but many states deprive former felons of their right to vote after they have served their time. Overall, almost 6 million people, black and white, cannot vote because they are incarcerated, but blacks constitute the largest proportion of those in or out of jail that are banned from political participation.[24]

The surge in imprisonment of blacks that began in the late 1970s coincided with increased economic deprivation in poor neighborhoods that already were at risk for crime. From 1980 to 2006, the rate of imprisonment for blacks increased four times as much as that for whites. States and the federal government embraced harsh punitive policies in an overheated climate of opinion demanding "law and order." An economic downturn that disproportionately impacted blacks came together with racially punitive policies and became self-reinforcing. The heightened "war on drugs" during the Reagan administration bore down particularly hard on poor black men who lived in inner cities. As historian David Courtwright has put it, "mass incarceration meant, for all practical purposes, the institutional resegregation of surplus black laborers made idle by agricultural mechanization and industrial decline, unemployable by poor education and self-defeating attitudes, and dangerous by worsening ghetto conditions."[25]

Because one in three black men has had a felony conviction, his chances of finding a stable, good-paying job are much lower than those for white men, including white males who also have had felony convictions. In 1987, the Equal Employment Opportunity Commission issued guidelines declaring that not hiring people with criminal records violated the Civil Rights Act, because it had the effect of reinforcing racial disparities. But after 9/11, Congress undermined the EEOC by banning former felons from working in many transportation jobs; then most states, concerned about drug theft and health-care issues (among many others), made it difficult for ex-felons to find jobs in education, government, the postal service, and occupations requiring licenses issued by the state. While some states are relaxing such restrictions, the 650,000 people released from prison every year who face starkly diminished opportunities are disproportionately African American and Hispanic. The consequences spread far beyond these groups' already impoverished neighborhoods: "billions of dollars in lost productivity, forfeited tax revenue for cities, rampant exploitation by employers, and a cascading series of bans and exclusions from civic life that make it almost impossible for these [potential] workers to achieve a stable economic existence."[26]

Do Americans care about their prisons and ex-felons, not to mention their inner cities? The answer seems to be no. In the current climate of opinion and gridlock in Washington, D.C., the plight of inner cities and the growth of a prison-industrial complex seem to be off the radar, absent from the nation's political agenda.

SOME ARE MORE
UNEQUAL THAN OTHERS

In December 2013, Obama not only returned to the issues of inequality of income and opportunity but also declared that he would spend the rest of his presidency taking up "the defining challenge of our time" in an effort to reduce economic inequality and improve upward mobility. The president's broad-ranging speech showed his awareness of the dimensions of heightened inequality and declining mobility, even if many of his fellow Americans remained unengaged by the erosion of America's promise. He directly confronted "the myth that this is a problem restricted to a small share of predominantly minority poor." Conceding "a painful legacy of discrimination" that continued to hurt African Americans, Latinos, and Native Americans, and the fact that women still made seventy-seven cents on the dollar compared to men, Obama nevertheless insisted (accurately) that "decades-long shifts in the economy have hurt all groups: poor and middle class; inner city and rural folks; men and women; and Americans of all races."[27]

The ramifications of inequality and the policies and conditions that have created it do indeed extend far beyond minorities, the poor, and the disadvantaged, and they diminish the quality of life for all but the very wealthy few. A ramshackle tax system permitting hugely profitable corporations to pay few or no taxes and allowing the income and wealth of the top 0.01, 1, and 10 percent to grow while everyone else bears the brunt of the tax burden has helped drive the impoverishment of the public sector and created a substantial reduction in the quality of life for millions of Americans in all walks of life. States lack funding to support education at all levels, the nation's transportation infrastructure crumbles, and public services of all kinds are cut. Food insecurity stalks the lives of millions, and tens of thousands of the poor, the elderly, and children chronically experience hunger. Unemployment, under-employment, and part-time employment are a fact of life for tens of millions. In 2012, six in ten workers expressed worry about losing their jobs; their quality of life clearly is diminished, and they are not thinking about realizing "the American Dream."

The average workers with jobs can hardly be unaware of the millions without jobs, of the underemployed, of declining wages, and of the disappearance of benefits and retirement security. The official unemployment rate of 7 percent at the end of 2013 vastly understated the actual number of unemployed. According to former political strategist and historian Kevin Phillips, what economist John Williams labeled "Pollyanna creep" has been at work at least since the 1960s in successive presidential administrations to make yardstick numbers about the economy look better than they are. The lowering of the unemployment rate has come about by redefinitions of what constitutes the jobless, progressively excluding long-term job seekers. The number of *under*employed at the end of 2013 remained at just over 13 percent of the workforce. The climate thus created for even those holding jobs is what Paul Krugman calls the "fear economy," because when the recession hit in 2007, the number of workers voluntarily leaving their job plunged—and has remained low. They know that if they leave their current job, finding another could be very difficult. By 2014, with the economy slowly improving, a Gallup poll found that workers were less scared of being laid off, though confidence had not returned to its pre-crisis levels.[28]

"Workers with jobs," however, is fast becoming a figure of speech, at least for the low-income wage earners in the bottom third of the workforce. According to a recent survey by the Federal Reserve, 30 percent of the respondents who had jobs reported that their incomes went up and down through the year, due to irregular work schedules and periods without a job or with seasonal employment. When asked how they were balancing income and expenses, 23 percent of the households said they were "living comfortably," 37 percent answered that they were "doing okay," while 25 percent reported they were "just getting by," and 13 percent admitted they were "finding it difficult to get by." Thus a total of 38 percent essentially were *struggling to make ends meet*.[29]

"Pollyanna creep" hides too many realities creating economic insecurity for millions of Americans: the undercounted jobless;

the underemployed; income volatility for the lower portion of the workforce; seven million part-time workers, most of whom prefer full-time jobs. Together with stagnant or falling wages, the result is lower consumer spending and an economy still plodding out of the recession.

Robert Kuttner, author, editor, and a keen observer of the political economy, describes the destructive loop: "Widened income inequality is not just socially unattractive or morally repugnant. It has real macroeconomic effects. As wealth concentrates, the very rich can't possibly spend it all. Much of their income is saved or invested. The rest of us, meanwhile, have deficient purchasing power relative to the economy's capacity. As wages are constrained, the economy remains in a self-reinforcing slump."[30]

Francis, the pope elected in 2013 who took the name of a saint who embraced the poor, has condemned "trickle-down economics." President Obama returned to the topic of inequality in his January 2014 State of the Union address. In October of that year, Janet L. Yellen, the new chair of the Federal Reserve, called attention to growing inequality and Americans' declining chances for economic advancement. Yet Ms. Yellen is continuing her predecessor's policy of low interest rates, which allows big banks and Wall Street firms to become even richer while the savings accounts of ordinary people stagnate and mortgages and small-business loans remain hard to get.[31] Thus inequality of income and wealth are getting worse, despite alarms sounded by powerful and knowledgeable government leaders, and despite a blizzard of information about inequality as "the root of social ills."

Compassion and empathy for those left out seems to reside mostly outside the political class; many of the rich and powerful (and their media flacks) even express disdain for the continually poor, the working poor asking for higher wages, and formerly middle-class people who have lost jobs and slipped down the socioeconomic ladder. Concern to restore fairness to the economy seems limited to most of the ordinary Democrats, liberal intellectuals, some Republicans, religious people, and professionals who work with the casualties of inequality. Many of these concerned Americans hope for a political reaction to move a largely dysfunctional national government into addressing the inequities that have created a society far removed from the kind intended by the country's founders. As long as those unaware or unconcerned remain that way about the harmful effects of inequality on the nation's entire society, attempts to get their attention must continue. Given the disjunction between what Americans *think* about inequality and how *bad it really is*, efforts to expose it must continue.

What many Americans *think* about opportunity and social mobility, examined in the next chapter, also tends to be far from the reality.

THE MYTH OF OPPORTUNITY

*America's overconfidence in upward mobility . . . has become the
rationale for indifference toward income inequality—a rationale
built on a demonstrably false premise.*

TIMOTHY NOAH, The Great Divergence

Long-cherished convictions among a people die hard, and the belief
in the American Dream—the United States as the land of opportunity—
has enjoyed a particularly durable afterlife. That its mystique extends
well beyond the nation's borders probably has added to its longevity.
But the dream, once a reality, has become a myth.

MOBILITY

Noble laureate Joseph E. Stiglitz, summarizing the work of economists, observed that presently "the United States has less equality
of opportunity than almost any other advanced industrial country.
Study after study has exposed the myth that America is a land of
opportunity." While social mobility is still possible, "the upwardly
mobile American is becoming a statistical oddity." Economic mobility in the United States is less than in most of Europe. And beyond
Europe, countries as diverse as Japan, New Zealand, Singapore, and
Pakistan have higher degrees of income mobility than the United
States. The life chances of an American child are more dependent on
the income and education of her or his parents than in most other advanced countries for which there is data. This relationship increased

after 1980, and cross-national comparisons indicate that the "more inequality, the less social mobility."[1]

Class mobility in the United States displays what demographers call "stickiness," namely, those born into the top fifth of incomes and those born into the bottom fifth tend to stay there. The Economic Mobility Project of the Pew Charitable Trusts found that about 62 percent of children born in the top fifth stay in the top two-fifths, while 65 percent born in the bottom fifth stay in the bottom two-fifths. More mobility occurs in the middle, but not as much as in comparable countries.[2]

Diminished mobility in the United States flows from inequality, which "lowers mobility because it shapes opportunity. It heightens the income consequences of innate differences between individuals; it also changes opportunities, incentives, and institutions that form, develop, and transmit characteristics and skills valued in the labor market; and it shifts the balance of power so that some groups are in a position to structure policies or otherwise support their children's achievement independent of talent." Indeed, their parents' position in the United States "explains around half of the differences in adult children's incomes, much more than in Canada, and more than in any European country except Italy and Britain."[3]

F. Scott Fitzgerald famously told Ernest Hemingway that "the rich are different from you and me," to which Hemingway replied, "Yes, they have more money." The 1 percent are also different, mobility studies show, "in the way advantages are passed on to the next generation, which certainly involves much higher-quality schooling and other investments of human capital from the early years onward, but may well also involve nepotism in the allocation of jobs. Children of top earners are more likely to grow up to be top earners."[4]

Yet expectations of social mobility remain resilient and impervious to reality. A survey of twenty-seven nations between 1998 and 2001 found that 69 percent of Americans agreed with the proposition that "people are rewarded for intelligence and skill," the highest proportion among the countries surveyed. The median for other countries was 40 percent. Similarly, asked if "people get rewarded for their effort," 60 percent of American agreed, compared with the median of 40 percent. Even in response to the question of whether coming from a wealthy family is "essential" or "very important" to getting ahead, Americans displayed less belief in socioeconomic advantage than the international median: 19 percent compared with 28 percent.[5]

In 2013, Hollywood made yet another film based on F. Scott Fitzgerald's *The Great Gatsby*, a novel set in the 1920s amid that decade's extremes of wealth and luxury and a desperate striving for status. Predictably, the 2013 version, released in the midst of a New Gilded Age, wallowed in the garish excesses of wealth far more than previous productions, such as those made in 1974 and 1949. Meanwhile, the chairman of President Obama's council of economic advisors, economist Alan Krueger, gave a speech at the Rock and Roll Hall of Fame in which he compared the winner-take-all economy of the music industry with the contemporary American economy. Krueger had already attracted attention among inequality specialists for his creation of what he called the "Great Gatsby curve," a chart showing countries along an axis of inequality, demonstrating that those nations with high inequality also have less economic mobility across generations. Krueger borrowed the title of Fitzgerald's novel precisely because it "explored class and inequality in the 1920s." On Krueger's curve, the United States falls at a point of both high inequality and low social mobility.[6]

A 2007 study by the Organisation for Economic Co-operation and Development combined several previous estimates and found income heritability to be higher and economic mobility lower in the United States than in Denmark, Australia, Norway, Finland, Canada, Sweden, Spain, and France. Italy has somewhat less mobility than the United States, and the United Kingdom ranked lowest. Thus, generally "western and northern European countries provide, in fact, greater opportunity than the United States to move up the economic ladder." Advanced studies of *intergenerational inequality* confirm that, contrary to Americans' strong belief in equality of opportunity, unequal chances are real and persistent across generations.[7]

EDUCATION

Inequality and diminishing mobility are reflected in—and caused by—growing inequalities in the U.S. system of secondary and higher education. High school graduation rates have improved in recent years, with the national rate going from 71.1 percent in 2001 to 78.2 percent in 2010 (in 2008 it was 85 percent in the European Union). Some states have attained rates of 90 percent, but minority students still lag well behind whites, with one-third of African American and 29 percent of Hispanic students dropping out. Graduation rates also stayed lower among Native Americans. Educators attribute the overall increase to efforts to keep students in school, while economists also point to the lack of jobs as a motivating factor.[8]

More importantly, during the last decade the number of high-poverty schools has risen, and many students in these schools remain trapped in a self-perpetuating set of disadvantages that significantly lower their chances of improving their lives. (High-poverty schools are defined as having at least 75 percent of their students enrolled in free or reduced-cost lunch programs.) For decades studies have shown that students in high-poverty schools perform poorly, compared with those in better-off districts. And that gap has not been decreasing, but growing. High-poverty high schools have a graduation rate of 68 percent, and only 28 percent of their graduates attend four-year colleges, compared with 52 percent of the graduates from low-poverty schools. The homes of low-income students contain fewer resources to enhance their education, and they suffer from lesser-quality materials available in their classrooms. Schools in affluent neighborhoods enjoy abundant resources and more qualified personnel.[9]

The high-poverty label for schools increasingly has come to mean those segregated by income and race. Since the 1990s, white flight and black middle-class flight, along with a series of decisions by a conservative U.S. Supreme Court majority hostile to desegregation remedies, has led to the rapid resegregation by race in schools across the country. Consequently, dozens of school districts have been released from court-ordered desegregation, especially during the presidency of George W. Bush. Studies of large school districts that had been removed from these court orders found that they steadily lost white students and became increasingly segregated after the release—isolated by both income and race.

Scholars of segregation now use the term "apartheid schools" to refer to those whose white population is 1 percent or less. Most are in the Northeast and Midwest, and they are increasing in the

South. In 1988, these pockets of underachievement numbered 2,762; in 2011, they rose to 6,727. These schools are surely separate but not equal. According to ProPublica, an independent nonprofit devoted to investigative journalism, many are no better or are worse than the segregated schools of the 1950s. "High-poverty, segregated black and Latino schools account for the majority of the roughly 1,400 schools nationwide labeled 'dropout factories'—meaning fewer than 60 percent of the students graduate." Nikole Hannah-Jones, who wrote the joint *Atlantic*–ProPublica report "Segregation Now," comments that not just poverty, but "the concentration of poor students in the same school hurts them the most."[10]

As Suzanne Mettler notes in *Degrees of Inequality,* "our system of higher education contributes, increasingly, to rising inequality, as it stratifies Americans by income group rather than providing them with ladders of opportunity." Inequalities, beginning in the household, strongly influence how high school graduates fare at four-year and community colleges. Over 40 percent of the students entering college do not get a degree within six years; over half do not when community colleges are counted in the mix. Whether or not a student graduates seems to depend largely on how much money her or his parents make. Paul Tough put it in blunt terms in the *New York Times Magazine*: "Rich kids graduate; poor and working-class kids don't." Just one-fourth of college freshmen born into the bottom half of the income distribution will earn a degree by age twenty-four, while almost 90 percent of students from the top quartile will graduate. Tough adds that this difference has little to do with ability; comparing students with the same standardized-test scores, "you find that their educational outcomes reflect their parents' income, not their test scores."[11]

High-income students increasingly attend elite private universities and colleges as well as the best public universities. Rising inequality and intensified competition for entrance into selective colleges has skewed those institutions' populations toward youths from families in the upper income brackets. Researchers at Stanford University found that low-income and middle-income students, regardless of race, are significantly underrepresented in highly selective colleges and universities: "Almost three-fifths (58%) of the students in these universities come from families in the top quartile of the income distribution, overwhelmingly white, while only 6 percent come from families in the bottom quartile of the income distribution." Over the last thirty years, "more and more seats" in the top schools "have been occupied by students from high-income families." Black and Hispanic students remain substantially underrepresented, and racial disparities in enrollment have increased. In 2004, "white students were five times as likely as black students to enroll in a highly selective college and almost three times as likely as Hispanic students."[12]

The Stanford group commented that the American educational system is often seen as a pyramid, with "many low-status, broad-access institutions at the bottom and fewer high-status, narrow-access universities at the top. Students who attend the few elite schools . . . enjoy larger tuition subsidies, disproportionately extensive resources, and more focused faculty attention." Surrounded by high-achieving peers from affluent, educated families, these privileged few move into social networks that continue to pay off for them. Elite graduate schools, financial institutions, and high-status law firms recruit exclusively at these colleges, and "evaluators at elite firms routinely use school prestige as a key factor when screening resumes. Indeed, nearly half of all Fortune 500 CEOs have degrees from one of thirteen schools, twelve of which are highly selective."[13]

While elite universities are becoming precincts of privilege, tuition at public universities, which educate 70 percent of the nation's students, has skyrocketed at a rate faster than medical care, gasoline, and all consumer items. Since 1985, the cost of college tuition and fees has increased by 559 percent, far outpacing family income. From just the years 2006 to 2011, as a major recession depleted family resources and income, tuition at four-year public colleges went up 18 percent. Although schools have been adding services, huge cuts in state funding have shifted the financial burden onto students. Every time state legislatures face a budget squeeze, they look to education as a convenient target where they can cut back on discretionary spending, in contrast to something like Medicaid. Between 2008 and 2012, states provided 28 percent less financing for education, and students have borrowed more to compensate, so that in the decade before 2012, federal college-loan debt more than doubled, from $41 billion to $103 billion.[14]

Yet students with federal debts enjoy flexibility in avoiding default and harming their credit history by making lower or even delayed payments. The private-loan industry of banks and other college-loan agencies usually provide their borrowers with no recourse other than to go into default. During 2013–2014, the Consumer Financial Protection Bureau saw a 38 percent increase in the number of complaints from borrowers with loans from private institutions. Members of Congress and federal regulators have been lobbying private lenders to adjust their Dickensian approach, but to no avail, according to an October 2014 report from the CFPB ombudsman.[15]

"No Rich Child Left Behind" is the wry comment of Stanford University researcher Sean F. Reardon on yet another dimension of inequality in higher education. The 10 percent and 1 percent are using their resources for their children's educational enrichment to further pave the road to plutocracy, if not aristocracy—at least this is the way aristocracies used to work. Hence children from wealthy families get better grades, have higher standardized-test scores, and even have higher rates of participation in extracurricular activities, along with higher graduation rates. The scores of wealthy and poor students on standardized math and reading tests have diverged over the past fifty years: the average difference is around 125 points, compared with about 90 points in the 1980s. The gap has grown not because poor students' scores are falling, but because rich children are performing so much better from kindergarten on.

Reardon and his colleagues tie this directly to growing income inequality. The rich now use their money differently regarding their children's education, "increasingly focusing their resources—their money, their time, and knowledge of what it takes to be successful in school—on their children's cognitive development and educational success." With educational success becoming ever more important, middle-class and poor families are trying to do the same thing but with fewer resources. "Relative differences can have absolute consequences," comments James Lardner. "When some people enroll their children in high-priced test-taking courses or hire 'private guidance counselors,' the landscape is changed for everybody, like it or not."

That changing landscape now contains private groups of parents in affluent communities, organizing themselves as nonprofits, who are raising and pouring money into their neighborhood schools to pay for extra programs and equipment. Between 1995 and 2010, the number of school-supporting nonprofits increased from 3,500 to 11,500, springing up mostly in communities with higher median incomes. These fund-raising efforts have the salutary effect of encouraging affluent families to keep their children in public schools, rather than sending them to private schools; but the support groups contribute to greater inequality between wealthy and less well-off school districts.[16]

The United States leads the world in educating the wealthy. Children of the 10 percent are receiving "some of the best [education] in the world, and the quality keeps getting better." For the 90 percent, not so much, as the average global standing of the United States in educational achievement keeps falling behind because of wide funding gaps between the rich and everyone else. Ironically, the federal government's efforts to close achievement gaps are actually backfiring, according to Rebecca Strauss of the Council on Foreign Relations. Intentionally or not, the government has actually funneled more money to the least needy, reinforcing inequities. In easing repayment terms for student debt, the government bestowed the biggest gains on those with the most debt, individuals who tend to be in graduate or professional programs that offer increased earning potential. These "winners" could get a federal subsidy four times larger than that provided to low-income debtors through Pell Grants. The government also gave a new, more generous tax credit to families earning between $120,000 and $180,000, amounting to $10 billion in annual benefits.[17]

State university systems have compounded inequity by shifting financial aid away from needy students and toward those with sparkling resumes—who tend to come from more affluent families with greater resources. High SAT scores and other merit-based criteria correlate closely with family income, with the result that state aid to the *non-needy* has tripled in the last two decades—to 29 percent per full-time student in 2010–2011. States also promote this shift in an effort to motivate students and keep them in-state once they graduate. About one in five students from households earning over $250,000 receive merit aid, while one in ten students from families making less than $30,000 receive aid.

In Kentucky, a state that lags behind in educating its youth, two of its three financial aid programs "primarily benefit middle- to upper-income students." In 2013, the state denied aid to 86,000 students who qualified by need. It should be noted, however, that while merit aid is increasing, 71 percent of educational aid nationally is based on financial need.[18]

The many dimensions of inequality in American higher education seem to proliferate. The dearth of low-income students at elite universities results in part from high-achieving poorer students not applying to selective colleges—although many of these institutions might cost them less, since they offer generous financial aid—whereas the two-year and nonselective colleges to which they do apply and get accepted lack resources to give adequate aid. But low-income high achievers typically live in small school districts, lack a critical mass of talented students in their schools, and are unlikely to encounter a teacher or friend from an older cohort who attended a selective college.[19]

Some educators do not see this as a problem. They point out that "students of any background can—and do—get a top-quality education at lots of non-name-brand institutions." Further, high-achieving students in working-class or rural regions do not just apply to places close to home because of ignorance of opportunities at selective institutions, but also because of loyalty to parents, "family ties, cultural fears, and economic pressures." Although they can receive "a top-notch education" close to home, they are also likely to incur a great deal of debt in those institutions lacking financial-aid resources.[20]

THE FOR-PROFITS

For-profit colleges far too often lead low-income students into debt rather than toward graduation or careers. Their marketing claims hold out the promise of certain jobs and upward mobility, but too many deliver the reverse and deepen inequality. The for-profits have grown rapidly in recent years since they offer flexible, market-oriented programs of vocational training. According to recent studies, some students and alumni are satisfied with the training they receive and may gain employment, but most end up wondering if the cost has been worth it. Many prospective employers are either uninformed about for-profit degrees or prefer graduates of public community or four-year colleges. Almost all students at for-profits are financed with loans or grants, and graduates with bachelor's degrees have taken on a median debt of $33,000 per student, compared with $18,000 at nonprofits and $22,000 at public institutions.[21]

For-profits have also proliferated because a federal spigot of tax-payer money—more than $30 billion a year—helped create them, with 90 percent of their income derived from federal aid. Thus taxpayer money has created what are often money-making machines for unscrupulous administrators and Wall Street investors.

While nonprofits have expanded the supply of skilled workers and have accommodated nontraditional students and underserved populations, their overall impact has not alleviated—and has probably deepened—inequality. From 1998 to 2008, enrollment at for-profit colleges rose by 225 percent, accounting for 10–13 percent of all college students as these institutions aggressively targeted non-traditional students, low-income students, and veterans through promises of secure employment. At least half of for-profit enrollees, however, do not know they are attending a for-profit school. Nor did most do any comparison shopping for an education: only four in ten considered other schools before attending a for-profit. Graduates also "end up with higher unemployment and 'idleness' rates and lower earnings six years after entering [for-profit] programs than do comparable students from other schools." Their default rates on student loans are the highest, accounting for nearly half of all defaults.[22] In 2013, attorneys general in thirty states began cooperating to stem abuses in the industry. The U.S. Senate had already conducted a two-year investigation and issued a report in 2012 accusing thirty for-profit colleges of paying out more for marketing than instruction, using "troubling" recruiting tactics, wasting taxpayer money, and failing to graduate half or more of their students. The for-profits, while spending very little to recruit qualified staff at any level, generally garnered more in tuition and fees than public colleges, helping to make the enterprise highly lucrative for its executives.

Senator Tom Harkin (D-IA), long associated with populist causes, declared that the practices of the for-profit colleges the Senate investigated typified most of the remainder: "They are systemic throughout the industry, with very few individual exceptions." The Senate report, endorsed only by the Democrats on the investigating committee, said that more than half of the nearly 1.1 million students enrolled in the thirty for-profits examined in 2008–2009 left without a diploma. Many who had graduated often found no promised job waiting for them and were burdened with significant debt, sometimes amounting to tens of thousands of dollars. Julie Kampschroeder, a high school guidance counselor in the St. Louis area, warns students about entering for-profits and winding up bankrupt: "They will go after your Social Security, your paycheck; they will not stop."[23]

Congress made matters worse for indebted students with the 2005 Bankruptcy Reform Act, which made it almost impossible for students to discharge their debts by declaring bankruptcy. The law treated in-debt students as if they were no different from people who went on credit card binges. Consumer advocate Elizabeth Warren, now a senator (D-MA), observed that the law treated all bankrupts as if they were cheaters.

General David Petraeus and his wife Holly have often criticized for-profits for taking advantage of veterans aided by the 9/11 G.I. Bill. The law provides financial assistance for education and housing to anyone serving in the armed forces for at least ninety days after 9/11, and as soon as it was passed, for-profit colleges began targeting veterans with often-deceptive advertising and promises. At the for-profits with the highest veteran enrollments in bachelor's degree programs, 53 percent of the veterans withdrew within two years, compared with 20 percent of the veterans attending public universities. Another adversary of the for-profits has been Kentucky's attorney general, Jack Conway, who wondered why a state with 4.5 million people contained 141 for-profit colleges. Conway relentlessly has brought consumer-protection and other suits against for-profits in his state, earning the ire of the industry. When he ran for reelection in 2011, his opponent—whom he defeated—received "scores" of donations from administrators at for-profits such as ATA College, Northwestern College (not to be confused with nonprofit Northwestern University), Sullivan University, Harrison College, Herzing College, Keiser University, National College, Daymar College, and Bryan College Online.

In bringing suit against Spencerian College's Louisville branch, Conway provided specifics on that college's advertised rate of placing graduates in occupations such as phlebotomy, medical transcription, and other areas contrasted with the actual rate of placement—with discrepancies of 30 to 40 percent in some cases.[24]

The largest for-profits are publically traded on Wall Street and are enormously profitable for their owners and shareholders. Even during the 2008 financial crisis, "the top nine companies enjoyed a 4 percent growth in their stocks, while the S&P 500 declined by 39 percent." Most taxpayers are the unwitting underwriters of this bonanza. The post-9/11 G.I. Bill, for example, allowed the for-profits to increase their income from military benefits from $66.6 million in 2006 to $521.2 million in 2010, while revenue from expanded Pell Grant funding went from $2.5 billion in 2006–2007 to $7.5 billion in 2009–2010.[25]

For-profits wield enormous influence by contributing heavily to Republican and Democratic candidates at the state and federal levels. Some congressmen and senators, along with Wall Street firms, are investors in or proprietors of these institutions, reaping millions of dollars. In early 2012, when moderate senator Olympia Snowe (R-ME) announced she would not run for reelection, she attributed her decision to Congress's hyperpartisanship and dysfunction and promptly cashed in on her reputation for bipartisanship by publishing a book, *Fighting for Common Ground: How We Can Break the Stalemate in Congress.* Unremarked in almost every news story about her retirement was the fact that she and her politico husband, former Maine governor John McKernan, had made several million dollars from Education Management Corporation, which had just become the target of a class-action lawsuit initiated by whistleblowers. In 2012 McKernan held almost $15 million worth of the company's shares, and Wall Street's Goldman Sachs owns 43 percent.[26]

The debt piled up by for-profit students, graduates, and nongraduates has consequences for the U.S. economy and for the nation's taxpayers. Some economists believe that the $1 trillion in overall student debt has inhibited recovery from the financiers' economic debacle of 2008–2009 by causing indebted former students to delay purchasing big-ticket items, instead conserving their resources and paying off debt. A Brookings Institution study, however, argues that student borrowers who graduate from traditional institutions are no worse off than those a generation ago. But the students leaving for-profits with or without a degree or certificate are usually burdened with debt and struggling to recoup in a weak economy.[27] More of the age eighteen-to-twenty-four cohort are in poverty now than in 1990, more are in families with lower incomes and resources, and more young adults are living with their parents: 55.3 percent, compared with 52.8 percent in 1990.

In 2014, Education Management Corporation and several other large, publically traded for-profits faced renewed investigations from a network of state attorneys general working with the new federal Consumer Financial Protection Bureau. Former employees of one large, private for-profit—the Harris School of Business and its parent company, Premier Education Group—filed a federal lawsuit accusing school officials of fraudulent recruiting and falsifying records in order to enroll students and keep receiving federal grant and student-loan money. As opportunity and mobility decline, profiteers that are in bed with politicians and large financial institutions continuously emit false promises, leading low-income aspirants into debt.[28]

The Obama administration has taken an aggressive approach to for-profits by proposing standards that would deny federal funds to programs whose graduates fail to make enough money to pay back their loans. Though this effort is tied up in court, the administration has acted against institutions that would not satisfy new regulations if they were to be put in effect. One of them, Corinthian Colleges, a publically traded for-profit with 72,000 students at over a hundred campuses, went bankrupt in June 2014. At the time, most of its $1.6 billion in annual revenue came from federal student aid. The U.S. Department of Education had demanded information about Corinthian "falsifying job-placement data" and engaging in other shady practices. Given this institution's dubious track record in placing students, Kevin Carey of the *New York Times* commented that "its students may very well be better off" with Corinthian's closing.[29]

Although under siege, the for-profits retain enormous influence in Congress and have managed to prevent the Obama administration and the Department of Education from imposing restrictions.

Congressional Republicans—who, in the 1980s, included critics who labeled for-profit institutions "diploma mills designed to trick the poor into taking on federally backed debt"—now constitute a block of staunch champions. In 2012, presidential candidate Mitt Romney praised specific for-profits whose owners and investors contributed to his campaign. But many Democratic legislators join their Republicans cohorts in votes against more regulation, while the efforts of Democratic lobbyists and prominent politicians, including former president Bill Clinton and personal friends of President Barack Obama, supplement the stepped-up spending of the industry to ward off restrictions. A phalanx of money, partisans, and personal relationships, concludes Mettler, allows the schools "to exist primarily to take advantage of opportunities to milk the system," at the expense of taxpayers and "disadvantaged Americans."[30]

EATING TUITION

While students are paying more for tuition and going increasingly into debt, college presidents and a ballooning number of administrators are doing very well financially. As recently as 2004, no college president earned more than $1 million in annual compensation, but the CEO ethos and the market model have been occupying academia in many ways. In 2010, as one story line put it, "three dozen private college presidents earned over $1 million." In 2011, that number climbed to forty-two, and the total median compensation for this group rose by 3.2 percent, compared with a 1.7 percent increase for average wage and salaried workers. Another headline announced that "colleges pay presidents millions while raising tuition." In 2011, University of Chicago president Robert Zimmer led the pack, at $3.4 million in total compensation. The heads of public universities were not far behind the privates, with foot-in-mouth E. Gordon Gee of Ohio State University (known for his offensive verbal gaffes) out in front with $1,999,221 in compensation in 2011. Pennsylvania State University's Graham Spanier, who was forced to resign in the wake of the university's sex abuse scandal that also brought down football coach Joe Paterno, enjoyed a soft landing with total compensation of $2.9 million.[31]

Perhaps Spanier, as penance, could contribute to the National Association for the Education of Homeless Children and Youth, which recently took up the cause of the growing number of homeless college students who have nowhere to go during school breaks. A survey in 2011 found that 7 percent of college students had been or were currently experiencing homelessness while enrolled. Colleges from Georgia to South Dakota have started offering support for such students, and Senator Patty Murray (D-WA) has introduced legislation requiring colleges to provide housing for homeless students.

Defenders of high administrative salaries argue that such compensation is not increasing as fast as tuition and makes up only about 0.4 percent of a college's budget, as well as point out that the sticker price for tuition and fees may not represent what students actually pay, given the increasing amount of financial aid. Vanderbilt University's chancellor, Nicholas Zeppos, made $1.9 million in 2009; the chair of the Board of Trustees defended this salary, saying Zeppos was "a highly attractive candidate for other top universities seeking, new, vibrant leadership." The same rationale was used by AIG, Goldman Sachs, and other Wall Street firms that took taxpayer-funded bailouts but gave "retention bonuses" to employees who helped cause the 2008 financial meltdown.[32]

In a recent book, Libertarian political scientist Benjamin Ginsberg suggested that galloping tuition and fees resulted in part from colleges and universities having bloated numbers of administrators. From 1975 to 2005, Ginsberg pointed out, the faculty-student ratio remained fairly constant, at about one per fifteen to sixteen students. But the administrator-student ratio underwent a large change, from about one administrator per eighty-four students and one professional staffer for every fifty students in 1975 to an administrator-student ratio in 2005 of one to sixty-eight, and an even more dramatic rise in the better-paid professional staff to a student ratio of one to twenty-one. A Delta Cost Project study reported that between 1998 and 2008, private colleges increased their spending on instruction by 22 percent, while hiking up their expenditures on administrators and staff by 36 percent.

Amazingly, administrators and staffers now outnumber full-time faculty members on campus, due in part to the hiring of more adjunct, or part-time, faculty, while the proportion of part-time staffers has declined. "As a result," says Ginsberg, "universities are now filled with armies of functionaries—vice presidents, associate vice presidents, assistant vice presidents, provosts, associate provosts, vice provosts, assistant provosts, deans, deanlets, and deanlings, each commanding staffers and assistants—who, more and more, direct the operations of every school." Between 1947 and 1995, administrative costs outdistanced the funds devoted to instruction, increasing from barely 9 percent to nearly 15 percent of college and university budgets. Ginsberg attributes this development to several causes but leans toward the notion that administrators have acted to "aggrandize their own role in academic life," even by way of meaningless makework, since their excess numbers mean there is often not enough work to keep them busy.[33]

Bloated administrations and grandly paid presidents on university campuses promote inequality that mirrors to a lesser degree—for now—the disparities between a financially strapped Main Street and a hugely prosperous Wall Street. Escalating pay for university presidents lies most heavily on the backs of student debtors and underpaid part-time faculty. A report from the Institute for Policy Studies found that from 2005 to 2012, student debt and the number of low-wage faculty rose fastest at the twenty-five universities with grandly compensated presidents. As student debt increased, "administrative spending outstripped scholarship spending by more than two to one at schools with the highest-paid presidents." Meanwhile, adjuncts swelled the faculty at these institutions at a rate 22 percent faster than the average at all universities; permanent faculty declined "dramatically."[34]

College presidents and administrators increasingly emulate the corporate and financial elites with whom they interact when fundraising. University presidents and their highest-paid associates now tend to set themselves off from their faculty and students, while living large and dipping freely into their schools' coffers.

Take the case of Benjamin Ladner, who became president of American University (in Washington, D.C.) in 1994. He and his wife, the "first lady," quickly decided that the official residence for the president was inadequate, so they persuaded the university to build an expensive new house, with a price tag of $1.45 million, and to pay $30,000 for landscaping, which included a waterfall, patio, and pond. "The Ladners outfitted the house with expensive china and stemware to host elegant dinners for donors and dignitaries." They served fine wine in crystal glasses costing $100 per glass, poured by tuxedo-clad waiters. Their staff included a chauffeur, a cook, a social secretary, and numerous others. Travelling abroad frequently, they usually charged first-class tickets to the university. Students and faculty, however, rarely glimpsed the Ladners' domain or the president himself. Their chauffeur-driven car, however, was often seen idling outside the residence.[35]

By 2004, Ladner's total compensation had risen to $880,750, but in March 2005, as he pressured the Board of Trustees for even more pay, a whistleblower wrote to the trustees regarding the Ladners' "severe expense-account violations." A subsequent audit revealed hundreds of thousands of dollars in questionable spending. Some expenses were said to be for "image polishing" for the president and first lady, something they may have needed during their final months at the university, when their former workers began to accuse the Ladners of abusive behavior. The Ladners' charges to the university included $6,000 for club dues, $54,000 for drivers' costs, $220,000 for chefs and catering, $44,000 for alcohol, and $100,000 for their social secretary. There were also numerous splurges in expensive restaurants, such as $1,285 for meals during two nights in Rome, all charged to the university. One critic said that Ladner had "an imperial presidency with a mentality of 'L'état, c'est moi.'"[36]

The Ladners' years of living large came while faculty and staff received miserly raises and tuition rose every year. Ladner hired a lawyer and fought dismissal. Despite the revelations of the audit, he retained significant support from a board that included wealthy realtors, lawyers, and others attuned to the same ethics as the governing boards overseeing corporate CEOs. One dissident board member called it a "cocktail board." In October 2005, the university finally got Ladner to resign, rather than firing him, which allowed his board supporters to cobble together a very generous severance package worth $3.7 million. The protests and outrage of students, faculty, deans, staff, and alumni counted for nothing.[37]

By all accounts, John Lombardi, president of the University of Florida from 1990 to 1999, did not live as lavishly as the Ladners. For him and his family, the president's dwelling provided by the university was enough, and he liked students and the public to know that he drove a red pickup truck. Before he resigned in 1999, however, Lombardi was accused of misusing state resources and using university money for his daughter's 1997 wedding, which cost $73,612. Subsequently, Lombardi released personal checks showing that he had reimbursed all university personnel who had worked on the wedding. The sanitized Wikipedia entry for Lombardi does not mention these allegations, nor his near ouster in 1997 over a report that at a private dinner party, he had used a "racial slur" in reference to the newly appointed chancellor of the state university system, Adam Herbert, an African American.[38] (In the Wikipedia entry for "oreo," meaning an African American who is black on the outside but white on the inside, Lombadi's use of it to refer to Herbert is mentioned.)

More seriously, Lombardi had antagonized the Florida Board of Regents by often ignoring it and dealing directly with the state legislature, and he received negative publicity for granting five-figure raises to his university's top administrators without informing Herbert, the head of the entire state university system. Meanwhile, faculty and staff were getting no or only miniscule raises (and were so informed by three-by-six-inch computer-generated slips in their campus mailboxes). Particularly objectionable was a $28,789 raise to University of Florida provost Elizabeth Capaldi (his second-in-command), boosting her salary to $260,000, $5,000 more than Herbert was making. The largest raise, for Gerald Schaffer, the vice president for administrative affairs, totaled $39,143. As Lombardi resigned, the chair of the Board of Regents commented that "clearly, the salary issue was a big issue for the Chancellor and the Board." It was also reported that after the attempt to oust him following the "oreo" scandal, Lombardi had tried to put two new positions for himself and Capaldi into the university's budget, ones that would cost the institution several hundred thousand dollars, presumably to provide safe havens should the enemies he had made be successful in ousting him the next time around. Newspapers around the state also attributed his forced 1999 resignation to his bullying and arrogant style.[39]

A particularly egregious case of what Benjamin Ginsberg would call "administrators eating tuition" occurred under the guidance of University of California president Mark Yudof (in office from 2008 to 2013). Yudof became president as the state's economy plunged and the California legislature cut the university budget by nearly $800 million. Yudof responded with "draconian" cuts: eliminating jobs and courses, imposing unpaid days and furloughs for faculty, cutting salaries for nonfaculty employees, raising student fees, and initiating a series of hikes that increased tuition from $7,517 in 2007 to $12,192 in 2012–2013.

As Yudof was defending his "system-wide belt tightening," it came out that contrary to announced pay cuts for administrators, the University of California Board of Regents had quietly approved raises and bonuses for more than two dozen executives. In what became known as San Francisco Gate, the press learned that the chief financial officer at the University of California, San Francisco, was getting a 6.5 percent boost to his stipend, upping it to $500,763; another financial officer received a 25 percent raise, increasing her salary to $293,125; and three new administrative positions had been created, with potential salaries between $239,700 and $420,100, plus benefits. In 2009, the regents also approved other campuses' requests to pay new deans and vice chancellors higher salaries than their predecessors had earned, justifying the action with the Wall Street argument of needing to offer retention pay to keep the theoretically ablest persons. These revelations led to faculty, staff, and student outrage and to walkouts and demonstrations on the university system's ten campuses.[40]

One of the more ironic recent episodes revealing administrative excess involved the now former president of the American Academy of Arts and Sciences, a 223-year-old society (founded during the American Revolution) to promote scholarship. Just as a bipartisan U.S. Senate report was about to be published regarding the crisis facing liberal arts education, due to severe budget cuts to universities throughout the nation, the *Boston Globe* revealed that the Academy's president, Leslie Cohen Berlowitz, had misrepresented her credentials for years. Moreover, she was receiving a total compensation of over $598,000, far greater than that of the head of any other scholarly society and more than many college presidents. Berlowitz claimed to have a Ph.D. from New York University (her resumé used the British abbreviation D.Phil.), but university representatives said that she never received one; she also misstated job titles she had while at that institution. She made these false claims when applying for federal funds, a potentially serious offense. As the story unfolded, Berlowitz's personality and allegedly abusive management style stirred controversy, but what added to the irony of her bloated pay—given the financial crisis facing the "at risk" humanities disciplines that was about to be recognized in the Senate report—was her high-spending lifestyle. Members of her staff (the Academy has forty-four employees, some part time) told the *Boston Globe* that Berlowitz always flew first class, stayed at luxury hotels, ordered catered meals at work, and required staff to chauffeur her between her office and a high-rent apartment on the Charles River.[41]

RISE OF THE ADJUNCTS: "TEACHERS ON WHEELS"

While the Ladners and Berkowitzs of academia emulated Wall Street millionaires, the foot soldiers of colleges and universities experienced very different lifestyles—and rewards. "Professor: Staff" became a ubiquitous fixture in the class schedules on most campuses, and students wondered, "who is Professor Staff and how can this person teach so many classes?" Professor Staff especially dominated the course offerings of two-year community colleges, where 70 percent or more of faculty were part-time, or contingent, faculty. The proportion of contingent faculty also increased at four-year institutions, and by 2012 about half to two-thirds or more of all faculty members were contingent. These educated professionals in what were once middle-class jobs earn low salaries with virtually no benefits. A report by the Democratic staff of the House Committee on Education and the Workforce commented: "Having played by the rules and obtained employment in a highly skilled in-demand field, these workers should be living middle-class lives. But . . . many often live on the edge of poverty."[42]

Political leaders, including President Obama, frequently point to community colleges as gateways to opportunity and social mobility, but "just-in-time" hiring practices of adjuncts and a lack of pedagogical support severely diminish the quality of education delivered. Contingent faculty often are hired just weeks or days before they begin teaching, usually affording them scant time to prepare their courses. They receive no logistical or technical support and no office space. With a median pay of $2,700 for a three-credit course in 2010, contingents often race from campus to campus to increase their earnings, as pointed out in a 2003 documentary, "Teachers on Wheels." Anonymous and interchangeable, these "Road Scholars" receive no wage premium based on their credentials, and their "damaging working conditions" often translates into a second-rate education for their students. Campaigns to unionize adjuncts have emerged throughout the country, and advocacy groups (such as the New Faculty Majority) have formed to publicize the adjuncts' plight.[43]

As many educational institutions have funneled money to administrators or used funds to pay for expensive dorms and other infrastructure to attract middle-class students, the number of adjuncts has grown. Research shows a negative impact on students at both two- and four-year colleges as an overreliance on contingent faculty leads to fewer students continuing past their freshmen year and lower graduation rates even for those who do stay on. These patterns form part of a broad trend toward the corporatization of higher education over the past thirty years.

Corporatization has reorganized many of America's national resources, "including higher education, in accordance with a short-sighted business model. Three decades of decline in public funding for higher education opened the door for increasing corporate influence, and since then the work of the university has been redirected to suit the corporate vision."[44]

DEATH OF A CONTINGENT: "SHE WAS A PROFESSOR?"

One wonders if "D.Phil." Berlowitz has ever heard of Margaret Mary Vojtko, who taught French for twenty-five years as an adjunct professor at Duquesne University in Pittsburgh and died on September 1, 2013. Vojtko, age eighty-three, had been terminated by Dusquesne while living in poverty and being in debt for her cancer treatment. Vojtko earned $3,500 per three-credit course, more than many other adjuncts around the country are paid, but she never made more than $25,000 a year and, like other contingents, had no benefits. Nor did Duquesne give her any severance pay.

Before her death she turned for help to Daniel Kovalik, a United Steelworkers Union official who had been working to organize Duquesne's adjunct teachers, asking him to intervene with the university to help her with her bills for radiation therapy. After her funeral, Kovalik published her story in the *Pittsburgh Post-Gazette*, and it quickly went viral. Maria Maisto, president of the New Faculty Majority, said it should be a "rallying cry" for all faculty members, not just adjuncts.

Duquesne officials and others have challenged parts of Kovalik's account of Vojtko's final months and accused Kovalik of exploiting her death for his own agenda. The university chaplain, who claimed to know Vojtko well, stated that she had been offered some help and had stayed for several weeks at a community house on campus.[45] The university's provost, Timothy Austin, pointed out that Duquesne pays its adjuncts more than most institutions do. But no one has disputed the fact that Vojtko, like other contingent faculty, earned wages close to the poverty line, received no benefits or severance pay, and worked for the university for twenty-five years yet ended up destitute and living a miserable existence.

"She was a professor?" That was the question a caseworker asked Kovalik after he contacted Adult Protective Services following Ms. Vojtko's first appeal to him. "The caseworker was shocked," he said. "This was not the usual type of person for whom she was called in to help." The caseworker did not know of the circumstances that are now normal for contingent faculty.

But the question also pointed to what has happened to the American middle class over the past three or four decades.

THE SHRINKING
MIDDLE CLASS

*It is therefore the greater of blessings for a state that its members
should possess a moderate and adequate property. Here some
have great possessions, and others have nothing at all, the result
is either democracy or an unmixed oligarchy. . . . Where democracies have no middle class, and the poor are greatly superior in
number, trouble ensues, and they are speedily ruined.*

ARISTOTLE, *Politics*

*The simple story of America is this: the rich are getting richer, the
richest of the rich are getting still richer, the poor are becoming
poorer and more numerous, and the middle class is being hollowed
out. The incomes of the middle class are stagnating or falling, and
the difference between them and the truly rich is increasing.*

JOSEPH STIGLITZ, *The Price of Inequality*

The signs of America's middle-class decline can be seen throughout
the land. Who has not encountered a man or woman who previously
held a professional or semiprofessional job now mired in a service or
retail occupation with low pay and scant or no benefits? Who does
not know of the millions of blue-collar workers whose manufacturing jobs once paid enough for them to see themselves as middle class,
but whose jobs got shipped overseas along with their middle-class
status and sense of self-worth? Factory workers still lucky enough
to be employed earn pay and benefits that are considerably less than
their counterparts received a generation ago.

The American middle class was once the envy of the world, *and* the richest, even into the 1990s, although inequality was growing. Political scientists boasted that it was the bedrock of American democracy. But by 2010, middle-class incomes in the United States lagged well behind those in most of Europe and Canada. The American poor are even worse off, earning much less than the poor in most European countries. Although U.S. economic growth compares favorably with that of many other countries, the lion's share of the gains go to top executives and corporate profits, not to middle-class wages; the minimum wage is lower, and unions are weaker.[1]

THE LOST DECADE

The period from 2000 to 2010 has gone into history as the "lost decade of the middle class," during which the middle class became "fewer, poorer, [and] gloomier," according to a Pew Research Center survey. Economists say the middle class was "hollowed out," hardly a term suggesting health for what once was America's strength. During the 2000s, the middle-income tier of Americans actually shrank in size—the only one to do so—continuing a trend of the past four decades. In 1971, the middle-income group included 61 percent of all adults; in 2011, just 51 percent. A lucky few of those leaving the middle sector did better, as the percentage of those in the upper tier rose slightly, while others joined the lower-income tier, where the numbers went from 25 to 29 percent. Pew found that an overwhelming 85 percent of adults describing themselves as middle class complained of greater difficulty maintaining their standard of living.

In a separate poll a year later, middle-class anxiety surfaced again. Although 56 percent of the adults surveyed said they believed they would eventually better themselves economically, 59 percent said they worried about dropping out of their current class. When asked to define middle class, a majority of respondents picked "having the ability to keep up with expenses and hold a steady job while not falling behind or taking on too much debt." Thus "resilient optimism about rising was matched by a widespread fear of falling." The biggest fear? Losing one's job.[2]

While the "morose middle class," as one columnist termed it, grew smaller and less well off, many families and individuals, men and women, suffered blows to their confidence and emotional well-being. Their tangible losses—jobs, homes, health insurance, benefits—have diminished them in their own eyes. Inequality presses down on them. They certainly know that the rich live in worlds very different from their own. As Ralph Waldo Emerson put it in the early nineteenth century, "'Tis very certain that each man carries in his eye the exact indication of his rank in the immense scale of men, and we are always learning to read it."[3]

In 2012 in Santa Barbara, California, 150 people who no longer had homes or apartments spent their nights in 113 vehicles in twenty-three parking lots designated as Safe Parking, a program run by a local nonprofit. One of them was fifty-six-year-old Janis Adkins, who grew up in a middle-class family in Santa Barbara. Before the 2008 recession, she ran a successful plant nursery in Moab, Utah. Now she was spending her nights in her Toyota Sienna van, doing odd jobs while continuously looking for work and volunteering at a wildlife shelter, where she had permission to pick fruit from the shelter's orange and avocado trees.[4]

Adkins's saga reflects numbers that tell a stark story of middle-class decline. While the Great Recession hammered middle-class incomes, they had already been declining for decades. In 1968, a then-robust middle class earned 53.2 percent of the nation's total income. In 2012, the share of the middle 60 percent of households fell to 45.7 percent. In the lost decade of the George W. Bush presidency, the middle class experienced a decline in overall wealth, not just an immediate income loss. The collapse of the housing bubble resulted in the loss of homes and equity—in effect, much of the middle class's assets. In 2012, the Federal Reserve reported that the steep recession had wiped out 39 percent of Americans' wealth, with middle-class families losing the most.[5]

From 2005 to 2011, the number of home-owning households with children under age eighteen declined by15 percent, with decreases of 20 percent or more in Michigan, Arizona, California, and Ohio. More mothers entered the workforce, and more people applied for food stamps. Jamie Lewis, coauthor of a U.S. Census Bureau report, stated the obvious: during the Great Recession, "economic well-being worsened for families with children," and it has not improved much since.[6]

American home ownership, promoted by Congress and federal agencies, peaked around 2004. But the unscrupulous exploitation of new buyers by investment houses, banks, brokers, and complicit regulators devastated much of the middle class when the recent recession struck. Millions of families went underwater, ending up with houses worth less than they paid for them. In 2008, U.S. householders lost $3.6 trillion in the value of their homes. By December 2011, 31 percent of mortgage holders were underwater; a year later, 27.5 percent. Las Vegas had become the "underwater capitol of the nation," with 59 percent of the city's homes worth less than their mortgages. In 2013, 10 million homes across the country remained underwater, and 5 million householders had lost their homes.

Some observers of declining home ownership point to young people deciding against buying real estate as either too risky or as a lifestyle choice, but that ignores the extent to which many of the millennials (those born between 1980 and 2000) took on debt getting a college education(see chapter 2). And with young and minority families' wealth concentrated in housing, they suffered much more than older families in the real estate bust.[7]

Compared with whites, minorities absorbed heavier losses in the housing collapse. From 2005 to 2009, "inflation-adjusted median wealth fell by 66% among Hispanic households and 53% among black households, compared with just 16% among white households." From 1984 to 2009, the wealth gap between whites and blacks nearly tripled, and in 2009, about a third of both black (35%) and Hispanic (31%) households had zero or negative worth, compared with 15 percent of white households. The evaporation of African American wealth during the Great Recession led to a "titanic wealth gap" between blacks and whites. By 2013, the median wealth of white households was thirteen times the wealth of black households, and more than ten times the wealth of Hispanic households.[8]

The housing stock available to African Americans factors into their net worth. Blacks fleeing Detroit's inner city, for example, generally wind up in "secondhand suburbs." Moreover, mortgage lenders often charge minority home buyers higher fees and interest rates than whites, and African Americans still encounter discrimination in housing markets. In tests of realtors' practices, advocacy groups and academic researchers have sent out white and black couples or individuals to look at the same houses or apartments and have found that these units are often available to whites but not to blacks.[9]

THE GEOGRAPHIC DIMENSION

As the middle class shrank, residential segregation *by income increased.* Neighborhoods across the country became less diverse, with fewer middle-class families living next to low-income families. From 1980 to 2010, the number of low-income households living in majority low-income neighborhoods rose from 23 to 28 percent. A parallel shift took place in upper-income neighborhoods, where affluent households doubled, from 9 to 18 percent. Income segregation by neighborhood grew in almost all of the nation's thirty largest cities.[10] This trend deepens inequality and erodes social well-being and civic life.

The growing absence of middle-class neighbors for poor and racially segregated families has a depressing effect on intergenerational mobility: it correlates with educational underachievement (lower test scores and higher dropout rates), more poor single parents, and families below the poverty line. Not surprisingly, residential segregation increased more rapidly for low-income African American and Hispanic families than for whites.

Larger numbers of well-off families have also segregated themselves. This "sorting" of the affluent is not without consequences for everyone else. As Stanford University researchers Sean Reardon and Kendra Bischoff point out, the rich take resources with them: better schools, parks, and public services gravitate to upscale neighborhoods, resulting in "greater disadvantages for the remaining neighborhoods where low- and middle-income families live."[11] When Fitzgerald quipped to Hemingway that the rich are different from you and me, he might have added that they really did not want to be around nonrich people, except when employing them as faceless gardeners or maids.

Residential segregation has not been confined to urban areas. Scholars use "suburban disequilibrium" as a term to describe the phenomenon of suburban enclaves close to one another that represent extremes of income and wealth. In Los Angeles County, for example, the town of Bradbury is one of the richest zip codes in the region, with one house on the market for $68.8 million. A couple of miles away is the suburb of Azusa, with a more than two-thirds Latino and working-class population. Their disparate profiles are no recent development, but instead have evolved over decades. "Patterns are established, and successive waves of pressure—fiscal, political, social—tend to keep things moving in the same direction." Each suburb creates reinforcing advantages and disadvantages. In the case of Azusa, inferior schools result from racial redlining that depresses property values and limits investment in the schools. Rich and poor do not live in different places simply through class sorting. "The places themselves help to create wealth and poverty."[12]

On the opposite coast, DUMBO is an acronym for a neighborhood in New York City that is "Down Under the Brooklyn Bridge." At one time a manufacturing district, the area began to be gentrified in the 1970s. It now houses some of the city's highest concentrations of technology firms, and Wikipedia calls it "one of New York City's premier art districts." It is home to affluent residents with a median income of $168,000 who enjoy fancy boutiques, cafes, gourmet restaurants, and Bargemusic, a floating stage for classical musicians.

Not far away, however, DUMBO's cobblestone streets vanish and ten rust-colored towers named Farragut Houses loom into sight. They are among the city's 334 public housing projects chronically afflicted by budget cuts, so that their elevators are unreliable; trash bags litter the area. The median income there is $17,000. For over four years, its residents had to walk four miles to a laundry facility. Some improvements have been made recently and security cameras have been installed, but crime and guns are still a problem. New York City abounds with such different worlds: one of the country's poorest Congressional districts in the South Bronx lies less than a mile from one of the wealthiest, on Manhattan's Upper East Side.[13]

RUNNING IN PLACE
AND FALLING BEHIND

The economic crisis of 2008–2009 revealed other dimensions of the harm that inequality causes to middle-class Americans. The housing bubble prompted more people to tap into their temporarily rising housing equity to "go shopping," as President George W. Bush urged after 9/11, and funds put into household saving fell across the country, especially among low-income households. More perilously, with wages remaining stagnant or falling, the American middle class used "debt as a substitute for income. People lacked adequate earnings, but felt wealthier." When the Great Recession set in, getting credit became more difficult, and families' losses pushed them back to saving more and consuming less. Worse, as housing prices plummeted, "the use of debt to finance consumption did not just halt; the process went into reverse as households had to pay down the debt. Rising unemployment compounded the damage. Consumer purchasing power took a big hit," recovery remained sluggish, and many were still jobless.[14]

While the party—and spending—lasted, however, consumption at the top (by the 20, 10, and 5 percent) radiated down the income ladder, creating what Cornell University economist and *New York Times* contributor Robert H. Frank has called "expenditure cascades." Viewing keeping up with the Joneses in a new light, Frank argues that it functions as a contemporary driver of inequality that, in turn, creates "enormous losses and few gains, even for its ostensible beneficiaries."[15]

Elsewhere, Frank and his colleagues assert that the consumption patterns of one group are heavily influenced by that of the group either just above or of equal status. Over the last three decades, the rich have been doing better than ever, and thus spending more. Greater purchasing at the top spurs the group just below to buy more to keep up, and so on down the income scale. Individuals and families susceptible to this syndrome "are caught up in a race where everybody is running to keep in the same place." These cascades have made it more expensive for middle-class families to achieve their lifestyle goals.[16]

In an earlier book, Frank called this phenomenon "luxury fever." One result has been a substantial increase in the size of houses people buy—not just the McMansions of the rich, but middle-class dwellings, too. From 1980 to 2001, the median size of a newly constructed house grew from approximately 1,600 square feet to over 2,100 square feet, "more than twice [the] corresponding growth in family earnings." In 2007, a typical new home covered about 2,500 square feet, with the median family now spending much more on housing and living well beyond its means. Frank and his colleagues argue that these kinds of consumption decisions "ripple through the entire economy."[17] Aspiring middle-class families often pay for more floor space in pursuit of better schools, which are closely linked to property taxes, "which in turn depend on local real estate prices," so the bigger-than-needed house is a way to avoid sending their children to below-average schools.[18]

According to Avner Offner, when people decide to consume more and take on more debt, their "frames of reference are very local." Other social scientists agree that an individual's measure of status, which Emerson referred to as what "each man carries in his eye," is made in one's locality. So it is with families: those in greater-inequality areas will find it harder to live within their means than those in lesser-inequality ones.[19] Indeed, state and county data show that the growth in inequality "is positively linked" with low savings and financial troubles (such as bankruptcy), as well as with longer commute times, stress in personal relationships, and, thus, higher rates of divorce. Middle-class families are simply better off living in a place with less economic inequality.[20]

"Trickle-Down Consumption" is the title of a research paper by Marianne Bertrand and Adair Morse that reinforces the findings of the Frank group and adds another rubric to express the same idea as "expenditure cascades": conspicuous consumption among the rich induces the nonrich to buy more and save less. In a detailed study of counties and cities across the United States, Bertrand and Morse also find that nonwealthy families exposed to greater spending by the rich experience more financial distress and personal bankruptcy. It's not just the McMansions, but also the exposure to "rich goods" in upscale shops, chichi bars and cafes, expensive restaurants, and pricier grocery stores like Whole Foods. Rich goods cover a range of services and recreational activities besides buying a Mercedes or other luxury car: yoga lessons and a health club membership, horseback riding for the kids, and the most expensive country club for golf.[21] Moreover, to run in place uses lots of energy without the satisfaction of feeling as if one is getting ahead. Chapter 4 will explore the effects of this situation on many Americans' health.

JOBS AND WAGES

Ronald Reagan quipped: "Recession is when a neighbor loses a job. Depression is when you lose yours." During the Great Recession, unemployment rose rapidly, hitting 10 percent in October 2009, with an estimated 9 million jobs lost in 2008–2009. For most of 2010, unemployment hovered just under 10 percent; in 2011, just under 9 percent. According to the U.S. Department of Labor Statistics, it was 7.6 percent in May 2013, and just under 6 percent in October 2014, but there is good reason to believe that the unemployed, underemployed, and those who have simply given up are substantially undercounted. Millions stopped looking for work, hordes of the young decided to stay in school, and, since 1994, long-term discouraged workers have been defined out of existence and thus do not get counted as being unemployed. Indeed, the "labor force participation rate" of 62.8 percent is the lowest it has been in more than three and a half decades.[22] Perhaps 6 million (or more) workers out there are not looking for a job; most are without employment opportunities yet are not counted among the unemployed.

When Henry David Thoreau observed that most men lead lives of "quiet desperation," he referred to an anxious striving to get ahead, but his phrase could well apply to those men and women today who have lost jobs, income, and status and become emotionally depressed. "Surveys of well-being show that by far the most potent of general causes of unhappiness is unemployment. Low rank induces misery."[23]

Loss of work often devastates older employees. A study done by economists at Wellesley College found that workers in their late fifties or early sixties who lost jobs and employer-provided health insurance can also suffer up to a three-year reduction in their life expectancy. They are in a kind of no-man's-land age cohort of not qualifying for Social Security until age sixty-two and Medicare until age sixty-five and thus are in the most peril. The effects of sudden unemployment in that group can linger well beyond the loss of meaningful work.[24]

Sudden unemployment has haunted white- and blue-collar workers at least since the 1970s. While corporate layoffs of white-collar workers marked the 1980s and 1990s, the loss of manufacturing jobs began as early as the 1960s. The U.S. economy had created new jobs, but not during the lost decade of the middle class. From the 1940s through the 1990s, each decade saw at least a 20 percent increase in the number of jobs, but between 1999 and 2009 the net gain in jobs was zero. The reasons for this are complex, including the real estate collapse, technology-caused job loss, free trade deals that result in sending jobs overseas, too little investment by the federal government in research and development, foreign competition, and unfair trade practices. Between 2001 and 2009, the latter bore down particularly hard on minority workers. An estimated 1 million minority workers with good jobs and benefits suffered displacement during that lost decade, resulting in major wage reductions for them from lower-paying work.[25]

Barry Lynn and Phillip Longman single out another culprit that has conspicuously escaped notice: monopolization. "Four great waves of mergers and acquisitions" from the 1980s to the 2000s "transformed America's industrial landscape at least as much as globalization." "Evidence is growing," they argue, "that the radical wide-ranging consolidation of recent years has reduced job creation at both big and small firms simultaneously."[26]

Combine the causes driving job loss with the lack of job creation and the stagnation of wages, and the result is a perfect storm for middle-class workers and those trying to ascend into the middle class. Indeed, during the Great Recession, workers in the United States, as in other developed countries, suffered a double dip, with wages going down in 2008 and again in 2011. Wages have remained stagnant: in 2013 they theoretically rose 1.9 percent, but in practice increased just 0.4 percent (after accounting for inflation), even less than in 2012. Until the economy resumes robust growth and full employment becomes a serious goal of government policy, wages will stay stuck and purchasing power will languish.[27]

Well-paying manufacturing jobs once provided a pathway into the middle class; no longer. According to a recent study by the National Employment Law Project, a workers' rights advocacy organization, "the public assumes that manufacturing jobs are highly paid, but the reality is that millions of manufacturing workers are at the bottom of the wage scale." In the 1980s and 1990s, factory work did indeed provide good pay for many men and women without much education, but in the 2000s, manufacturing wages plunged. Now "more than 600,000 manufacturing workers make just $9.60 an hour or less"; one in every four such workers—more than 1.5 million—make $11.91 an hour or less. Meanwhile, the federal government pours tens of millions of dollars into grants for factory innovation—and expected job creation—and state and local governments bestow tax breaks and credits to attract companies. Foreign auto manufacturers that moved into the South in recent years are increasing the number of low-paid workers they employ and often relying on staffing agencies to provide workers.[28]

WAGE-PRODUCTIVITY GAP

What economists term the "wage-productivity gap" has continued as the great wage slowdown of the twenty-first century, depressing the wages of low-income and middle-class workers and contributing to Americans' sense that the country is headed in the wrong direction.[29] Up until the 1970s, the growth of productivity and compensation in the United States were both robust. But as American workers became more productive, their real hourly compensation since the late 1970s lagged well behind. During the last three decades, the gap between workers' productivity and their wages widened. According to the *Monthly Labor Review*, from 2000 to 2009 "an unprecedented decline" in workers' wages, salaries, and benefits "accounted for most of the gap." This translates into American families making less than they did fifteen years ago.

Meanwhile, top CEOs' salaries and compensation rose to record highs, becoming the foremost driver of inequality in the United States. Extraordinary compensation for the heads of large firms had "spillover effects in pulling up the pay of other executives and managers," a major cause of the doubling of salaries for the top 1.0 percent and top 0.1 percent between 1979 and 2007. Soaring riches for executives and managers came at the expense of labor's share of the fruits of production, and depressed the chances of those workers who hope to make their way up the ladder into the middle class.

FIGURE 3.1. The wage-productivity gap

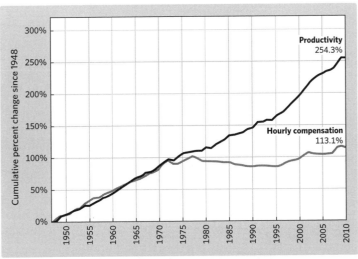

Adapted with permission from "The Root of American Inequality" (graph) in "The 13 Most Important Charts of 2013," Economic Policy Institute, December 20, 2013.

Low-earning workers in the United States have a steep road to climb, since they are "worse off than low-earning workers in all but seven peer countries [out of nineteen]." That inequality gap continually widens, because workers with the least education and low wages lag far behind as technological change pushes up educated workers, who earn higher pay.[30]

CEO salaries are enhanced by more than stagnant wages, since millions of American workers suffer from "an epidemic of wage theft, as large numbers of employers violate minimum-wage, overtime, and other wage and hour laws with virtual impunity. . . . Fully 64 percent of low-wage workers have some amount of pay stolen out of their paychecks by their employer every week," according to a 2009 multicity study. In 2012, robberies of banks, gas stations, and convenience stores grossed $139 million. The U.S. Department of Labor, however, recovered $280 million in 2012 from companies violating wage and labor laws. That, sadly, is but the tip of the iceberg. Data from the 2009 National Employment Law Project multicity study suggests that as much as $3 billion per year was withheld in the three cities studied (New York, Chicago, and Los Angeles); nationally, that could amount to a whopping $40–$60 billion. Perhaps the most distressing wage theft, from the point of view of taxpayers, is committed by companies receiving contracts from the federal government. Wage and safety violations are common among many of the firms receiving as much as $500 billion yearly in federal contracts. In 2012, forty-nine companies that received $81 billion in federal funds "were assessed $196 million in penalties for neglecting to pay workers earned wages or failing to uphold safe working conditions." These lawbreaking companies are aided by chambers of commerce and corporate lobbies working through the American Legislative Exchange Council to fight tenaciously against the enforcement of existing wage laws. ALEC, funded by some of the most antiunion and reactionary corporations, has infiltrated many state legislatures and provides compliant representatives with "model laws" written by corporate flacks.[31] The flow of corporate profits toward the top and away from earned wages hardly results from a free market.

Taxpayer money also fattens the salaries of the CEOs who run the companies that increasingly have taken over the work that federal employees once did—or should be doing. Their executives can make up to $763,039, while many of their employees—560,000 of them—earn twelve dollars an hour or less. According to the Government Accountability Office, in 2013 the U.S. government laid out about $23.9 billion in compensation for these top executives, who additionally benefited from their companies' stock awards. "Commonsense Contractor Act" bills have been introduced in Congress to raise the pay of workers and cap executive pay at the $230,700 figure earned by the vice president, but they have gone nowhere in the Republican-controlled House.[32]

"WHY SCREWING UNIONS SCREWS THE ENTIRE MIDDLE CLASS"

Conservative politicians still reflexively complain about "Big Labor," yet union membership has been declining; in 2013, it accounted for just 11.3 percent of wage and salaried workers. Unions have lost their once-prominent position in the American economy for a complex set of reasons, not least of which was a concerted effort by businesses and hostile politicians to crush them. But organized labor's loss of economic and political power has contributed substantially to lowering the wages for all workers and worsening inequality.[33]

Any doubt that the decline of labor unions intensified inequality should be dispelled by Jake Rosenfeld's new book, *What Unions No Longer Do*, a persuasive empirical study of the causal relationship between deunionization and rising inequality. Rosenfeld shows that unions served as a "core equalizing institution" whose effect "was strongest for society's most vulnerable and historically disadvantaged workers."[34]

Wages of most workers, including those in the middle class, have suffered from the decline of labor unions. At their height in the 1950s, unions enrolled 35 percent of the workforce and already had contributed substantially to building the American middle class. Although a Gallup poll in 2013 reported that 54 percent of adults age eighteen and over approved of unions, up from a historic low of 48 percent in 2008, considerable amnesia exists among middle- and lower-income Americans regarding the role of unions in the Great Prosperity of the post–World War II era.[35]

Most Americans perhaps hardly realize that it is more difficult to form a union in the United States than in any other country with an advanced economy and a supposed democratic system. In recent years, conservative reactionaries like the Koch brothers and their political allies have launched a war on public-sector unions. After Republicans took control of several states in the 2010 elections, they introduced legislation depriving public-sector unions of bargaining rights, succeeding even in traditionally progressive Wisconsin. Budget cuts and freezes at the state and federal levels led to layoffs of federal and state workers, so while unions in the private sector added about 282,000 members, public-sector membership declined by almost 120,000. Moreover, ignorance about and hostility toward unions extends beyond Republican politicians, as millions of Americans are hardly aware of the unions' historic and central role in helping create a broad middle class that characterized the decades of the Great Prosperity. Much of the middle class really doesn't get "why screwing unions screws the entire middle class."[36]

Since at least the 1970s, a business-corporate offensive launched from conservative think tanks has ginned up hostility towards unions. The New Left of the 1960s tended to ignore economic issues, and the rise of identity politics led to the foregrounding of cultural issues among progressives. As organized labor lost members and political clout, a "new liberalism" arose in the form of citizens' groups focused on specific issues, such as women's rights, the environment, gun control, and civil rights. These groups deflected the Democratic Party's attention away from issues of economic justice that affected the less affluent and gained traction as Congressional Democrats turned away from union interests in the late 1970s and welcomed corporate and Wall Street money. Meanwhile, right-wing economists and propagandists relentlessly promoted (a faux) free-market ideology, a dogma that corporations conveniently set aside whenever they seek government subsidies.[37] True, some unions, by their irresponsible actions or corruption, helped create negative public opinion, but it would be difficult to argue that overall, misconduct and self-serving practices by unions have done anywhere near the damage to the economy as that wrought by the financial industry in recent years.

The contemporary weakness of labor unions was reflected in a 2009 Pew Research Center study of how the media covered economic news during the Great Recession, focusing on who "triggered" stories and "whose voices were heard." Not surprisingly, the Obama administration sparked most of the stories (49%), followed by the press itself (23%) and then business (21%). The pattern was similar with regard to who dominated conversations, with government officials (including Congressional representatives) followed by spokespersons from business and industry, academics, and independent observers. Ordinary citizens and workers lagged far behind, making cameo appearances in about one out of five stories. And what about representatives of labor unions? They served as sources in a mere 2 percent of all stories Pew studied about the economy. As Timothy Noah observed, "labor's decline was as much cultural as it was quantifiably economic," recalling that labor in its heyday "played a large role in shaping societal attitudes." In negotiations with industry and government, labor once was "an inevitable component to the modern industrial economy."[38] No longer.

What the media do not report and politicians (including Democrats) fail to emphasize is that higher union wages translate into *higher wages for nonunion workers, especially low- and middle-wage workers.* The decline of labor unions over the past forty years has closely paralleled the rampant rise of inequality in the United States. Middle-class shrinkage and its reduced share of the nation's total income correlate closely with falling union membership, but the relationship is not merely coincidental. Wages have stagnated as the union wage premium—the raising of wages by about 20 percent and of benefits by around 28 percent due to the influence of unions—has fled with the unions' decline. Rosenfeld makes clear how "the collapse of private-sector unions eliminated a tested pathway to the middle class for millions of immigrants and their offspring" and exacerbated racial inequality when unions began to crumble just as African American men and women were joining them in large numbers. Unions "helped equalize [voter] participation across SES [socioeconomic status] divides," and powerful unions once "moderated the impact of the introduction of new technologies in the workplace."[39]

According to a study by the Center for American Progress Action Fund, in states with more union members, the middle class earns significantly more income than in states with low union membership. In the ten most-unionized states, "households in the middle class received 47.4 percent of total state income . . . [and] in the bottom 10 states, households in the middle class received only 46.8 percent." That seemingly insignificant difference of 0.6 percent can amount to real money: in 2012, 0.6 percent of Pennsylvania's aggregate income equaled over $2 billion, or about $700 per middle-class household. The bottom line? More-unionized states have stronger middle classes.[40]

Unions reduce inequality through collective bargaining agreements that deliver higher wages and (often) benefits such as employer-provided health insurance. Moreover, in places where they are present, unions also tend to raise the wages and benefits of nonunion workers fortunate enough to be in the vicinity. This happens when nonunion employers frequently decide to meet union standards for their own workers, or at least to improve their companies'

FIGURE 3.2. Unions and shared prosperity

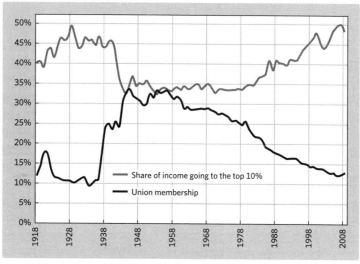

Adapted with permission from Ross Eisenbrey and Colin Gordon, "As Unions Decline, Inequality Rises," Economic Policy Institute, June 6, 2012.

compensation and labor practices beyond what they otherwise would have provided. "This dynamic is sometimes called the 'union threat effect,' the degree to which nonunion workers are paid more because their employers are trying to forestall unionization."[41] Even without this threat effect, the presence of unions has created gains for workers throughout the economy—especially for low-wage workers—by establishing norms and practices that improve pay and working conditions for everyone. The roughly 70 percent of workers who are not college educated benefited from the influence of unions by gaining fringe benefits, such as pensions and health insurance, as well as grievance procedures.

But since the 1980s, this spillover effect has weakened considerably. "Together with other laissez-faire policies such as globalization, deregulation, and lower labor standards such as a weaker minimum wage, deunionization has strengthened the hands of employers and undercut the ability of low- and middle-wage workers to have good jobs and economic security." The causal relationship between the decline of unions and the rise of inequality could not be clearer, but antiunion elements in corporate-political America have been successful in erasing the memory of labor unions' historic building of a middle class.[42]

STAYING AFLOAT / SINKING IN THE NEW ECONOMY

"Golden Opps"

A typical American path into the middle class historically has been starting a small business or taking on a franchise from a large industry and becoming your own boss. But that was before McDonald's pioneered the transfer of all the risk of a startup enterprise to the franchisee. "McDonald's is Your Golden Opportunity" announces the McDonald's website. "Owning a McDonald's restaurant is a tremendous opportunity. We are seeking individuals with significant business experience who have successfully owned or managed multiple business units or have led multiple departments. And who have significant financial resources."

Franchising schemes had been around since the nineteenth century, with the automobile, soft drink, oil, and motel industries relying on franchising for much of their early growth. But, as Eric Schlosser explained so well in *Fast Food Nation*, "it was the fast food industry that turned franchising into a business model soon emulated by retail chains throughout the United States." Franchising greased the wheels for rapid expansion and attracted capital from banks wary of a brand-new industry. While the system itself was widespread, "it was McDonald's that perfected new franchising techniques, increasing the chain's size while maintaining strict control of its products."

The McDonald's model spawned many imitators, particularly after the Small Business Administration began financing new franchises, creating "free enterprise with federal loans." Subway led the way among many chains that expanded using government-backed loans, and federal money thus flowed to the fast food industry, "thereby turning a federal agency that was created to help independent, small businesses into one that eliminates them." These "golden opportunities," however, have a high rate of failure compared with independent small restaurants; when the franchises close, McDonald's,

Subway, and Burger King corporations do not lose. Instead, "American taxpayers had covered the franchise fees, paid for the buildings, real estate, equipment, and supplies." Thus all the risk has devolved on the aspiring small businessman seeking middle-class status.[43] And many do not make it.

Retirement and the New Economy

From the 1940s to the1980s, when middle-class workers retired they could usually count on staying in the middle class. A private pension plan with a guaranteed payout became a standard of worker compensation for millions. No longer. The traditional employer-provided plans, known as defined-benefit pensions, have, according to the U.S. Bureau of Labor Statistics, become "rare" in private industry. In 2011, just 18 percent of private-industry employees enjoyed such coverage; it has steadily declined over the past four decades, down from over 60 percent in the early 1980s. This change has increased economic insecurity for millions of Americans. It forms just part of what Jacob S. Hacker has called the "great risk shift," where "more and more economic risk has been offloaded by government and corporations onto the increasingly fragile balance sheets of workers and their families."[44] During the 2000s, employers accelerated their switch to defined-contribution pension plans such as 401(k)s, IRAs, and the like. Most of these rely on worker contributions and are much riskier and less predictable for the employee; employers may—or may not—match employees' contributions. In businesses with fewer than fifty workers, only 8 percent offered a defined-benefit plan.[45]

Except for government workers at all levels, the vast majority of whom have defined-benefit plans, an assured system through which retirees can stay in the middle class has been rapidly disappearing. Further, great disparities now prevail, in line with a person's income, race and ethnicity, education, gender, and marital status. Even before the 2008 recession, many employers who offered defined-benefit plans began to freeze them and instead offered new hires only defined-contribution plans. Some younger workers who anticipate career moves actually prefer the latter, but for middle-aged and older workers, defined-contribution plans are bad news. The entire American retirement system has been shaken up, and, like franchising, risk has been shifted onto the individual employee, who must rely heavily on his or her own contributions and the unpredictability of the stock market.[46] Worse, corporations' raids on pension funds—debts they owed their workers—have exacerbated the peeling away of middle-class income and accelerated its flow up to the corporate elite.

During the 1980s, corporations used takeovers of other companies and bankruptcy laws written in their favor to offload their pension obligations onto workers and the federal Pension Benefit Guarantee Corporation. Over 2,000 firms used complex accounting strategies to avoid the 1974 Employee Retirement Income Security Act by changing ownership and transferring the money they owed their workers to the PBGC, with employees ending up shortchanged and savings going to corporate "financial engineers."

In the 1990s, a booming stock market created enormous surpluses in corporate pension funds: $25 billion at General Motors, $24 billion at Verizon, and $20 billion at AT&T. Dozens of corporations then restructured these funds to divert the money to their companies. General Electric, for example, in a sale of one of its aerospace units—including its employees and their pension fund, which had a surplus of $531 million—added that surplus into the sale price and pocketed the money that had belonged to its employees. Other big firms plundered their employees' pension funds to the tune of tens of billions of dollars, but when the stock market crashed, they began to plead that they could no longer afford expensive pension benefits, and they often blamed unions for any financial distress. Corporations have also used bankruptcy laws to their advantage in ways that individuals cannot, avoiding pension obligations by diverting them to the government. Ellen E. Schultz, who covers the topic of pensions for the *Wall Street Journal*, called her detailed account of the corporate looting of employees' nest eggs *Retirement Heist*.[47]

The rush of companies switching from defined-benefit to defined-contribution plans has been supplanted by a new approach, appropriately called "de-risking." Firms are now offering lump-sum buyouts of pensions or transferring their pension obligations to insurance companies. General Motors, Ford, Archer Daniels Midland, and many other corporations are using this method to reduce their own risk, but the change may be riskier for the retirees. Although some retirees are not concerned, many others are, and a portion of the 40,000 Verizon retirees affected by such a switch are suing the company. Since benefits will no longer be guaranteed by the PBGC, Deborah Chalfie, senior legislative representative for AARP, says: "It's really not de-risking. It's transferring the risk."[48]

In 2010, higher-income households—the top fifth—held 72 percent of their total savings in retirement accounts, but almost half (48%) of middle-income households did not have retirement savings accounts. The retirement savings of African American and Hispanic workers (the latter have traditionally had low participation rates) have fallen well behind those of whites. Individuals lacking college degrees and unmarried women are particularly ill-prepared with savings for retirement.[49]

Although public employees have defined-benefit plans, in recent years public pensions have become political footballs. Republican politicians, as well as business groups, have criticized these pensions as being too generous and have blamed unions for driving up costs and adding to states' budget problems. While many state and local governments' "defined-benefit plans are fiscal debacles," many are in good shape. Yet in 2012, thirty-four states failed to meet their pension obligations. While unions often have resisted cuts, the problem is overwhelmingly political, with plenty of blame to go around.

State legislators delay putting money into pension funds to use it for other purposes and tend to overestimate how much pension investments will earn. Fearing voter reprisals, and with many public-sector unions retaining political influence, these legislators refuse to make tough political decisions to raise taxes or cut future benefits. The editors of *BloombergView* recommend that governments "stop lying to themselves. Money that's slated to cover annual pension and health-care fund contributions but is instead siphoned away to cover other costs won't magically reappear in later budgets."[50]

The problem is not with defined-benefit plans, which tend to be more efficient than defined-contribution plans, but mostly with "elected officials operating on limited time spans in office to kick fiscal consequences down the road," according to political scientist Patrick McGuinn of Drew University, a specialist in the politics of pension shortfalls. Almost any actuary will tell you that "the worst defined-benefit plan is more efficient than the best defined-contribution plan." The former tend to be better managed and earn higher investment returns, since defined-benefit plans "take advantage of the law of averages."[51] Members of public-employee unions and union members in the private sector who have defined-benefit plans likely will remain middle class. Chalk up another way in which unions shore up a dwindling middle-class America.[52]

Another hallmark of the New Economy that separates many employees from assured benefits and good pay is the rise of freelance workers. Employers increasingly rely on independent contractors, temporary workers, contract employees, and freelancers. The federal government estimates that there are now more than 20 million freelancers and independent workers, and professionals possess no immunity from this status.

At a Manhattan law firm twenty years ago, Sara Horowitz found herself a freelancer, dismayed and angry, with no health coverage, no pension, and no paid vacation. Half seriously, she and two other young lawyers formed the "Transient Workers Union" with the facetious motto "The union makes us not so weak." But Horowitz knew a thing or two about real unions: her grandfather had been a vice president of the International Ladies Garment Workers' Union and her father was a labor lawyer. What began as a morale booster evolved into a fast-growing labor organization, the Freelancers Union, with 200,000 members in early 2013, over half of them in New York State. (By comparison, the United Auto Workers has 380,000 members.) The Freelancers' Union set up a health-insurance company that covered 23,000 workers in New York in 2013, and the Obama administration recently awarded this union $340 million in low-interest loans to establish cooperatives in New York, New Jersey, and Oregon to provide health coverage to tens of thousands more workers.[53] So goes the middle class in the New Economy.

Some economists on both the Left and Right predict the middle class will just keep going—away. One grim (or realistic) forecast comes from Libertarian economist Tyler Cowen, who argues that the Great Prosperity of the post–World War II era was an anomaly, middle-level jobs will continue to disappear, and the standard of living of the middle class will steadily decline.[54] America will continue to become a society very different from what it was when it boasted of a prospering and optimistic middle class, the foundation of the nation's democratic culture.

The continued disappearance of the middle class may be moot, but corporate America has rendered its verdict as to that class's decline, one that should remove any doubts. It has recognized that the customer base for middle-level businesses is steadily eroding. Upscale retailers and restaurants are thriving, while Sears and J. C. Penney are closing stores and fewer people are dining at Olive Garden and Red Lobster. General Electric is expanding its array of luxury appliances that sell for $1,700 to $3,000 as the demand for mass-market models tails off.

The *New York Times*' Nelson Schwartz breezily reported this story as "The Middle Class Steadily Eroding." Referring to a recent paper by St. Louis Federal Reserve economists Barry Cynamon and Steven Fazzari, Schwartz told readers that in 2012, "the top 5 percent of earners were responsible for 38 percent of domestic consumption, up from 28 percent in 1995" and that since 2009, "top echelon" spending rose by 17 percent, compared with just 1 percent for the bottom 95 percent.

What the *New York Times* did not reveal in the article—since it was not the main point—was that the Cynamon and Fazzari paper focused on how "rising inequality" has created a drag on consumer spending; that spending by the bottom 95 percent before 2008 relied heavily on going into debt and was "unsustainable"; that during the Great Recession, spending by the 95 percent *collapsed*; and, above all, that the declining share of income going to the bottom 95 percent from 1989 on (i.e., rising inequality) contributed both to the recession and to the economy's failure to recover.[55] So the backstory, of far greater significance than Schwartz's focus on spending, is rising inequality: a shift of income from the bottom 95 percent to the top that has deprived the American economy of adequate purchasing power.

As the middle class shrinks, the American socioeconomic distribution resembles a distorted hourglass, with an enlarging bottom, shrinking middle, and slightly expanding narrow top.

KEEPING THE RICH (FILTHY) RICH AND THE POOR (DIRT) POOR

Under this ancient distinction the worthy employments are those which may be classed as exploit; unworthy are those necessary everyday employments into which no appreciable element of exploit exists.

THORSTEIN VEBLEN, *The Theory of the Leisure Class*

In 2012, income inequality in the United States reached a historic high, with the top-decile income share equal to 50.4 percent, the most ever since 1917 (when such information first became available). The top 1 percent, according to economist Emmanuel Saez, took in nearly one-fifth (19.3%) of overall income in 2012. Wealth also continued to flow to the top, with the richest 400 people owning more wealth than the bottom 150 million combined. The 1 percent made famous/notorious by Occupy Wall Street control 40 percent of the nation's wealth, while the bottom 40 percent barely own 1 percent. The United States truly is the land of the free to be unequal.

In the U.S. economy's "jobless recovery" from the Great Recession, the rich got even richer. The top 1 percent took in 93 percent of all income gains, the wealthiest 7 percent saw the mean value of their assets grow by 29 percent (from $2.48 million to $3.17 million), while the bottom 93 percent had their net worth drop by 4 percent (from $139,896 to $133,816). Saez echoes a chorus of social scientists in observing that the current record-breaking inequality culminates roughly thirty years of economic productivity gains going to the top of American society. This trend seems likely to continue, he concludes, along with further deterioration of the middle class.[1]

RENT SEEKING AND GEORGE WASHINGTON PLUNKITT

Most Americans are not well informed about how extremes of wealth are coming into being. They probably are unfamiliar with the term "rent seeking," used by economists and political scientists to describe activities of those at the top who have "inordinate political power" and not only use but shape the rules of the game (with their enablers in the political class), limiting redistribution "to extract from the public what can only be called 'gifts.'" So what economists call rent seeking means getting income not as a reward for creating wealth but for grabbing a larger share of the wealth than would otherwise have been produced by one's own efforts. An early twentieth-century ward boss of New York City's Tammany Hall described something similar to a reporter: "Everybody is talkin' these days about Tammany men growin' rich on graft, but nobody thinks of drawin' the distinction between honest graft and dishonest graft." Professing to practice only "honest graft," George Washington Plunkitt summed up his way of "gettin' richer every day" with a comment many contemporary Wall Street manipulators—especially the flash traders—could make a mantra of their own: "I seen my opportunities an' I took 'em."[2]

TWO TAX SYSTEMS

Inequality of income and wealth has been created in part by grossly unequal and unfair systems of taxation at the federal and state levels that give more generous tax breaks to the wealthy and allow rent-seeking opportunities by the 1 percent. The Tea Party slogan of "taxed enough already" could not be further from the truth, particularly as it applies to the wealthy, to corporations, and even to the middle class relative to lower-income and poor families.

David Cay Johnston, Pulitzer Prize–winning financial reporter for the *New York Times*, notes that the federal tax code "is shaped by elected officials beholden to the corporations and wealthy individuals who make up America's political donor class. Through a swirl of lobbying activities and campaign contributions, they have swept the interests of average working Americans aside while galvanizing support for a series of self-serving changes in the rates and rules, many of which the politicians do not even understand." Johnston further describes the reality of American taxation that is ordinarily obscured by media reportage on the American tax system:[3]

> What is commonly referred to as the tax code might be better described as two codes: one that forces most Americans to account for every nickel of income they earn, and another that allows the wealthy to reveal or conceal [income] at their discretion. Every April 15, local television news teams set up camp at post offices to film Americans mailing in their last-minute tax returns. For the most part, those taxes have already been reported, paid, and spent by Uncle Sam. If you are a wage earner, your employer reports to the IRS your income down to the penny, withholding from every paycheck the amount due (and usually a bit more) and sending it on to the Treasury. Most wage-earning Americans couldn't significantly cheat on their taxes if they wanted to.

The political capture of the tax code has been well documented. In the 1960s and early 1970s, the business community suffered a series of defeats, culminating in Republican president Richard Nixon promoting progressive policies in a turbulent climate of movements challenging all orthodoxy and authority, including the American economic system. Before Nixon left office, business groups mounted an "organizational counterattack . . . [that] was swift and sweeping." Between 1968 and 1978, the number of corporations with public-affairs offices in Washington rose from 100 to over 500; in 1971, 175 firms employed registered lobbyists in the capitol; by 1982, that number climbed to almost 2,500.[4]

Powerful and well-financed elements of corporate America moved to acquire political power and change the climate of opinion by promoting free-market ideology. They also began to invest in political giving—not just to Republicans, but also to Democrats—with a huge payoff in the late 1970s during the Carter administration, when Congressional Democrats became more probusiness and hostile to unions. Politicized business interests hit the jackpot in 1978 with a tax bill that "signaled a dramatic shift in governance in Washington." Three years later, the Reagan administration's tax bill "was an astonishing acceleration of the 1978 formula of big tax cuts for business and the affluent."[5]

While market forces and other government policies have driven rising inequality, tax policy has exacerbated after-tax income inequality since the late 1970s and has promoted the shift of pretax income toward high-income households. The top federal tax rate averaged 80.6 percent from 1947 to 1979. Under Reagan the top rate came down from 70 percent to 28 percent; then Clinton raised the top rate to 39.6 percent in 1993. George W. Bush, as a self-proclaimed friend of the "haves and have-mores," pushed the top marginal rate down to 35 percent. The tax rates on capital gains income, which is received mostly by the wealthy, are especially beneficial: more than half of the capital gains in America go to the top 0.1 percent. "The bottom 90 percent of the population gets less than 10 percent of all capital gains." Clinton reduced that tax rate to 20 percent in 1997, and G. W. Bush dropped it to 15 percent. The interest accrued on municipal bonds, another large holding of the wealthy, is not even taxed.

One result of all this bipartisan beneficence toward the most privileged (and privilege does accompany wealth) was that in 2009, the top 400 earners (the superrich .01 percent) paid an average tax rate of just 19.9 percent on the income they reported, and the richest 1 percent now pay effective tax rates in the low twentieth percentile.[6]

In the 1980s the rich got richer, but in the 1990s "the extraordinary transfer of income to the top truly shifted into high gear." The bonanza for the wealthy then continued under both Democratic and Republican presidents. Congressional Democrats aided the process, particularly those that political scientists Jacob S. Hacker and Paul Pierson describe as "Republicans for a day." While "Republicans for a lifetime" infrequently break ranks to vote against the party line, many Democrats often cross over to cater to wealthy constituents or corporate interests ready with checkbooks to contribute to their re-election campaigns.[7]

Even the *Economist*, a conservative magazine, opines that "America's Byzantine tax system does hardly anything to redistribute income." It is "riddled with deductions and loopholes, most of which favour the wealthy." Tax breaks, a form of government spending—and regarded as such by Congress's Joint Committee on Taxation—benefit mainly the wealthy and the upper middle class. "These exemptions, which include interest paid on mortgages up to $1m [*sic*] and contributions to gold-plated health insurance, are now worth some $1.3 trillion." Between 60 and 70 percent of these "tax preferences" flow to the top one-fifth of taxpayers, and only 3 percent to the bottom quintile. "Successful professionals do not see themselves as beneficiaries of government largesse, but the government in effect subsidizes their big houses, expensive health care, and retirement savings." Conservative defenders of low income-tax rates for the richest point to the top fifth of taxpayers paying three-fourths of the federal tax burden, while receiving "only" ten percent of federal entitlements. But consideration of tax breaks, as *New York Times* economics columnist Eduardo Porter commented, "creates an entirely different landscape of winners and losers of the government's largesse." The big bucks flow upward—almost $25,000 in tax breaks for the top fifth and $447,259 for families earning $1 million before taxes—while taxpayers earning $10,000 or less get chump change: $427.[8]

The payroll-tax cap illustrates another way wealthy individuals with large salaries pay less in taxes than less-affluent citizens. The payroll tax, which funds Social Security and Medicare, takes 6.2 percent of income from everyone's paycheck, with an additional 6.2 percent coming from one's employer. Since 2010, the payroll tax applies only to the first $106,800 in earned income, however. This means that a person earning $1 million has the same amount deducted in payroll taxes as someone earning $106,800. Thus an ordinary couple, if each of their salaries is at the cap, has twice as much taken out of their paychecks as Mitt Romney or Bill Gates.[9]

The 15 percent tax rate on capital gains is a pillar of inequality and a gift to the wealthy that keeps on giving. As investment income has risen, labor income has declined. Recent research suggests that the transfer of income from labor "results from bargaining by executives and managers—at the expense of other workers." Thus such transfers "are zero-sum . . . with no gains to productivity." In addition, the exemption from estate tax, which is levied on large fortunes passed on to beneficiaries after a person's death, has risen to "an extremely generous $5.25 million per person" (set at $5 million for 2013 and adjusted up for inflation). This means very few of the assets passed on after a person's death will be subject to the tax, since a couple can jointly exclude $10.5 million of their estate from this tax, as well as put assets into escape mechanisms, such as an irrevocable trust. President George W. Bush succeeded in getting the rich a one-year total exemption from the tax in 2010. In 2013, the Tax Policy Center expected an estimated 3,800 estates to be subject to this tax. Nothing does more, perhaps, to create and maintain an aristocracy of wealth in the United States.

Among this group, the twenty-five highest-paid hedge-fund managers had their already-large fortunes grow by a combined $21 billion in 2013. As Paul Krugman observed, they made more than twice as much as all the kindergarten teachers in the nation. These twenty-five men—no women—are not job creators, but financial speculators enjoying favorable tax rates. It is only a matter of time, Krugman observed, "before inheritance [itself] becomes the biggest source of inherited wealth."[10]

CORPORATE TAXES AND CEO COMPENSATION

George Lefebvre's comment about taxation in his book *The Coming of the French Revolution* can be applied to the United States today: "The *taille* (the word originally meant the 'cut' taken by the lord from the subject) was the basic tax of the French monarchy before the Revolution. It . . . was never paid by anyone who because of class status, regional privilege, or personal influence could obtain exemption, so that not to be taillable was . . . one of the most common of privileges, and to be taillable was not only a financial expense but a social indignity." Corporations, as well as the rich, did better than everyone else in America during the recent so-called recovery. By 2013, with a soaring stock market, they entered "a golden age for corporate profits." In the third quarter of 2012, corporate profits reached $1.75 trillion, a share of national income higher than at any time since 1950 and the greatest share of GDP in history. The portion of that income going to employees, however, dropped to its lowest since 1966. Corporations also enjoyed a plunge in corporate tax rates. The stated federal tax rate on a corporation's income is 35 percent, but the tax code for corporations, according to Allan Sloan, senior editor at *Forbes*, has "more holes than Swiss cheese."[11]

Offshore tax havens for businesses deprive the government of billions of dollars in revenue and deepen inequality. One study estimates that at least 20 percent of all corporate profits are shifted to low-tax countries and bilk the U.S. government of one-third of its potential corporate-tax revenue. Everyone else pays the piper, but multinationals with at least $50 million in assets easily outmaneuver the Internal Revenue Service. The 2010 Foreign Account Tax Compliance Act, imposing sanctions on foreign banks that keep secret accounts held by American citizens, makes it more difficult for even moderately wealthy individuals to evade taxes.[12] Nonetheless, many of them still benefit from the 15 percent capital-gains tax rate.

In early 2011, the billionaire investor and philanthropist Warren Buffet set off a debate about the fairness of taxes when he declared that his tax rate of 17 percent was about half the rate his secretary paid, and less than that of thirty people in his offices. Later that year, the nonpartisan Citizens for Tax Justice and the Institute on Taxation and Economic Policy published a joint report on corporate taxes that also sparked controversy about the unfairness of the U.S. tax system. A study of 280 of the largest and most profitable American companies over a three-year period (2008–2010) revealed that with pretax profits of $1.4 trillion, these firms at most paid about half of the 35 percent corporate-tax rate on that income; some of them paid even less than half; and others paid nothing at all. Overall, tax breaks for corporations reduces their on-paper tax rate of 35 percent to an actual rate of around 13–15 percent.

One-fourth of these companies owed less than 10 percent, almost equal to the number—"the good news" said the report—that paid close to the full 35 percent tax rate. One of the report's authors, Robert S. McIntyre, commented that those paying "their fair share ought to demand that the tax-dodging companies pay their fair share too. So should the public, which is subsidizing them in terms of increased federal debt." Most startling were the thirty companies that paid less than zero percent, an effective rate that averaged minus 6.7 percent over the three years. Corporate tax loopholes, according to the report, "are so out of control that most Americans can rightfully complain, 'I pay more federal income taxes than General Electric, Boeing, DuPont, Wells Fargo, Verizon, etc., etc., all put together.'"[13]

Most Americans are unaware of how much corporate taxes have fallen over the past fifty years, nor do they know that many corporations pay no taxes at all. In the 1950s, the amount big business rendered in taxes was about 6 percent of the nation's gross domestic product; in 2010, only 1.6 percent. A principal reason is that multinational corporations "now enjoy an unprecedented ability to move their capital around the world, and the corporate tax code has not kept up with the changes." A *Washington Post* study in 2013 found that most of the thirty industrial companies listed on the Dow Jones stock index were paying a "dramatically smaller percentage of their profits" into the U.S. Treasury. The majority had shifted their income overseas, where they paid much lighter taxes, thus depriving the American government of revenue for investment in infrastructure, education, and research that would be beneficial to U.S. corporations as well as to the public welfare. The middle class has made up for what the corporate giants no longer pay, and about 20 percent of the corporate income tax has been shifted to workers.[14]

Meanwhile, corporate executives' compensation has reached mind-boggling heights and, in dwarfing the pay of average workers, has led to an inequality ratio larger than in any other advanced economy. In 2013, the median compensation for the 100 top CEOs was $13.9 million, up 9 percent from 2012. These supersalaried executives pocketed a total of $1.5 billion. The biggest winner in 2013 was Lawrence J. Ellison of Oracle, at $78.4 million (down from $96.1 million in 2012); Robert A. Igger of Walt Disney took second place, at $34.3 million; and David M. Cole of Emerson Electric rose to fourth place, with a 264 percent pay raise bringing his salary to $25.4 million.

FIGURE 4.1. Corporate income tax as a share of GDP, 1946–2012

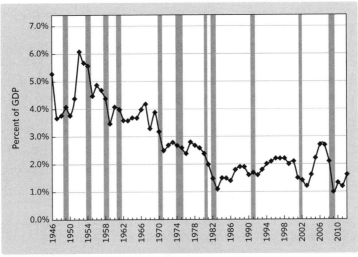

Reproduced with permission from "Tax Facts—Overview: Composition of Taxes,"
Tax Policy Center, Urban Institute and Brookings Institution.

In the 1950s and 1960s, CEO pay was about twenty to thirty times that of the average worker. The rapid upward trend for CEO compensation (salary plus multiple forms of benefits and bonuses) at major companies began in the 1970s and 1980s, according to the Economic Policy Institute, and "surged in the 1990s" to go over 400-to-1 in 2000. The ratio has gone up and down since then, and in 2012 it was 273-to-1. Between 1978 and 2011, CEO compensation grew by 876 percent, while that of the typical private-sector worker rose by just 5.4 percent.

Depending on the measures used and the companies studied, the rise in CEO compensation has been variously reported. According to the Institute for Policy Studies, the ratio in 2010 was 325-to-1. Some unfounded reports of larger ratios have gone viral. But one thing is certain, as the Economic Policy Institute commented: CEO compensation "has grown faster than **the stock market or the productivity of the economy**. This extraordinary growth of pay for executives has been a **major factor fueling the growth of incomes for the top one percent**" (boldface in the original).[15] It is the major factor driving the growth of inequality.

FIGURE 4.2. CEO-to-worker compensation ratio, 1965–2012

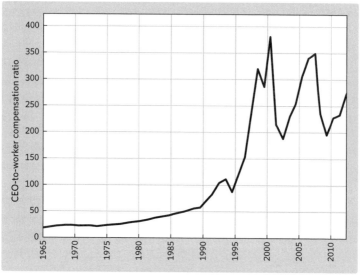

Reproduced with permission from "The Disparity between CEO Pay and Typical Worker Wages
Is Climbing Back Up into the Stratosphere" (graph) in "The 13 Most Important Charts of 2013,"
Economic Policy Institute, December 20, 2013.

The media too seldom has remarked that CEO compensation has become detached from a company's success or failure. The CEOs of the fifty firms that laid off the most workers during the depths of the Great Recession took home nearly $12 million (on average) in 2009, 42 percent more than the CEO pay average at S&P 500 firms as a whole. Fred Hassan of Schering-Plough received a golden parachute after laying off 16,000 workers when his firm merged with Merck, getting almost $50 million in compensation. And five of the top fifty layoff leaders received financial bailouts provided by taxpayers. American Express's Kenneth Chenault, for example, pocketed $16.6 million, including a $5 million cash bonus, after his company received $3.4 billion in bailout money. Meanwhile, American Express laid off 4,000 employees. According to *Forbes*, of the 697,448 layoffs between November 2008 and April 2010, more than three-quarters of those firings occurred at just fifty firms, companies that mirrored corporate America's "relentless squeezing of worker jobs, pay, and benefits to boost corporate earnings and maintain corporate executive paychecks at their recent bloated levels."[16]

Other top executives at firms that received billions of dollars in bailout money during the financial crisis garnered government-approved compensation packages. Sixty-eight out of sixty-nine executives at three companies benefiting from the Troubled Asset Relief Program, or TARP, received packages of $1 million or more; sixteen top executives at Ally Financial, General Motors, and the (notorious) American International Group took home a combined pay of more than $100 million. These companies convinced the U.S. Treasury Department to set aside its guidelines designed to keep exorbitant salaries and raises in check.[17]

The bailouts (thus far) have been a one-time deal. But corporate welfare that also enhances CEO salaries is a long-standing routine of government beneficence. Even the Cato Institute, a conservative think tank, has become a critic of corporate welfare—such as unneeded tax breaks or subsidies for "clean coal" or for agribusiness to produce ethanol—though its recent claim of governmental assistance amounting to $100 billion a year rises to that total by including many worthy government programs. Cato publicists argue that corporate welfare does not aid economic growth, but the institute's opposition to all forms of governmental intervention in the economy prompts it to criticize aid to small businesses that do produce jobs, as well as funding for worthy federal programs.[18]

CEOs collecting large paychecks, stock options, bonuses, and luxury toys are completely insulated from the havoc wrought on their watch in the lives of employees who lose their jobs. The National Bureau of Economic Research has calculated the "large and persistent effects [of job loss] on workers' lives." The most senior seem to suffer the most, as they "tend to experience long-term earnings losses, reduced employment rates, early retirement, increased job instability, lower consumption, and loss of health-insurance coverage." Younger and lower-skilled workers who are suddenly let go also see their earnings decline, but the worst effect is the damage done to the health of older workers.

Job loss increases mortality. Displacement of older workers leads to a 15–20 percent increase in death rates during the years thereafter, with a drop of 1.5 years in life expectancy for those losing jobs at forty years of age or older. Likely causes of this effect are loss of health insurance, employment insecurity, unhappiness, and emotional distress.[19]

CEOs, their publicists, and their compliant boards of trustees defend supersized compensation packages as necessary to retain top talent and provide performance incentives. "Of course, much of what is called incentive pay isn't really that," comments Joseph Stiglitz. "It's just a name given to justify the huge inequality, and to delude the innocent to think that without such inequality our economic system wouldn't work." Economists have shown that excessive CEO compensation is not the result of a competitive market, but is due in large part to the rents described in chapter 3: add-ons, or freebies or "gifts." CEO packages "grew far faster than compensation for other highly paid workers" and were not the result of a magic black box known as "market forces." Economists have another term for gratuitous excess: "skimming."[20]

The incentive-pay fig leaf covers up the realities of how this supposedly top talent actually performs. Of the 241 executives who have ranked among the highest paid in one or more of the past 20 years, nearly 40 percent of them were eventually "bailed out, booted, or busted." Research by the Institute for Policy Studies found that CEOs "performing poorly—and blatantly so—have consistently populated the ranks of our nation's top-paid CEOs over the last two decades." The poster boy for these underachieving millionaires and billionaires has to be Richard Fuld, chief of Lehman Brothers Holdings when this financial-services firm crashed in 2008 and helped set off a global economic meltdown. From 2000 to 2007, Fuld took around $529 million in salary, cash bonuses, and shares out of Lehman Brothers and became notorious for using the firm's money to furnish his office with items such as a $16,000 umbrella stand. When Fuld and his henchman Joe Gregory, in reckless pursuit of personal wealth, ran the firm into bankruptcy, "they very nearly collapsed the world economy." After giving themselves hefty bonuses, they transferred billions of dollars of other people's money to a potential buyer, "leaving tens of thousands of people and institutions to which Lehman owed money—from foreign orphanages to the city of Long Beach, California—high and dry." In 2013 Fuld, unlike many Lehman employees who lost their jobs, still owned several palatial residences and had a reported net worth of $160 million.[21]

In 2012, seventy-one of Fuld's former brethren responded to Washington's wrangling over spending and taxes by launching a campaign to "Fix the Debt," proposing sharp cuts in Social Security and Medicare. The integrity of their proposals, which would have ordinary Americans tightening their belts, was undercut by an IPS investigation revealing that these executives were sitting on an average of $9 million in their own retirement funds. A dozen had more than $20 million in their accounts. Forty-one of the seventy-one companies involved had offered their employees pension funds, yet only two had sufficient assets to meet their pension obligations. The other thirty-nine had a total deficit of $103 billion, or about $2.5 billion per firm, on average. A "pension deficit disorder" indeed.

The experience of other rich nations shows that "extraordinary executive salaries" in the United States are not the inevitable result of impersonal market forces, but are made possible by government policies—such as the bailouts for big banks—and cozy corporate governance.[22]

THE 47 PERCENT

During the 2012 election campaign, comments by Republican presidential candidate Mitt Romney to wealthy donors who shared the "Fix the Debt" mind-set were secretly recorded:

> There are 47 percent of the people who will vote for the president no matter what. All right, there are 47 percent who are with him, who are dependent on government, who believe that they are victims, who believe the government has a responsibility to care for them, who believe that they are entitled to health care, to food, to housing, to you-name-it. That that's an entitlement. And the government should give it to them. And they will vote for this president no matter what.... These are the [low-income] people who pay no income tax.

The backlash from this gift to President Obama's reelection campaign came swiftly, and not just from liberals. Even the *New York*

Times' conservative columnist David Brooks was withering in his criticism. The comment suggests, Brooks said, "that he [Romney] really doesn't know much about the country he inhabits. Who are these freeloaders? Is it the Iraq war veteran who goes to the VA? Is it the student getting a loan to go to college? Is it the retiree on Social Security or Medicare?"[23]

Actually, according to the Tax Policy Center, two-thirds of the 47 percent who, because of their low income levels, paid no federal income tax in 2011 still did contribute through the payroll taxes taken from their paychecks. The rest were mostly the elderly or retired receiving Social Security payments, or households earning less than $20,000. In fact, in 2011 only 18.1 percent of American households paid neither payroll nor federal taxes and, of that group, 10.3 percent were elderly and 6.9 percent earned less than $20,000 per year.

Although their numbers were much smaller, Romney surely did not have in mind the high-income earners who did not pay federal taxes in 2011: 78,000 with incomes between $211,000 and $533,000; 24,000 with incomes from $533,000 to $2.2 million; and 3,000 with incomes above $2.2 million. Romney was probably unaware that the ten states with the greatest number of wealthy residents who avoided paying federal income taxes were mostly southern, and Republican, and likely to vote for him (and did).[24]

At times during his campaign, Romney indicated his concern regarding increasing poverty in the United States but blamed the government for creating a culture of poverty by providing too generous a safety net (his vice-presidential running mate, Paul Ryan, called it a "hammock"). But a major reason that the United States ranked second in having the most child poverty among thirty-five economically developed countries in 2012 is precisely because what Romney thinks of as holes in the safety net are really yawning chasms.

Economist magazine has observed that "for all the conservatives' insinuations of loafers living on handouts, America spends less than half as much as the average OECD country on cash transfers for people of working age." The poor get little. "Around 10% of the total goes to the richest fifth of Americans, almost 60% to the middle three-fifths, and only 30% to the poorest fifth." The top fifth also benefits substantially from the mortgage-interest deduction from federal income taxes: the amount saved by the richest 20 percent amounts to four times what the government spends on public housing for the poorest fifth. Other developed countries do much more to alleviate poverty through social expenditures, transfer programs, and tax policy. Thus the United States "stands out" among most of its peer countries because of its soaring poverty rate "and one of the lowest levels of social expenditure" as a percentage of GDP.[25]

KEEPING THE POOR POOR

Taxation

While CEOs and the most-affluent Americans benefit from tax laws rigged in their favor, state tax systems help guarantee the persistence of poverty. Many states perpetuate inequality and keep the poor down and struggling by putting the heaviest tax burden on middle- and lower-income groups. Since 2010, some states with Republican governors and legislatures have moved to eliminate state income taxes and shift even more of their tax revenues from the wealthy to middle- and lower-income people.

According to a 2013 report by the Institute on Taxation and Economic Policy, "virtually every state's tax system is fundamentally unfair, taking a much greater share of income from middle- and low-income families than from wealthy families." Many states make this situation worse by having no graduated personal income tax and relying heavily on consumption taxes. "Combining all of the state and local income, property, sales, and excise taxes state residents pay, the average overall effective tax rates by income groups nationwide are 11.1 percent for the bottom 20 percent, 9.4 percent for the middle 20 percent, and 5.6 percent for the top 1 percent." The most affluent families do not pay at a rate "at least equal to what low- and middle-income families pay."[26]

Southern and western states increase the burden of poverty by garnering revenue primarily through sales taxes. Over the past thirty years, southern states have increasingly collected revenue from their poorest citizens though sales taxes that fall on the essentials of life: food, clothing, medicine, bus fare, and the like. A sales tax takes a larger chunk of a poor family's income than that of well-off families.

Katherine Newman and Rourke O'Brien, the authors of *Taxing the Poor: Doing Damage to the Truly Disadvantaged*, demonstrate that the regressive taxation of the states from the Old Confederacy plays a role in early mortality, out-of-wedlock births, high school dropouts, and crimes against property and persons. "Over time, the more the poor are taxed, the worse these outcomes look within states." Ironically, although the U.S. government—the same one demonized by red-state politicians—has poured billions of dollars into southern states to combat poverty, their legislatures and governors have taken them in the opposite direction, so poverty remains pervasive throughout the South. "With the exception of Virginia and Florida, no southern state had less than 13 percent of the population below the federal poverty line in 2008. . . . Louisiana, Arkansas, Kentucky, Texas, Georgia, and Mississippi all weigh in with more than 15 percent below the poverty line"; so too with their rates of extreme poverty and children in poverty. Ohio, New York, and Michigan also have high child-poverty rates, as do some southwestern states with large immigrant populations, "but the most serious concentration of poor children remains in the Deep South."[27] One byproduct of these systems is a needy workforce willing to work for minimum wages. Another result: the social costs of the southern states' regressive taxes are passed on to the federal government and middle-class taxpayers elsewhere.

Six out of the nine states *receiving* the most federal dollars compared with taxes *paid* to the federal government are southern. For every tax dollar sent to Washington, D.C., these states obtain an average of about $1.40 in federal funding: Medicaid matching funds, welfare block grants, disability payments, food stamps, and housing assistance. The federal government pours money into a region ringing with denunciations of "big government" and "socialism." For a long time, southern Congressional leaders have used their influence to prop up their states' economies by getting military bases for their districts, while federal safety-net programs financed by taxpayers throughout the nation try to provide "poverty relief . . . to close the gap created, in part, by the unwillingness of the states to fund poverty relief themselves."[28]

Predators

The poor are also kept poor by a host of predators taking advantage of their lack of resources: the thousands of storefronts across the country that promise quick cash through payday loans; tax-preparation offices that charge high fees and take big cuts from any tax refunds due to poor families; businesses that offer easy-payment car-title loans that come with hefty interest rates; rent-to-buy contracts for cars, cell phones, refrigerators, and other essential products that ensnare poor families into paying far more than the advertised original cost; scam artists offering government "grants"; employers who do not pay extra for overtime work or skim from their employees' tips; pension-advance companies that prey on low-income retirees by persuading them to sign over all or part of their monthly pensions; and subprime credit card companies that offer their cards to those with questionable or poor credit ratings. The list of predators is long because, as David Shipler put it, "at the confluence of private industry and government, American society devises numerous techniques of separating the working poor from their meager cash." Researchers are finding that at times, even the poor exploit the poor: cab drivers, for example, who buy SNAP (Supplemental Nutrition Assistance Program) food-stamp cards at half their value from homeless people desperate for any cash to buy drugs or alcohol.[29]

The most-adept are payday lenders, who entrap the poor in a cycle of ever-increasing debt and interest. Most of these businesses do not "replace loan sharks" as some of their Congressional defenders claim; they *are* the loan sharks. According to the Center for Responsible Lending, the typical two-week payday loan has an annual interest rate averaging 300 percent. The churning, or average repetition rate, of nine loans per borrower per year results in $3.4 billion in fees annually. The CRL, a nonpartisan, nonprofit research group located in North Carolina, judges these loans to be "simply unaffordable." The typical borrower makes $35,000 a year, cannot repay the loan on time and still meet other monthly expenses, and gets caught in a debt trap for months.[30]

On shabby streets in depressed cities and towns, these loan stores—more than 22,000 of them, two for every Starbucks—are often local chains, but the ranks of paycheck predators have included big banks such as Wells Fargo, Bank of America, and JPMorgan Chase. Their loans are tied to checking accounts from which the borrower withdraws money to be repaid within a short term, often ten days. Fees are steep—Wells Fargo charged $1.50 for every $20 borrowed—and the annual interest can soar to 365 percent. At the prompting of the Center for Responsible Lending, two federal government agencies warned the banks about these practices, and in early 2014, Wells Fargo, Fifth Third, U.S. Bank, and Regions announced they would discontinue what they euphemistically call "deposit advance products": more accurately, quicksand for the working poor. Payday lending has been expanding in a tough economy. In 2014, twenty-five states allowed stand-alone payday lenders within their borders, while fifteen states have banned them. But these lenders evade regulation by setting up business in other states or in offshore venues such as Belize, Malta, and the West Indies, although they can do so only with the help of large banks like JPMorgan Chase and Bank of America.[31]

At the same time, however, the new Consumer Financial Protection Bureau is moving against payday-loan abuses, and it required ACE Cash Express, a company with 1,500 storefronts in 36 states, to pay refunds and penalties of $12 million for illegal practices. In early 2014, the CFPB released a study showing that out of 12 million loans during one year, only 15 percent of the borrowers could raise the money to repay the original debt without borrowing again within fourteen days. CFPB director Richard Cordray observed that most borrowers get caught in a "revolving door of debt," with 20 percent of them defaulting and almost two-thirds renewing their loans multiple times, with escalating fees. Almost half the business of the payday-loan firms, he said, "comes from people who are basically paying high-cost rent on the amount of the original loan."[32]

Lenders also target states with large military populations. A few years ago, when the North Carolina legislature considered increasing the amount of interest the loan companies could charge, military commanders fought successfully to block these rates going up. Army generals argued that the lenders took advantage of young, low-income servicemen and -women, and that huge debts endangered their security clearances. Commanders eventually gave in as campaign cash from payday companies poured in to lawmakers. Recently, the Obama administration and the Defense Department have recognized the problem and have sought changes to the Military Lending

Act of 2006 that would extend the 36 percent interest cap on short-term loans to cover the many variations on lending to members of the military that lenders have used to get around the law.[33]

Exploitive and fraudulent predators on the poor also populate the tax-preparation business, lured by figures such as the $63 billion in tax refunds in 2013 returned to low-income people through the Earned Income Tax Credit. Millions of individual tax returns are "prepared" every year (42 million in 2011) by unlicensed preparers. Only four states regulate these individuals, who are often incompetent and charge their clients hundreds of dollars each. When the Obama administration tried to require preparers to prove their competency and undergo a criminal background check, a Libertarian institute founded by the Koch brothers challenged the regulations in court and won. Meanwhile, these tax preparers can be found alongside payday lenders throughout low-income neighborhoods.[34]

Keeping up with the latest variants, or "lucrative splinters," of what Gary Rivlin, author of *Broke, USA*, calls the "poverty industry" seems impossible. New methods of bilking, cheating, and crushing the lives of the working poor constantly come to light across the country. Nationally, the number of subprime auto loans, not a new swindle in the repertoire of predatory lending, have skyrocketed more than 130 percent in the last five years. About one out of four auto loans in 2013 went to borrowers with subprime credit scores (at or below 640). Private equity firms and some of the biggest banks are investing heavily in ways to cash in on fraudulent loans with high interest rates, with many such loans bundled into bonds and sold as securities. The lenders and debt-buyers profit handsomely, while the low-income borrowers can quickly lose their cars—many of which are worn out—and fall into years of debt.

Then there are place-specific collusions between local public officials and out-of-town sharks. In Washington, D.C., bureaucrats at the federal tax office changed what had been a fairly benign system of putting liens on the property of delinquent homeowners, with the liens then sold at auction to investors who charged interest until the debt was paid. Now well-financed companies have taken over, turned delinquencies of under $1,000 into debts of $5,000 or more, and then rapidly foreclosed on the homes. A *Washington Post* investigation found that out of nearly 200 homeowners who lost properties in recent years, one out of three had liens of less than $1,000; more than half of the foreclosures were in the city's two poorest wards; and more than forty houses were taken by companies that had broken laws in other states to acquire liens. The *Washington Post* began its report with the distressing tale of Bennie Coleman, a seventy-six-year-old retired marine sergeant and widower who suffered eviction by armed U.S. marshals and the loss of his home in 2011 because of an unpaid $134 tax bill.[35]

Rivlin describes the staggering profitability of "Poverty, Inc." In 2008, payday lenders "charged their customers a collective $7 billion in fees. . . . Rent-to-own shops collectively took in about $7 billion in revenues. . . . The pawnbrokers booked roughly $4 billion in revenues that year and the check cashers $3 billion. Toss in businesses like the auto-title lenders . . . and that adds up to $25 billion." Include the money-wiring business and all those billions of dollars banks and debit-card companies charge for services, "and revenues in the poverty industry easily exceed those of the booze business." Rivlin calculates that the money extracted from a worker supporting a family on $25,000 a year works out to a 15 percent "poverty tax" on his income.[36]

MINIMUM-WAGE WELFARE QUEENS: MCDONALDS AND WALMART

Walmart's 2014 corporate annual report to the U.S. Securities and Exchange Commission noted: "Our business operations are subject to permanent risks, factors and uncertainties, domestically and internationally, which are outside our control. . . . These factors include . . . changes in the amount of payments made under the Supplement[al] Nutrition Assistance Plan and other public assistance plans, [and] changes in the eligibility requirements of public assistance plans." In the South and throughout the nation, the low federal minimum wage contributes powerfully to keeping the poor in their place and ensuring many businesses a low-wage and docile workforce. Low wages also make for a sluggish economy, because of limited consumption. Large numbers of men and women without work, chasing after too few jobs that pay well, put employers in the driver's seat and help keep the poor down. The fast-food, service, and retail industries that pay nonliving wages also cost taxpayers billions of dollars every year. The average middle-class family that treats the kids to McDonald's for a quick meal does not realize that their tax dollars are subsidizing the fast-food business.

Minimum-wage workers are not just teenagers, who now account for only 17 percent of the total; the average age is thirty-five. Nearly 25 million workers in the United States earn less than $10.10 an hour, and 3.5 million of them make the federal minimum of $7.25. Among minimum-wage workers, 79 percent of them have a high school degree; over 40 percent have attended college for a period of time or have a college degree; and many are the primary earners in their families, whose income is usually supplemented with safety-net programs. People of color make up 42 percent of minimum-wage workers.

Congress last raised the minimum wage in 2009, to $7.25 an hour—which, adjusted for inflation, makes it worth less than it was in 1968. In early 2014, President Obama, by executive action, raised the minimum wage for businesses with new or renewed federal contracts to $10.10 per hour, an amount barely above the real value of the minimum wage in 1968. By international standards, America's minimum wage is one of the lowest in the OECD, just 38 percent of the median in 2011. Almost 25 million workers earn less than $10.10 an hour and, of those, 3.5 million make $7.25 or less. These figures, however, do not measure how this low minimum depresses wages throughout the labor force. The proportion of poor, working-age Americans is at its highest since 1967. Raising the minimum wage to $10.10 for all workers would affect an estimated 27.8 million people.[37]

A majority of Americans favors raising the federal minimum. In 2014, over 600 economists signed an open letter to President Obama advocating an increase in the minimum wage and advising him that doing so would not hurt employment; a short time later the National Restaurant Association rounded up 500 economists to send the president a letter urging him *not* to do so. Economists may differ, but two-thirds of the people polled in repeated surveys favor lifting the minimum-wage amount. During 2013, Obama had used his bully pulpit to urge Congress to increase the minimum wage, but the Republican-controlled House refused to consider it. The next year, the president issued an executive order raising the minimum wage for workers under federal contracts to $10.10 an hour. Meanwhile, states and cities are deciding that both equity and economic growth will be served by raising their minimum wages higher than the federal level. In 2014, Seattle led the way by upping its minimum wage to $15 an hour. In the November 2014 midterm elections, four Republican-leaning states approved referendums increasing the minimum wage: Alaska (by 69 percent!), Arkansas, Nebraska, and South Dakota. Heavily Democratic San Francisco did the same, joining the more than 120 cities and counties with minimums greater than the federal standard. In 2015, when a higher minimum wage goes into effect in Hawaii, Maryland, and West Virginia, 29 states and Washington, D.C. ,will have acted independently to surpass the $7.25 amount still mired in federal law.[38]

Since some cities and states have had higher minimums for several years, researchers have been able to examine their effects on employment, and specifically on whether raising the minimum wage "costs jobs." Most studies have found "little to no adverse impact." Many small businesses, as well as the CEO of COSTCO, one of the nation's largest retailers, favor a higher minimum. These employers, and several studies of localities where they do business, point to savings through increased employee loyalty, less turnover, and more production. The latest research also shows that a 10 percent increase in the minimum wage would reduce the U.S. poverty rate by about 2 percent. What is indisputable is that a low minimum wage that has not caught up to inflation helps keep millions of the working poor in poverty or just above it.[39]

So too does many large employers' evasion of the seventy-five-year-old Fair Labor Standards Act outlawing child labor, establishing a forty-hour work week with overtime compensation for anything more, and guaranteeing a minimum wage. But in the New Economy, an increasing number of businesses are classifying their employees as exempt from these provisions by shifting their jobs, but not their pay, to artificial categories that do not relate to the actual work performed, thus avoiding the necessity to pay overtime or even minimum wages. These tactics now make even white-collar workers vulnerable to wage theft. In 2010, the U.S. Justice Department brought an antitrust suit against Google, Apple, Intel, and Adobe for colluding in a conspiracy not to hire one another's workers, a scheme affecting 64,643 software engineers. The engineers claim that the companies' collusion from 2005 to 2009 kept the engineers' pay lower than it would have been and thus cost them $3.5 billion in lost wages.[40]

The high turnover rate in fast-food restaurants is not accidental. McDonalds has become notorious for using software to shuffle the schedules of its workers to prevent them from acquiring higher wages or benefits. But McDonalds wants them to know that it cares. In 2013, the company partnered with VISA to launch a website to show its workers a budget for living on wages of $8.50 hour, based on a monthly take-home pay of $2,060 by working two jobs! This magical budget allocated $20 a month for health care, nothing for heating, and nothing for food or clothing. Meanwhile, McDonalds' CEO Don Thompson took home $13.8 million in 2012.[41]

During 2012–2013 in cities across the country, fast-food workers—with median pay nationwide of $9.05 an hour—began walking out of McDonalds, Taco Bell, KFC, and other chains at peak mealtimes to demand higher wages. One of them was Terrence Wise, who earned $9.30 an hour after working for eight years at a Burger King in Kansas City, plus $7.40 an hour from his second job at Pizza Hut. Another was Sharise Stitt, age twenty-seven, who made $8.09 an hour after five years at Taco Bell. Evicted from her Detroit apartment, Sharise and her three children moved to her sister's house, a forty-five-minute commute to work. After taxes, she has about $900 a month plus food stamps to feed and clothe her children. Wonder how the McDonalds budget is working out for these families?[42]

Many of these workers—and others in retail and health-care jobs—cannot make a living wage because employers, benefiting from the scarcity of good jobs and high unemployment, keep their workers as part-timers, subject to calls to work on short notice. Nearly 28 million workers are part time, with almost 8 million wanting, and needing, full-time work, including many low-wage women and people of color. They lack benefits and lead furtive lives, unsure of which days or how many hours they will be requested to work.[43]

The fast-food industry makes big money—the seven publicly traded corporations made $7.44 billion in profits in 2012—and it pays its executives in princely fashion: $52.7 million to the highest paid, and $7.7 billion distributed in dividends and buybacks. But this success costs taxpayers billions of dollars. According to a study by economists at the University of California, Berkeley, over half (52%) of front-line fast-food workers need to rely on at least one public-assistance program, compared with 25 percent in the workforce as a whole. In other industries, far fewer workers rely on public assistance: the next-highest is agriculture; then forestry and fisheries at 34 percent; followed by leisure and hospitality, retail, and construction, all at 30 percent. Given a workplace with low wages, no benefits, and limited or staggered work hours, the fast-food industry's average cost to taxpayers amounts to nearly $7 billion per year. Over half of that sum, on average $3.9 billion every year, comes from two federal support programs: Medicaid and the Children's Health Insurance Program. Families dependent on fast-food wages receive around $1.04 billion in food stamps and $1.91 billion from the Earned Income Tax Credit. One out of five families with a member employed by a fast-food chain has an income below the federal poverty level, and 43 percent have an income two times or less below that level.[44] Among the ten largest fast-food companies draining federal funds, McDonalds heads the list, with an estimated average cost to taxpayers of $11.2 billion in public assistance for its employees; Domino's Pizza occupies the tenth spot, with an average cost of $126 million.[45]

Next to fast-food chains, Walmart leads the pack as the company doing most to keep low-income workers poor. Indeed, in November 2012 it ranked first among the twelve companies paying the least, as reported on the 24/7 Wall Street website. One source has Walmart's pay averaging $8.81 per hour, with its affiliated Sam's Club workers making around $10.30. A 2005 New York University study found that Walmart employees earn an average of roughly 28 percent less than those of other large retailers. But in 2012, the company made $17 billion in profits, and from 2007 to 2010, as millions of Americans struggled through the recession, the wealth of the six Walmart heirs rose from $73.3 billion to $89.5 billion. The holdings of founder Sam Walton's descendants equaled that of the 48.8 million families at the bottom of the income-distribution scale.[46]

The low wages paid to most of Walmart's 1.4 million U.S. "associates" not only makes life difficult for them but also creates "downward pressure on wages throughout the retail sector and the broader economy." And the ripple effect from Walmart workers' wages, like those of low-level employees in fast-food chains, costs taxpayers hundreds of millions of dollars. A recent study of stores in the state of Wisconsin by the Democratic staff of the U.S. House Committee on Education and the Workforce measured the social costs that Walmart's "strictly controlled labor costs" passed on to taxpayers.[47] There are 100 Walmart stores in Wisconsin, 75 of them supercenters typically employing about 300 persons. Using data from Wisconsin's Medicaid program, BadgerCare+, the committee staff studied the extent to which Walmart employees needed to use a host of state and federal assistance programs. The company ranked first statewide in the number of its employees enrolled in BadgerCare+, with 3,216 in this program; including these employees' adult dependents and children brought the total to 9,204. Based on the actual enrollment in BadgerCare+, a single Walmart supercenter cost taxpayers an estimated $904,542. Since "the universe of recipients of all public benefit programs is likely larger than actual participation in Badger-Care+" (reduced-price lunches, reduced-price breakfasts, housing assistance, nutrition assistance [formerly known as food stamps], home-energy-use assistance, child care), adding this population raises the calculated cost borne by taxpayers from one Walmart supercenter to $1,744,590.[48]

In early 2014, Walmart unabashedly acknowledged the importance of public-assistance programs to its bottom line. The sentences from their 2014 annual report quoted at the head of this section refer not only to low-income families using their food stamps at Walmart but also to its wage structure being partly funded by taxpayers; indeed, the company coaches the 1.4 million employees classified in its "associates" category to use public-assistance programs. Economists, including Alan Krueger, former chair of President Obama's Council of Economic Advisors, "estimate that 20 to 30 percent of the rise of wage inequality in this country can be attributed to the decline of the real value of the minimum wage." The difference between the federal minimum wage and that of the average American worker used to be much smaller than it is today. In the 1970s and for many years later, the federal minimum wage was roughly half that of the typical worker, but today's minimum is only 36 percent of the average nonsupervisory wage.[49] The federal minimum-wage level has not kept pace with inflation out of "economic necessity," but because of political obstruction.

Walmart also has kept wages down through its notorious opposition to unions, at least in the United States. Walmart's company culture has been variously described as "patriarchal" and "authoritarian." Concomitantly, it has spent millions opposing unions and, over decades, refined union busting to a smooth, seamless operation. At the first signs of workers organizing or cooperating in any meaningful way, Walmart's headquarters flies in a special team by corporate jet to defuse the situation. Then, over weeks and months, the "troublemakers" eventually are fired or quit because their life at work has been made impossible. When the meat-cutting department of a Texas Walmart store organized, the company announced that it was phasing out that department in all of its stores.[50]

John Tate, the man who initially oversaw Walmart's union fighting for decades ("I hate unions with a passion"), appeared at a gathering of Walmart executives and managers in 2004, after he had retired. At age eighty-seven he had lost none of his vitriol toward unions. Tate reminded his audience that fifty years before, when he began his job, unions represented about a third of the private-sector workforce, but in 2004, just 9 percent. "Labor unions," he said, "are nothing but blood-sucking parasites living off the productive labor of people who work for a living." Company officials said Tate's views did not reflect Walmart's, but his audience of managers leapt to their feet in a frenzy of clapping and cheering.[51]

In observing the many dimensions of inequality in the United States, ironies continually emerge, but perhaps Walmart's recognition of unions in foreign countries is less an irony than a dirty secret. Walmart has been required by some foreign governments (such as China's) to play by a different set of rules than those that prevail in the United States. One probable reason why the firm complies is because, while its sales in the United States fell in 2010, it took in $100 billion in foreign sales, a quarter of its total income. Some Walmart employees are organized in the United Kingdom, Brazil, and Argentina; in Mexico, 18 percent of its employees belong to unions. In 2011, Walmart made a deal with South Africa's government and agreed to cooperate with a union, avoid worker layoffs, honor existing contracts, and establish a fund for supplier development. In contrast, in 2005, after workers at a Walmart store in Canada won union certification, the company soon closed the store.[52] In North America, Walmart prefers to have low-wage workers who, for all practical and profitable purposes, essentially form part of the Third World.

Walmart and McDonalds are models of how a major part of America's workforce has been financially squeezed to allow compensation to flow to the top, while the economy stagnates for lack of purchasing power. The top has plenty of the latter and uses too little of it to boost the economy; the middle and bottom don't have enough.

The consequences extend not just to consumption of ordinary goods or luxuries, but also to health, the quality of life, and life itself.

INEQUALITY, LIFE,
AND QUALITY OF LIFE

Inequality Kills.

GÖRAN THERBORN, The Killing Fields of Inequality

In America the passion for physical well-being is not always exclusive, but it is general; and if all do not feel it in the same manner, yet it is felt by all. The effort to satisfy even the least wants of the body and to provide the little conveniences of life is uppermost in every mind.

ALEXIS DE TOCQUEVILLE, Democracy in America

Inequality has consequences for both life and the quality of life. It impacts life expectancy, physical and emotional health, and the bonds of community, however thin and fragile the latter may be in the twenty-first century. It corrodes the ties that bind Americans as members of a common nation when the poor sink into what is more like a separate Third World nation. When Thomas Jefferson put the phrase "life, liberty, and the pursuit of happiness" into the Declaration of Independence, he understood the obvious: liberty and the pursuit of happiness depended on life itself.

A TALE OF TWO COUNTIES

In early 2013, the *Washington Post* reported on the contrast in life expectancy in two side-by-side Florida counties. In St. Johns County, well-off retirees enjoyed playing on the area's many golf courses and tennis courts and had access to its forty-one miles of Atlantic beaches. The women of St. Johns could expect to live to eighty-three years of age, four years longer than the average expectancy two decades earlier, and the men's life expectancy of age seventy-eight was six years higher.

In neighboring Putnam County, in the center of the state, life expectancy for men and women was markedly lower, just over age seventy-one for men and seventy-eight for women. Not surprisingly, almost one-quarter of Putnam County's population was below the poverty level, compared with 9.5 percent in St. Johns County. The median value of owner-occupied housing in 2007–2011 in the counties reflected the sharp economic contrast between the two: $105,000 in Putnam and $279,700 in St. Johns. Putnam County lacks the tax base and resources of St. Johns, and social ills in Putnam are as common as the hiking and biking trails in St. Johns. Smoking, obesity, diabetes, and high blood pressure are prevalent in Putnam, where access to health care can be a problem. St. Johns has one primary-care physician for every 1,067 residents, while in Putnam there is one for every 2,623 persons. Thus Putnam County—as do many other areas of poverty throughout the nation—stands apart from the national trend toward an increase in life expectancy. But these two Florida counties reflect "a growing body of research," as reporter Michael A. Fletcher put it, "that those gains are going mostly to those at the upper end of the income ladder."[1] Thus health and a longer life go hand in hand with income and wealth.

The life-expectancy research unfortunately is ignored by those who advocate raising the eligibility age for Social Security and Medicare. These budget cutters would compound the inequality that already exists between places like Putnam and St. Johns Counties by basing their argument on the overall rise in life expectancy. But having to be older before becoming eligible would mean that lower-income recipients would get fewer benefits, because they die at a younger age (as in Putnam County) than the affluent. Thus a bipartisan proposal to raise the regular retirement age from sixty-five to sixty-seven or seventy "will enlist the working poor to pay into the system for a few more years, curtailing their retirement years to the single digits, while the taxes they pay will flow into Social Security checks for the wealthier and healthier. A senior citizen with a fatter bank account wins twice—with greater longevity and more years drawing Social Security checks—while the poor work longer, live fewer years, and collect less in benefits."[2]

The gap in life expectancy between the rich and the poor diminishes the international standing of the United States when compared with peer countries. Among them, American life expectancy is decidedly lower than in at least sixteen other economically advanced nations. A 2013 report from the U.S. Institute of Medicine, "U.S. Health in International Perspective," observes that the United States has "a longstanding pattern of poorer health" that is "strikingly consistent" from birth to old age.

Yet in 2001, the United States devoted the highest proportion of its GDP to health care—which, at 13.9 percent, amounted to nearly $4,900 person—with the next-closest nation (Switzerland) spending 68 percent of U.S. outlays. While shelling out *about half of the total for all the rest of the world combined* on doctors, drugs, and other health costs, the United States does not even make the top twenty countries in terms of longevity and a low rate of infant mortality. And the bad news goes on. Measured against thirteen other countries that are "best at keeping their citizens alive," the United States also did worst in maternal mortality and deaths by noncommunicable diseases, and ranked among the highest in deaths from diabetes and cardiovascular and communicable diseases.[3]

A panel of experts convened by the Institute of Medicine and the National Research Council registered surprise at finding that Americans under age fifty experienced poorer health and shorter lives when compared with their cohorts in other developed countries. The high rate of U.S. gun-related deaths contributed to this result among the country's young people, as did car accidents and drug overdoses. Moreover, American youths have the highest rates of sexually transmitted diseases and teen pregnancy. The panelists were shaken by learning that their nation's younger people had the lowest chance of surviving to age fifty. Older Americans had lower death rates from cancers that can be readily detected with tests and better readings on cholesterol and high blood pressure measurements than their cohorts in other countries. But the United States had the second-highest death rates from heart disease related to heart attacks and from lung disease.[4]

Throughout the report's 374 pages of text, the authors considered various explanations of "the U.S. health disadvantage," with a fragmented health care system and millions of uninsured regarded as important causes. Poverty, of course, loomed large as a contributing cause, with the United States having the highest rate of poverty among the countries studied, though that statistic failed to explain why even people well above the poverty line also fared poorly in the international comparison.

The depressing finding regarding Americans under age fifty results in part from the United States having the highest infant mortality rate among its peer countries, more than twice that of Japan and Sweden, which have the lowest rates. Although the number of U.S. infant deaths fell from 2005 to 2010, it is worth noting that in 1960, before the Great Divergence, that rate was lower than the average among peer countries. The decline started in the 1980s, as inequality began to rise.[5]

Inequality as a pervasive presence throughout society, affecting not just the poorest but also those above the poverty line and in the middle class, provides another part of the explanation for the U.S. health disadvantage. A psychosocial interpretation argues that differing rates of life expectancy and disease are not simply a function of income. "Income is merely a proxy. It is the pain of inferiority, frustration, [and] lack of autonomy and control which adversely affect the immune system and lead to greater illness, and to shorter lives: that status 'complaints' are sufficiently stressful in themselves to generate ill health and extra mortality, over and above the effects of income."[6] According to the Institute's report, when a strong middle-class society was being created in the 1950s, the United States fared much better in international comparisons of health and mortality.

Relatively poorer health in the United States reflects the circumstance that, to cope with declining wages in the 2000s, many Americans were working more hours and sleeping less. By some estimates, sleep loss amounted to an average of one or two fewer hours each night than in the 1960s. A new industry has been created to help Americans get their rest: by 2007 they were spending a "whopping"

$23.9 billion on sleep-related products, "everything from white-noise machines and special sleep-inducing mattresses to drugs for insomnia," more than double what they spent on sleep aids a decade before. Americans' use of antidepressants also shot up during the same period. A 2009 government study found that one in ten Americans take antidepressants, with women two-and-a-half times more likely to do so than men.[7]

Various causes contributed to this development, with some mental-health professionals attributing the increase to aggressive drug company advertising or overprescription by physicians. Others have drawn a direct connection with unemployment and economic insecurity. Indeed, the rush to antidepressants has engulfed Europe as well, with reports of increased usage in the United Kingdom leading to headlines such as "Prozac Nation." A 2010 U.S. study found that 71 percent of those recently losing their jobs "had experienced symptoms of depression, while more than half had experienced stress and anxiety as a result of the recession." Even worried young adults from ages eighteen to thirty tended to show adverse emotional effects. The worsening economy during the 2000s and the economic collapse of 2008–2009 clearly intensified the skyrocketing use of Prozac, Celexa, Paxil, and Zoloft (among others). But what led antidepressants to be the third-most-prescribed drugs in the United States was a complex of causes that clearly antedated the specific economic conditions of 2000–2010. Indeed, their use has risen among all income levels.[8]

The malady of "luxury fever" perhaps helps account for Americans from various circumstance running, in the words of the Rolling Stones, "for the shelter of a mother's little helper." In part the doubling of antidepressant use after 1997 came "from trying to earn enough to afford everything that was considered the hallmark of a successful life," as Robert Reich has observed.[9] But, over the long haul, persisting economic insecurity and poverty mattered more.

STRUGGLING TO MAKE ENDS MEET

"Four out of five U.S. adults struggle with joblessness, near-poverty, or reliance on welfare for at least parts of their lives, a sign of deteriorating economic security and an elusive American dream. . . . Hardship is particularly on the rise among whites, based on several measures. Pessimism among that racial group about their families' economic futures has climbed to the highest point since at least 1987."[10] These findings from an Associated Press survey reinforce recent data from the U.S. Census Bureau revealing just how widespread economic hardship has become, as well as the growing numbers of both poor Americans and those in what is now termed "near-poverty." Galloping inequality and the loss of manufacturing and other middle-class jobs has made economic insecurity commonplace for millions of Americans.

By the time white adults turn sixty, about 76 percent of them will have experienced economic insecurity. Racial and ethnic minorities are still the most likely to live in poverty, but "race disparities . . . have narrowed substantially since the 1970s." The 19 million whites who now fall below the poverty line of $23,021 for a family of four constitute over 41 percent of the poor, but nearly double that number are blacks. The Census Bureau's figure simply captures the quantity of people at a particular point in time and does not reveal the numbers—of all races—that fall into poverty for at least a year of their lives. That much higher ratio is four in ten adults.[11]

The suburbs also contain a surprise. Once thought of as a bastion of middle-class stability, suburbs are now populated by millions of families *struggling to make ends meet*. These families fall into the new census category of "near-poor," and in 2012 the number of low-income families in this grouping grew by 200,000. There are now around 50 million people technically not in poverty but with incomes less than 50 percent above the poverty line, and half of these live in the suburbs. Added to the number of poor, that makes close to one in three Americans—100 million—subsisting either in poverty or just above it. About 20 percent of the near-poor would be below the poverty line if not for government benefits.

The suburban near-poor (49% of the total) defy conservative stereotyping: an astounding 28 percent of them work full time and year round; half live in households headed by a married couple; at least one parent, and often both, is employed; and, in racial composition, nearly half are non-Hispanic white, 18 percent are black, and 26 percent are Latinos. States in the South and West had the greatest increase in the number of working poor.[12] The denigration of low-income families as "takers" by Republicans such as Congressman Paul Ryan is completely belied by the information gathered by the Working Poor Families Project. The nonworking poor are favorite targets of conservatives, while the working poor go unnoticed in the sound-bite wars. Despite being employed, this class's economic status has declined over the past ten years, and "for most working families, the 21st century has been little more than a constant struggle to maintain employment, earnings, benefits, savings, and hard-earned assets." Members of more than seven in ten low-income families and half of all poor ones were working in 2011. Many formerly held middle-class jobs but have now been forced into lower-wage work, no benefits, and little security. These families are mostly headed by racial/ethnic minorities, with 59 percent having one or more minority parent; their households now total 47.5 million Americans.[13]

A consequence of the increase in the working poor has been a rise in the number of children living in near poverty. In 2011, the number of children forming part of such families had increased by 2.5 million from four years previously, with the total rising to about 23.5 million (37%) of U.S. children (compared with about 21 million in 2007). These children also tended to experience less-stable home situations, with parents typically working in the low-wage service sector or in retail jobs requiring long hours and weekends, making child care a struggle.[14]

These conditions lead to stress for millions: the families described above, as well as the (conservatively) estimated 3 million long-term unemployed and the 9 million unemployed (as of October 2014). But the government's figure of 9 million, for an unemployment rate of 5.8 percent fails to count those workers who, after being without a job for roughly a year, simply melt away from the statistics, so the true numbers are somewhere in a black hole. The Economic Policy Institute estimates that there are as many as 5,750,000 or more "missing workers." They have given up looking, because available jobs are few; if they were actively seeking work, the unemployment rate in late 2014 would have been 9.1 percent. The black unemployment rate (11.5%) is actually more than twice the *reported* rate for whites. EPI researcher Valerie Wilson has suggested that high black unemployment results not only because of historic causes such as "last hired, first fired," but also because black people keep looking for work longer and more persistently than whites and thus are counted among the unemployed.[15]

Poor, low-income, and unemployed Americans are highly vulnerable to stress, and it affects their physical as well as their emotional health. Scientists who study this issue say that feeling helpless when facing stress makes the condition "more toxic." The sense of control over one's life "tends to decline as one descends the socioeconomic ladder, with potentially grave consequences." Science journalist Moises Velasquez-Manoff adds that people who experience the stress of poverty early in life "may show persistent effects of early-life hardship" lingering through their later life. Poverty also disrupts the social bonds that help develop an individual's ability to learn. "If you're an underpaid, overworked parent—worried, behind on rent, living in a crime-ridden neighborhood—your parental skills are likely to be compromised."[16] Thus many children living in poverty now, even if they move up economically later in life, are dealt a double dose of bad luck.

FOOD INSECURITY, OR HUNGER AMID MOOCHER AGRIBUSINESS

In 2012, according to Feeding America, 49 million households—33.1 million adults and 15.9 million children—experienced food insecurity. Feeding America is a national network of over 200 food banks and the largest charity combating hunger in the United States. It classified some households as simply "food insecure" and others as having "very low food security," which the U.S. Department of Agriculture defines as households where "normal eating patterns of one or more household members were disrupted and food intake was reduced at times during the year because they had insufficient money or other resources for food." Seven million households met that definition, and households with children reported food insecurity at a higher rate than adult-only households.[17]

Many of these families depend on food stamps or SNAP, the federal Supplemental Nutrition Assistance Program, whose budget fell by $5 billion on November 1, 2013, because increases put into the 2009 stimulus bill expired. The reduction immediately affected 47 million people, such as Rafaela Rivera and her family of four in Charleston, South Carolina. Ms. Rivera earns $10 an hour as a home health aide, and her allotment of food stamps was reduced by $36, to $420 a month. Her income and her husband's disability check go to pay rent and other expenses, and they supplement their food stamps with fresh vegetables, chicken, and other groceries from a food pantry. She knows down to the dollar the amount they will have available for food at the end of the month.[18]

On a September morning several weeks before the SNAP cuts went into effect, hundreds of people, many of them food stamp recipients, in Dyersburg (a west Tennessee town of 17,000 next to the Forked Deer River) came to the county fairgrounds for boxes of free food trucked in from Memphis, about seventy-five miles away. After several nearby factories closed, the local Salvation Army started the Feed the Need program, which helps over 700 families every month. The median household income in Dyersburg is $28,232, with 20.5 percent of the population below the poverty line, including 29.5 percent of those under eighteen.[19]

The town, built on lands once owned by the Chickasaw Indian tribe, is surrounded by corn and soybean farms, including the 2,500-acre Fincher Farms, the family concern of local Republican congressman Stephen Fincher. In the Republican wave of 2010, Fincher won election in a traditionally Democratic district by promising to reduce federal spending. Fincher sees no conflict, however, in his family's agribusiness receiving close to $3.5 million in federal farm subsidies from 1999 to 2012 (altogether, Fincher-family enterprises received $8.9 million). Representative Fincher, a Tea Party zealot, would entirely eliminate food stamps from the farm bill and justifies his position by quoting the Bible: "Anyone unwilling to work should not eat." (Mark Bittman, a food and environmental writer, pointed out that this quote from 2 Thessalonians was not directed at the poor per se but at those who had stopped working while awaiting the Second Coming.)[20]

The Finchers are relatively small fry in the big scheme of welfare for agribusiness, not in terms of the amount they receive but in relation to billionaires also profiting from agricultural subsidies. The superrich receiving direct subsidies, or those who own companies that do, have a collective net worth of $316 billion; they include Microsoft cofounder Paul G. Allen, Wall Street tycoon Charles Schwab, and Chick-fil-A owner S. Truett Cathy. The total amount of agricultural benefits such individuals actually received is probably underestimated, according to the Environmental Working Group, because federal law prohibits the disclosure of crop-insurance subsidies, another gift to agribusiness. So House Republicans have worked hard to shift more taxpayer money from trackable direct subsidies into untraceable crop-insurance ones.

Congressmen eager to give handouts to corporate interests and billionaires cultivate the pastoral illusion that they are supporting "small farmers." In fact, eight out of every ten dollars in the billions of dollars' worth of subsidies go to fewer than a hundred agribusiness firms. From 1995 to 2012, around three-fourths of this taxpayer money went to just 10 percent of the "farms." This "crazy food policy" takes money necessary for the meager subsistence of "the poorest Americans and gives it to a small group of the undeserving rich."[21]

Food stamps kept about 5 million people above the poverty line in 2012; without SNAP, the child-poverty rate would have been 3 percent higher. That same year, 15 percent of the elderly nationally faced the threat of hunger, according to the National Foundation to End Senior Hunger. Meanwhile, Douglas LaMalfa (R-CA), when joining Representative Fincher's 2013 proposal to cut $40 billion from SNAP over ten years, also quoted the Bible. LaMalfa's family rice farm, however, has received over $5 million in subsidies since 1995, aid that was necessary, he told a California newspaper, to keep struggling farmers like him "on life support."[22]

The U.S. Conference of Mayors' Task Force on Hunger and Homelessness surveyed respondents in twenty-five cities on the extent of hunger and homelessness in their cities during 2011–2012. All but four cities in the survey reported substantial increases in requests for emergency food assistance. "In 95 percent of the survey cities, emergency kitchens and food pantries had to reduce the quantity of food persons can receive at each food pantry. . . . In 89 percent of the cities these facilities had to turn people away because of lack of resources." In food-insecure households all over urban and rural America, families missed meals and consumed less food. Meanwhile, the National Alliance to End Homelessness reported that 633,782 people "were experiencing homelessness" in January 2012.[23]

INEQUALITY AND HEALTH

The riposte to the old saw that "money can't buy happiness" goes, "The only thing money can't buy is poverty." In twenty-first-century America, the contrary wits have won the day. The rich are healthier than everyone else, and their money does indeed buy happiness, as well as a longer life. It does not begrudge the rich their health to observe that inequality creates poor health and higher mortality for millions of other Americans, especially African Americans. An August 2012 survey by the Pew Research Center found that "yes, the rich are different" in being generally happier, healthier, and more satisfied with their work that those in the middle and lower classes. Indeed, 44 percent of the wealthy stated they were in excellent health, compared with 32 percent of the middle class and 19 percent of the lower classes. Even with all their fast-lane, high-flying jobs, the rich reported experiencing far less *stress*: only 29 percent felt stressed, compared with 37 percent of the middle class and 58 percent of the lower classes. Very few of the wealthy reported enduring any economic stress during the Great Recession.[24]

For low-income people who live and work in unhealthy places, stress may be the least of their problems, since they are at greater risk of mortality, experience more unhealthy behaviors, and have less access to adequate health care. The U.S. Centers for Disease Control finds large disparities in health among racial and ethnic minorities and poorer and less-educated populations. Hispanics and African Americans tend to have less health insurance, leading to higher rates of health problems. Hispanics, according to the CDC, are more likely to inhabit living and work circumstances that expose them to disease, injury, death, and disability, when compared with whites.[25]

The CDC recognizes that poverty has continuous "effects on health that are cumulative over a lifetime," and unhealthy neighborhoods and workplaces have an even more substantial influence on health than low income alone. Noncompletion of high school emerges as a strong indicator of an individual's lack of access to health care. The CDC's 2013 analysis also revealed that residence in minority neighborhoods means a sharply decreased access to chain supermarkets, which the CDC deems to be likelier retailers of less-expensive and more-nutritious foods.[26]

Excellent health insurance helps keep the rich healthier (and happier), as well as increases their ability to pay out-of-pocket expenses for hospital and physician bills that are far outpacing inflation. In contrast, middle- and low-income people can be driven into poverty by medical expenses. The Census Bureau estimates that in 2012, about 10.6 million Americans "have been left broke by premiums, co-pays, and doctor's bills."[27]

The wealthy do not tend to have "crushing medical bills." A National Health Interview Survey found that in 2011, more than one in four families experienced financial burdens due to medical care, and one in five persons lived in families having problems paying medical bills. The poor and near-poor, not surprisingly, faced the most problems and the heaviest burdens, particularly families with children aged one to seventeen or with at least one family member who was uninsured. Hispanics and blacks also fared the worst in coping with medical bills.[28]

Bills levied by hospitals and doctors are skyrocketing, especially those from specialists, with health-care costs over recent decades rising twice as fast as general inflation. The long-standing problems with the standard fee-for-service payment model are well documented; this system rewards quantity over quality, and its difficulties are compounded by perverse incentives. "In health care, doctors can stimulate demand because (a) health insurance blinds most patients to the costs of services and (b) patients often don't know whether a complex procedure is as necessary as a non-invasive one." Thus the use of multiple (and usually more specialized) services has rapidly increased. Patients often assume that more care is better care and blithely suppose that added services are free. But complications from advanced procedures can drive medical costs through the roof, and nothing is free: health-care premiums have tripled over the past decade, on average more than salary bumps.[29]

The wave of hospital mergers in metropolitan areas has also driven up costs. One study found that after mergers, hospital prices rose by 40 percent. Cartels, in the form of giant purchasing combines, are raising costs artificially by keeping generic drugs and medical devices off the market. Several of these agglomerations are buying up billions of once-inexpensive items and then accepting kickbacks from vendors. Ironically, in rural areas, at a time when the Affordable Care Act has allowed more people to have health insurance, rising prices and the closing of small community hospitals are making it difficult for poorer patients to receive emergency care close to their homes.[30]

Improved medical devices and drugs now command prices that do indeed crush patients with staggering bills. As Elizabeth Rosenthal of the *New York Times* reported, "the routine care costs of many chronic illnesses eclipse that of acute care because new treatments that keep patients well have become a multibillion-dollar business opportunity for device and drug makers and medical providers." New treatments for chronic diseases such as diabetes, rheumatoid arthritis, and colitis emerge regularly, accompanied by higher price tags. Diabetes patients in particular confront updated and possibly unnecessary devices—some soon to be obsolete—that are heavily promoted by the industry. "Complication rates from diabetes in the United States," Rosenthal observed, "are generally higher than in other developed countries."[31]

Hospitals and high-salaried specialists in dermatology, orthopedics, cardiology, plastic surgery, gastroenterology, and similar areas have come under increasing criticism. The National Commission on Physician Payment Reform—headed by doctors—has weighed in with recommendations to lower fees. Abuses by physicians who invest in expensive machinery and overuse it to drive up their incomes have been well publicized. Medical schools and hospitals are training more specialists but not enough primary-care doctors; there is a greater need for the latter, but their incomes, especially if salaried, tend to be lower. The causes of America's $2.7 trillion in medical bills are complex, but they often add up to a financial disaster for middle- and low-income people struck with serious health problems. As one physician put it, "Medical care is intended to help people, not enrich providers."[32]

Since the passage of the Affordable Care Act, health-insurance executives are being paid millions, reaching Wall Street levels, mirroring the disproportionate compensation that prevails in the United States more than in any other advanced economy. Though they opposed the ACA's new regulations, the CEOs of the 11 largest for-profit companies hauled in packages in 2013 worth $125 million. The biggest winners were Mark Bertolini, CEO of Aetna, whose compensation totaled $30.7 million—a 131 percent increase from the year before—and Centene's CEO Michael Neirdorff, whose earnings climbed from $8.5 million to $14.5 million. Meanwhile, though they are turning large profits, these companies warned patients and businesses that premiums would probably rise in 2015.[33]

In 2009, insurance executive Wendell Potter became a whistleblower and began to expose profiteering in the health-insurance industry. He has collected data showing that the more health insurers deny claims, the higher their executives' pay. Other critics of soaring CEO salaries have pointed out that the chief administrator of Medicare—which is efficient, provides better financial protection, and gets more favorable ratings from patients than private insurers—is paid less than $200,000 per year. The outsize salaries of health executives reflect in part the consolidation of the health industry over the past two decades, and the lack of competition in an unhealthy health-insurance market. Obamacare did little to address that problem.[34]

TWO AMERICAS?

The divergence in life expectancy between better-educated whites and poorly educated blacks reveals that in this realm (as in others) there are "two 'Americas,' " concludes a team of researchers at the University of Illinois, headed by S. Jay Olshansky. Once again the inequalities in the nation's educational systems result in cascading consequences. Despite the overall improvement in life expectancy for most Americans, "alarming disparities persist": the largest exists between white men and women with sixteen or more years of education and black men and women with twelve or fewer years of education. Educational disadvantage produces as dramatic a finding regarding whites of low educational status. Their chances for longer lives have actually been *declining* over recent decades. Between 1990 and 2008, white women without a high school diploma lost five years off their expected life span, and white men without a diploma lost three years. Studies by other health researchers have found similar declines and point to a variety of possible causes to explain why this group is going backwards. The least-educated whites increasingly lack health insurance and are susceptible to prescription drug overdoses, obesity, and higher rates of smoking.[35]

More young women are bearing children outside of marriage and thus are more likely to be single parents. In 2012, one in four children in the United States were being raised in a single-parent household. Although greater numbers of single-parent families (a growing number of which are headed by fathers) were white, 72 percent of black children were being raised mostly by single mothers. The poverty and low income levels of many of those single-parent families has created steep learning difficulties and other educational disadvantages for their children. Indeed, a cross-national study finds that poverty and a heritage of poverty, rather than family structure (i.e., single parenthood), is the critical variable in causing children to achieve less educationally.[36]

The persisting residential segregation endured by low-income African Americans contributes substantially to their ill health and greater death rates. Lung cancer, one of the more preventable diseases, kills more blacks than whites wherever they live, but mortality is even higher among African Americans in the most highly segregated areas. This finding holds true regardless of the socioeconomic status of blacks.[37]

In predominantly black neighborhoods, overall health and life expectancy are also affected by the disproportionate presence of fast-food restaurants and the intensive advertising of alcoholic beverages. A recent joint study on child-directed marketing by researchers at the University of Illinois at Chicago and Arizona State University found that fast-food restaurants disproportionately appeal to children in low-income black neighborhoods, rural areas, and middle-income communities. Fast-food chains in disadvantaged black sections of towns and cities appealed to children with displays of celebrities and offers of toys 60 percent more than in mostly white areas. Similarly, a study conducted at Yale University's Rudd Center for Food Policy and Obesity described the multiple venues that beverage companies use to inundate Hispanic and African American youth with advertising for sugary soft drinks. Racially targeted marketing thus plays "a fundamental role in . . . the persistence of racial inequality and . . . health disparities." Fast food and alcohol consumption are associated with negative health conditions affecting blacks and low-income families and, in these cases, "race is the demographic axis along which marketing is deployed."[38]

Dysfunction and poverty persist in these neighborhoods from their being, as economist Paul Krugman puts it, "stranded by sprawl." In a city like Atlanta, "poor and rich neighborhoods are far apart because, basically, everything is far apart." Poor neighborhoods are also distant from where good jobs are, so disadvantaged workers often literally cannot get them. A generation ago, Krugman pointed out, sociologist William Julius Wilson argued that the migration of families and enterprises out to suburbs reduced economic opportunity for the African American poor left behind, which was a major cause of the social ills too common in urban ghettos. Krugman said this should be seen "in the large context of a nation that has lost its way, that preaches equality of opportunity while offering less and less opportunity to those who need it most."[39]

THE SPIRIT LEVEL

In a remarkable book, *The Spirit Level: Why Greater Equality Makes Societies Stronger*, Richard Wilkinson and Kate Pickett meticulously analyzed social science evidence to show the multiple ways in which inequality affects the well-being and quality of life in a society. Using comparative data for the fifty richest countries as well as the states of the United States, they showed that strong relationships exist between inequality and a striking set of health and social problems. The high average national income prevailing in the United States does not prevent it from having higher levels of dysfunction.[40]

To simplify, more inequality results in (1) a lower level of trust; (2) a greater prevalence of mental illness, including drug and alcohol addictions; (3) a lower life expectancy and higher infant mortality rate; (4) more obesity; (5) more damage to children's educational performance; (6) more teenage births; (7) more violence and homicides; (8) higher imprisonment rates; and (9) less social mobility (with data for this latter category not available for U.S. states). The authors repeatedly cautioned the reader that the correlations, however statistically significant, should not be assumed to "prove" causality, but just as frequently they commented that the patterns they observed, along with related considerations, could hardly be due to chance.

Wilkinson and Pickett bring their analysis down to the level of the individual psyche to show how, in effect, "inequality gets under the skin." They argue that inequality, especially among persons of low social status who have endured stress or hardship, creates low self-esteem, and what mental-health professionals call "(self-)evaluation anxieties," an emotional process observed in chapter 3.[41]

With regard to the correlations the authors found between inequality, disease, and social dis-ease, consider the data on mental illness. There is a "strong relationship: a much higher percentage of the population suffer from mental illness in more unequal countries. Such a close relationship cannot be due to chance, indeed the countries line up almost perfectly." And when new data regarding eight rich countries became available, presented in a postscript in the book's second edition, it confirmed the earlier findings.[42] Similarly, the close ties between inequality and educational achievement, on which a consensus already exists in social science literature, was "strong enough for us to be sure that they are not due to chance." While recognizing that the most important influence on educational attainment is family background, unequal status also seems to have a determinative impact.[43]

The bottom line: the more equality there is in a country, the better the physical and mental health of its citizens, the greater their degree of civility and positive social relations, and the greater the community spirit within it.

AFFLUENZA VERSUS THE "HIDDEN PROSPERITY OF THE POOR"

The Spirit Level's exploration of inequality and social ills resulted from a question haunting many thoughtful researchers and average citizens in the early twenty-first century. Why, in societies that have achieved great material and technological successes, are populations ridden with so much anxiety and mental affliction? Along with Robert Frank's concept of "luxury fever," the answer lies in an allied, somewhat broader condition social scientists have termed "affluenza." If it were in a dictionary, its definition would look something like: "affluenza, *n*. a painful, socially transmitted condition of overload, debt, anxiety, and waste resulting from the dogged pursuit of more." Among other meanings, it suggests that as Americans consume more and more, it makes them feel worse, not better.[44] Australians have also succumbed to this disease, and critics there give it this definition: "af-flu-en-za *n*. 1. The bloated, sluggish, and unfulfilled feeling that results from efforts to keep up with the Joneses. 2. An epidemic of stress, overwork, waste, and indebtedness caused by dogged pursuit of the Australian dream. 3. An unsustainable addiction to economic growth."[45]

As an affliction, affluenza is probably preferable to poverty. It affects the middle and upper-middle classes more than the poor and near-poor. It is stimulated, as noted earlier, by local inequalities. But an older person faced with choosing to pay for food or medication, or a single parent mired in debt and wondering whether to buy groceries or pay the heating bill, would readily trade places with anyone "suffering" from affluenza and having the wherewithal to go shopping for whatever they wanted.

Conservative economists and politicians frequently make the case that life for the poor and the middle class is not as bad as the data on income and wealth inequality suggest. This argument, "the hidden prosperity of the poor" (as Thomas B. Edsall has dubbed it), maintains that the middle class and the poor do not need as much income now as they did previously to buy necessities, so they actually have more money at their disposal for discretionary spending. They, too, participate in the consumer society and partake of a cornucopia of electronic goods, furniture, utensils, entertainment, sporting goods, cable television, and on and on. In fact, they even have refrigerators!

Persisting levels of poverty, and especially child poverty, in the United States belie (in a general way) the conservative dismissal of the deprivations of poverty and the diminished buying capacity of the middle class. But specific studies of consumption by the poor and the middle class have demolished the notion of their hidden prosperity. The median real middle-class family income has lagged well behind price inflation in key items such as housing, health care, and soaring college tuitions. The poor have fared even worse, since *their incomes have shrunk* as rising prices have forced them to scrape by in ways perhaps unfamiliar to columnists who write for the *Wall Street Journal*.

As long ago as 1962, Michael Harrington, in the book that prompted presidents Kennedy and Johnson to do something about poverty (*The Other America: Poverty in the United States*), unmasked the illogic of hidden prosperity apologists by declaring that the American poor "are not poor" compared with people in some undeveloped country or the poor in the sixteenth century; rather, "they are poor here and now in the United States. . . . They are dispossessed in terms of what the rest of the nation enjoys, in terms of what the society could provide if it had the will. The live on the fringe, the margin."[46]

In 2008 then-senator John Edwards, while campaigning for the Democratic nomination for president, made current the phrase "two Americas," referring to one that is affluent, "the haves," and another that is poor, "the have-nots." The latter were no longer gaining access to the American Dream, a term recognized around the world in reference to the United States as place of opportunity, where people can rise on the social scale and prosper. But it can be realistically said that there are more than two Americas: a nation stratified into a 1 percent accumulating ever more of the country's riches; a rising 10 to 20 percent; a stagnant middle; and a large bottom fifth, constituting in some ways a third-world country, figuratively a world apart, that grows invisible with increasing residential segregation. For the latter, inequality means shorter and more unhealthy lives.

Although too many Americans are able to keep the poor out of sight and out of mind, inequality is unhealthy for the great majority, and extreme inequality demeans and injures all of society. Rent-seeking plutocrats and the political class underestimate the dangers to the country as a whole. Politicians in Washington, D.C., for the most part demagogue and misinform the public about the true state of health and health care in the United States in comparison with other countries, proffering bogus claims that Americans have "the best health-care system in the world." The research on social distance suggests that "people with the most social power pay scant attention to those with little such power," and that the most powerful are "less compassionate toward the hardships described by the less powerful." For the wealthy and privileged who lack empathy for the less fortunate, the poor are either an inconvenience or maybe a source of cheap labor.[47]

Yet, as noted in the first part of this chapter, the 2013 report by the U.S. Institute of Medicine determined that even Americans in upper-income groups are in worse health than their peers in other wealthy countries. So is inequality perhaps not very important in creating "the U.S. health disadvantage"? On the contrary, additional studies are confirming that "the factor most responsible for the relatively poor health in the United States is the vast and rising inequality in wealth and income. . . . Inequality is the central element, the up-stream cause of the social disadvantage described in the IOM report. A political system that fosters inequality limits the attainment of health."[48]

Princeton University economist Angus Deaton observes that millions around the world have "escaped" from poverty and early death into better health, yet "health inequities are one of the great injustices of the world today." Such incongruities also prevail in the United States, but Deaton finds it ironic that life expectancy for Americans "is one of the lowest among the richest countries."[49]

Wealth (and family income) in the United States has become concentrated at the top, and it continues to move upward, facilitated by a political economy decades in the making.

POLITICAL
INEQUALITY

*Political voice is more unequal in the United States than in most
comparable affluent industrialized democracies. . . . It is a persistent problem, reproduced over time and across generations. It
is a violation of basic ideals of American democracy.*

KAY LEHMAN SCHLOZMAN, SIDNEY VERBA,
AND HENRY E. BRADY, *The Unheavenly Chorus*

Economist magazine's Intelligence Unit regularly analyzes 165 independent countries plus 2 territories and compiles a "Democracy
Index." In 2012 it found "global democracy . . . at a standstill," attributed in part to the economic crisis that began in 2008, but with
many other causes affecting different regions. The United States
ranks twenty-first on the list, well behind the leaders: four Scandi-
navian countries and New Zealand. America had slipped from its
seventeenth place in 2010, mainly because of low scores in "political participation" and "functioning of government." Moreover, the
United States remained at the bottom of the "full democracy category" because it "has been adversely affected by a deepening of the
polarization of the political scene and political brinksmanship and
paralysis."[1]

Political polarization worsens inequality. In 2011, the International Monetary Fund compiled a similar, more detailed index, along
with an Income Inequality Index comparing thirty-three advanced
nations. The United States did fairly well on criteria such as well-
being (in eleventh place) and level of democracy (in fifteenth place),

but on several other measures the country fared poorly. Not surprisingly, the United States fell near the bottom in life expectancy at birth, food insecurity, and income inequality. The most arresting ranking came in the United States' stratospheric incarceration lead over the thirty-two other countries, thanks to its massive prison population, more than double the ratios of four other countries joining it as the "worst of the worst" in this category[2]

Life expectancy, prison populations, and a faltering quality of life are tied to stark inequalities of income and wealth. And inequality diminishes democracy. These conditions, along with the level of poverty and relatively weak measures to combat it, foster growing *political inequality* in the United States.

PARTICIPATION AND *CITIZENS UNITED*

"The money power may win or lose a race, even an election year," as John Nichols and Robert W. McChesney observed in *Dollarocracy*. "But its authority is not conveyed via an election result. Its authority comes from its permanent presence. . . . Its permanence is what gives the biggest spenders their power." All forms of political participation—from voting to letter writing to knocking on doors—are heavily influenced by income and education. The rise in inequality that has increased residential segregation by income and class (see chapter 2) has heightened the tendency of poor and low-income voting-age adults to stay away from the polls, let alone engage in other forms of political activity. According to recent U.S. Census Bureau data, during the lost decade of the middle class, the number of people living in neighborhoods of extreme poverty grew by one-third. This development has political consequences: "When communities were more integrated along class lines, citizens with fewer political resources were more likely to benefit from their connections to the politically advantaged." The decline of unions and other civic organizations has had a similar effect. In short, disadvantaged community context matters because it reinforces existing inequalities.[3]

The hollowing out of the electorate parallels the hollowing out of the middle class and the decline of its lower ranks into near poverty. A study by the eminent political scientist Walter Dean Burnham shows that in the cities of Boston, Pittsburgh, and San Francisco, as the middle class declined and lost good jobs, the "party of nonvoters" increased during the decades after 1960 among what he termed the "solid ethnic working-class segment." In Boston, nonvoters within that group rose from 27.1 percent in 1960, to 59.5 percent in 1980, and to 74 percent in 1988. Burnham's findings reflect the overwhelming evidence showing that people with higher incomes and more education participate in politics far more than those with less education and lower incomes. People segregated into both urban and rural low-income areas possess weaker social ties and are less likely to be targeted for political activity by parties and candidates. These citizens are also more likely to be obstructed by felony disfranchisement laws, difficulties in voter registration, and their long daily work schedules when struggling to make ends meet.[4]

Elected officials tend to ignore the policy preferences of lower-income Americans. Political scientist Larry Bartels conducted a now well-known analysis of voting by Republican and Democratic senators and found that lawmakers of both parties "are consistently responsive to the views of affluent constituents but entirely *unre-*sponsive to those with low incomes." While Democratic senators listened somewhat to their middle-income constituents but not to their low-income ones, Republicans heeded only the preferences of their affluent constituents. The more comprehensive research of Martin Gilens, covering several decades, confirmed that government seldom follows the desires of poor and middle-class Americans. Leaders' routine responsiveness to the affluent is not, tellingly, a result of higher-income people having greater rates of voter turnout or campaign involvement. Rather, "money—the 'mother's milk' of politics—is the root of representational inequality." The cost of political campaigns has skyrocketed, and politicians' obsession with getting re-elected puts them in bed with the money-givers.[5]

The 1 percent have "access" to governmental policy-makers undreamed of by ordinary folk. A study, based largely on individual interviews of members of the wealthy elite in metropolitan Chicago, revealed that not only did the rich have an amplified political voice through using their money to make contributions, but they also candidly acknowledged the ease with which they reached public officials. Many often telephoned or emailed their senator or congressman directly, while "contacts with executive department officials, White House officials, and officials at regulatory agencies, though less frequent, were also common." In response to a question regarding the purpose of these interactions, 44 percent "acknowledged a focus on fairly narrow self-interest"; about half (56%) of the contacts involved "broader matters," but the study's authors thought it possible that the frequency of the self-interested contacts was underreported. In pursuit of narrow self-interest or broader common goals, the political activity of the top 1 percent far exceeds that of average Americans: in fund raising, campaigning, attending political meetings, and enjoying direct communication with elected officials.[6]

Corporate, financial, and wealthy elites also influence Congress, primarily through lobbying. Chrystia Freeland has summarized how most plutocrats translate their "vast economic power into political influence."[7] They pursue

> political lobbying strictly focused on the defense or expansion of their economic interests. This is very specific work, with each company or, at most, narrowly defined interest group advocating its self-interest: the hedge-fund industry protecting the carried-interest tax loophole from which it benefits, or agribusiness pushing for continued subsidies. Often, these are fights for lower taxes and less regulation, but they are motivated by the bottom line, not by strictly political ideals, and they benefit very specific business people and companies, not the business community as a whole.

Even when not focused on their particular interests, wealthy elites still differ widely from the general public in their policy preferences. They tend to be intensely concerned about federal and state budget deficits and much more willing to cut social welfare programs, including Social Security and health care; they are not interested in governmental spending to improve education or provide greater access to college; and they favor tax cuts and less regulation. They explicitly oppose policies to redistribute wealth and implicitly are against enhancing political equality.[8]

Political scientists use surveys to determine the policy preferences of the rich and influential, but the national political class knows the policies desired by the top 5 percent and 1 percent without the necessity of polling. Campaigning politicians assert a passionate concern for "the American people" or "the middle class" (the latter in part because Democratic candidates, especially, do not want to be thought of as catering to the undeserving poor, i.e., African Americans and people of color). Once most are in office, however, their campaign rhetoric translates into concern for the affluent.

While the political voice of ordinary citizens has been weakening for some time, the U.S. Supreme Court, under Chief Justice John Roberts, has acted to increase the influence of the wealthy and corporations in elections and in governmental policy, making it a court for the 1 percent. The Court's five conservative members, although self-proclaimed nonactivists and "originalists" (those claiming to follow the intent of the framers of the U.S. Constitution), struck down a century of laws attempting to limit the influence of money in elections by their 2010 *Citizens United v. Federal Election Commission* decision regarding advocacy campaign expenditures (e.g., television advertisements for or against a candidate) by corporations and organizations. A system of campaigning already awash in money raised by political action committees thus became even more of a "dollarocracy." Then the Roberts court pushed the maxim that "money is speech" even further in the 2014 *McCutcheon v. Federal Election Commission* decision that allowed individual donors to contribute to as many political candidates as they desired. Previously, not only was there a maximum dollar amount for individual contributions to a specific candidate or to a political party or committee, but also a limit on the total number of dollars that could be spent on those contributions over a two-year election cycle. Shaun McCutcheon, an Alabama "coal baron" and member of the Republican National Committee, brought a suit to remove those limits. He thought it unfair that his electoral contributions were restricted to a total of only $123,000 in any two-year period.

Although the *McCutcheon* ruling retains the previous limits on the size of direct contributions to individual candidates and political committees, fat cat donors no longer have restrictions on the number of candidates to whom they can make contributions, which can reach a total of as much as $3.5 million in any election cycle. The Court's majority expressed the belief—incredible to any informed citizen—that money influences politics only when one individual directly bribes an official in exchange for a vote, a "quid pro quo." Law professor (and New York Democratic-primary candidate for governor in 2014) Zephyr Teachout has criticized the Roberts court's narrow view of corruption as "bad law . . . [and] bad for politics, and displayed an even worse understanding of history." The classical American approach to corruption, Teachout observed, engages its complexity: "Like liberty, speech, or equality, corruption is an important concept with unclear boundaries. It refers to excessive private interests in the public sphere; an act is corrupt when private interests trump public ones in the exercise of public power, and a person is corrupt when they use public power for their own ends, disregarding others."[9]

Let's put this in a perspective other than that of hypocritical politicians who claim that the *McCutcheon* decision allowed more people to participate financially in election campaigns. In 2012, just 1,715 donors bumped up against the aggregate dollar limit on giving to political party committees, and another 600 plus hit the limit for individual candidates. Thus the Court has given a tiny slice of wealthy donors even greater political voice and influence over politicians. The editors of the *New York Times* commented that *McCutcheon* "is less about free speech than about giving those few people with the most money the loudest voice in politics."[10]

POLITICAL POLARIZATION

Economist magazine's Intelligence Unit wisely mentioned "a deepening of polarization" as a factor diminishing American democracy. Partisan polarization has also contributed powerfully to the rise of economic and political inequality. Since the 1970s, income inequality has widened steadily, as has political polarization, and time-series graphs show that measurements of each track closely together. As with the decline of unions, life expectancy, and rates of sickness, is there a cause-and-effect link between political polarization and the rise of inequality?

In *Polarized America: The Dance of Ideology and Unequal Riches*, Nolan McCarty, Keith T. Poole, and Howard Rosenthal find that this "causality can run both ways." Political polarization currently intensely divides political elites. In the U.S. Congress it manifests itself in a Republican Party that has moved far to the Right. When they are in the majority, Republicans enact policies—such as the tax bills of the Reagan and George W. Bush presidencies—that increased inequality; when in the minority, Republicans act to block changes to the status quo. Thus, "the political process [now] cannot be used to redress inequality that may arise from nonpolitical changes in technology, lifestyle, and compensation practices."[11]

Voters are not as polarized as political actors, but they have become increasingly aligned by income within the two major parties, with Democrats drawing support from lower-income groups and Republicans attracting the votes of the affluent and the rich. The high-income Republican nexus reinforces that party's swing to the Right, especially in the South and among white evangelicals. The rise in immigration has created another force for polarization. Republican elites and their constituencies adamantly resist redistribution policies that might ameliorate inequality, especially among the Hispanic and Asian immigrant poor, and, above all, they oppose aid to undocumented immigrants.[12]

DISENFRANCHISEMENT

Voter turnout in the United States is lower than in most other advanced countries. Australia's mandatory voting produces high turnouts, but elsewhere they result from greater ease both in registration and in access to the polls. Nonvoting in the United States occurs disproportionately among low-income and less-educated citizens. It does so because any difficulties involved in registering and voting fall to a much greater extent on them than on people who have higher incomes and are better educated.[13] Some individuals simply choose to avoid voting and lack interest in public affairs. (I know a well-educated older woman in a high-status job who does not vote and will have nothing to do with politics.) Others (across various income and educational levels) dislike the prospect of standing in line when large numbers of voters turn out in highly contested elections. Among high school dropouts (the group most disengaged from voting) and those in poverty there is also distrust, alienation, and disengagement from political life, and disadvantage clearly plays a role in creating these attitudes.

There has been a powerful mythology about voting and elections in the United States. Political scientist Richard K. Scher described this idealized version as having "few if any problems associated with casting ballots. . . . You register, you show up at your polling place on election day, you vote, the ballot is recorded and counted, and you go about your business. The whole process is said to be mechanical, neutral, and value free."[14] Scher commented that this sanitized picture of voting and elections ignores a long history—and continuation—of episodes of voter suppression, fraud, and manipulation of the rules by political elites to disenfranchise targeted voters or render their votes meaningless.

In America's first decades, many states imposed property or taxpaying requirements on adult white males that depressed voter turnout among the lower classes, although these restrictions were gradually eliminated. Gerrymandering, however, had an impact on voters across the socioeconomic spectrum. The word dates back to 1812, when partisan Jeffersonian Republicans won control of Massachusetts, a state that in the early republic usually voted for the Federalist Party. In an effort to consolidate power, the Jeffersonians created weirdly shaped legislative districts designed to dilute Federalist voting strength and maximize their own. Federalists gibed that one of those districts looked like a salamander, and when Jeffersonian governor Elbridge Gerry signed the bill, Federalists dubbed the distorted district a "gerrymander."

The practice continued, and spread, especially during times of close partisan balance between the two major parties. During the fierce political battles of the late nineteenth century, midwestern parties (and even factions of parties) created grossly malapportioned legislative districts with the same goal in mind: to tilt the outcome of elections in their favor and make the votes of opponents worthless. In the twenty-first century, multitudes of African American and Hispanic citizens, who now usually vote for Democrats, have been concentrated into heavily minority Congressional districts to dilute Democratic voting strength in other districts.[15]

In recent election cycles, Republicans and corporate PACs have strategically poured campaign funds into state elections and increased the number of state governments they control. They then moved to enact often-controversial policies that have stalled in Congress and to aggressively redraw—gerrymander—Congressional- and state-district lines to their advantage. By 2010, this campaign improved their occupancy of governors' offices from 23 to 29 and gave them majorities in 25 state legislatures, up from 14. Democrats, late to this game, began to play catch up, resulting in most state governments becoming thoroughly partisan. Meanwhile, the Supreme Court's 2010 *Citizens United* decision unleashed millions of dollars of "outside spending" into state and even local elections, and funds then were shuffled around by party committees, PACs, and big-spending oligarchs. Contrary to the conservative bloc of Supreme Court justices' willfully naïve assumption "that unlimited spending would happen *independent* of candidates, . . . outside spenders are working 'hand in glove' with candidates," according to the Brennan Center for Justice. After the 2014 midterm elections, Republicans dominated 68 out of 98 state legislative chambers, a legislative high. And across the country corporate-tax cuts, deregulation, voter ID laws, reductions in unemployment benefits, antichoice laws, and gerrymanders proliferate.[16]

For most of the previous post-1945 period, the Democrats had followed a similar policy, so much so that in 1987, then president Ronald Reagan declared "gerrymandering . . . a national scandal. . . . To look at the district lines shows how corrupt the whole process has become." Yet after several Supreme Court decisions regarding gerrymandering by the Rehnquist and Roberts courts' conservative majorities, who routinely favor Republican agendas, it has been said that those justices "have never seen a gerrymander they didn't like."[17]

Irregularities in presidential elections in 2000 and subsequently have gradually punctured two myths: that America enjoys elections that ensure equal access to all voters, and purity of the ballot box. The difficulties that Americans encounter in casting their votes are far from being isolated to a few locations; they are widespread and exist in rich and poor states, from New York to Mississippi, and from California to West Virginia.[18]

Republican control of many state governments has led also to systematic efforts to increase the disenfranchisement of African

Americans, Hispanics, Asians, people of color generally, the elderly poor, the young, college students, and the least well-off. It has been a concerted movement, thus far partially successful, to take away the vote of millions in the coalition who helped elect the nation's first black president in 2008.[19]

Well before the Bush/Gore presidential contest in 2000 and its aftermath, the structural impediments to a higher voter turnout and full and free voting bore down unequally on the groups now targeted by a new barrage of restrictive laws. In all but one state currently, voters must go through a separate registration process before voting, as most states do not allow election-day registration. Ease of registering in nations such as Britain, Canada, France, and Germany helps produce far larger turnouts that are not socioeconomically skewed toward the affluent. In 2000, voter turnout in the United States was 15 percent higher in states with same-day voting and registration.

The National Voter Registration Act of 1993 (the "Motor Voter Law") made registration easier for millions, and some states have taken it upon themselves to encourage those poor who receive public assistance to register. Still, in 2010 more whites were registered to vote (67%) than blacks (58.1%), Asians (34.1%), and Hispanics (33.8%), though the latter group was steadily increasing in both registering and voting. According to Census Bureau data, voters encountering the most problems with registering were in the eighteen-to-twenty-four age group (probably mostly college students) and, to a lesser extent, the twenty-five-to-forty-four age cohort. The basic fact remains, however, that "the nation's outdated registration system is among the most significant barriers to voting, resulting in the disenfranchisement of millions of Americans during every federal election." And those millions include disproportionate numbers of racial and ethnic minorities, low-income citizens, the elderly poor, students, and those with disabilities.[20]

THE ASSAULT ON VOTING

After 2010, Republican legislators in two-thirds of the states introduced various bills requiring voters to show photo IDs at the polls, curtailing early voting periods, demanding proof of citizenship, making registration more difficult, and tightening already draconian rules for former felons to regain their voting rights. According to the Brennan Center for Justice at New York University Law School, a nonpartisan public policy institute, as many as 11 percent of U.S. citizens—21 million people—do not have a current photo ID. Going into the 2012 election, restrictions on voting had been enacted in nineteen states by means of twenty-five laws and two executive actions.

Republicans pretend that voter ID laws are needed to prevent election fraud through impersonation. Yet detailed studies of alleged instances of voter fraud consistently have found them to be "extremely rare." One such study turned up a "handful of substantiated cases." An analysis of allegations of impersonation in Missouri in the 2000 election yielded typical results: six substantiated cases of ineligible voters out of 622,329 voters in St. Louis City and County, and a total 2,361,586 voters in the state, a rate of .0003 percent. A photo ID would not have prevented any of those six from voting. Richard L. Hasen, a professor of law and political science at the University of California, Irvine, has not found "a single election over the last few decades in which impersonation fraud had the slightest chance of changing an election outcome—unlike absentee ballot fraud, which changes election outcomes regularly." Hasen adds, "Let's face it: impersonation fraud is an exceedingly dumb way to try to steal an election." Republicans promoting voter ID laws have expressed little interest in curbing the real problem—absentee ballot fraud—while voter ID laws create additional harm by distracting attention from needed reforms.[21]

Courts and the U.S. Justice Department blocked or blunted several voter ID laws. In two states, citizens voting in referenda repealed the restrictions. In 2000, among many other malicious election practices, Florida's Republican state election officials became notorious for sending out a list purporting to contain the names of 57,000 felons that needed to be purged from the voting rolls. A Republican-connected software company had compiled the list, 90 percent of which was inaccurate. Half of the names on the list were African American and legal voters. In 2012, the state compiled an even larger list of 180,000 potential illegal voters, 75 percent of whom were blacks or Hispanics. After the state claimed to have found 2,600 suspicious names, it sent them to county supervisors, some of whom found the list "sloppy" or "embarrassing" and, as in 2000, refused to cooperate.[22]

In 2012, Florida's Republican legislature and Governor Rick Scott enacted legislation that severely limited the activities of civic-minded voter registration groups, leading the League of Women Voters to discontinue their registration drives; eliminated a long-standing policy of allowing voters to update a new address at the polls; reduced the early-voting period from two weeks to one; and, most egregiously, eliminated the Sunday before Election Day as an early-voting day.[23] But these efforts backfired.

Ever since the Voting Rights Act of 1965, the congregations of Florida's black churches traditionally have gone to the polls on the Sunday preceding Election Day. So in 2012 a wave of indignation and determination swept through black churches, and religious leaders launched a "Souls to the Polls" campaign. On the Sunday eight days before the election, which was the beginning of the early-voting period, black ministers shortened the length of their services, issued ringing calls to their parishioners to vote, and organized fleets of buses to get their now-aroused congregants to the polls. Any doubts regarding the intent of the Republican restrictions dissipated when Jim Greer, a dissident former chair of the state Republican Party, "blew the lid off what he claim[ed] was a systemic effort to suppress the black vote." Although Greer was on trial for corruption charges and in a vengeful mood toward his party, in a 630-page deposition he confirmed what many Democrats and minority voters believed.[24]

Despite Republican voter suppression, the nation's first black president carried Florida in 2012, as he had in 2008, though by a reduced margin of under a percentage point, compared with a 2.82 percent margin in 2008. Blacks and Hispanics voted heavily for Obama in 2012 (95 and 60 percent, respectively), with Latinos up three points from 2008, constituting 17 percent of all voters. Again, however, the election "reinforced Florida's image as being incapable of conducting fair and efficient elections." A study by the Advancement Project, in cooperation with the *Orlando Sentinel*, confirmed that polling places in counties with the highest concentrations of black and Hispanic voters had the latest closing times (the period extending past the official 7:00 p.m. end of voting so all those already in line were able to vote), which meant they had the longest lines and waits to vote. In Lee County, some citizens did not get to vote until after midnight. In Miami-Dade County, the wait at some precincts extended to a reported seven hours. The voting experience deviated wildly across the state, with many counties experiencing multiple problems and others having the voting go smoothly.[25]

Voters all over the United States encountered problems and delays at polling places, both during early-voting periods and on Election Day. Yet everywhere, those stains on the electoral process disproportionately troubled Democratic voters, notably black, Hispanic, Asian, and younger voters. "Long Lines, Demands for ID, and Provisional Ballots Mar Voting for Some," declared a headline in the *New York Times*. A number of voters encountered not just confusion but also intimidation and harassment, notably people of color.[26]

In his 2013 State of the Union address, President Obama mentioned these problems and added, "By the way, we have to fix that." He then singled out one of his invited guests in the audience, Desiline Victor, a 102-year-old Haitian American woman who waited four hours to vote on October 27 (during the early-voting period) at the North Miami Public Library polling place. A subsequent report by Florida's secretary of state, Ken Dentzer, concluded that "most, if not all [Florida] counties, experienced longer wait times than in previous elections due to . . . the record number of voters, a shortened early-voting schedule, inadequate voting locations, limited voting equipment, and a long ballot." Dentzer did not mention that he had been a strong supporter of Florida's new voting restrictions, including the "shortened early-voting schedule," and his claim that "all" counties experienced long waits was egregiously wrong.[27] (Obama later appointed a bipartisan commission that is still studying but not fixing the problem—yet.)

Another analysis of voting in Florida counties in 2012 confirmed that wide deviations existed in the voting experience. The study also made clear that in *some* favored locales, polling places operated smoothly, with minimal waiting times, few or no challenges to voters or removals from the rolls, and no citizens forced to use provisional ballots. These more-affluent precincts received no harassment from the Tea Party squads that made their intimidating presence felt in some minority precincts in a few states.[28]

Chapter 5 opened with a "tale of two counties" in Florida: coastal St. Johns County, inhabited by affluent retirees and others enjoying the good life; and next to it inland Putnam County, with a high poverty level, lower life expectancy, greater rates of disease, and inadequate educational and health facilities. According to a county-by-county analysis of the administration of Florida's 2012 elections, the voting experiences of the two counties mirrored their standing on the scale of quality of life. Based on a thorough examination of variables such as waiting time, the number of registered voters removed from the rolls, the amount of provisional ballots cast, and the number of rejected provisional ballots, St. Johns ranked number one in having the best election administration. Putnam was the second-worst-performing county, with the second-lowest percentage of overall voter registration, the third-lowest level of voter turnout, and the third-most voters removed from registration lists. St. Johns County had the highest turnout of voters in the state, at 83.6 percent, while Putnam, at 57.6 percent, fell well below the state average. The average waiting time for voters after the polls closed was not available for Putnam County, but for St. Johns that figure was a convenient zero minutes.[29]

Thus stark socioeconomic and demographic inequalities, creating a very different quality of life in Putnam and St. Johns Counties, found a hardly coincidental parallel in their political inequality. While the ability to exercise the right to vote in many Florida counties was impeded by restrictive state laws making it harder for people to vote, as well as by poor election administration, those obstructions bore down hardest on low-income and disadvantaged voters.

THE ASSAULT ON VOTING, CONTINUED

In the wake of the 2012 election embarrassments, legislators of both parties in ten states introduced bills to improve the ability for eligible citizens to register and vote; during the next two years, fifteen states made voter registration easier. Even Florida's Republican governor called for remedies, and in May the state legislature increased the number of early-voting days from eight to fourteen and provided many more sites that could be used as polling places. The secretary of state, however, announced that his office would resume efforts to review and purge voter-registration rolls, using a federal database to identify noncitizens illegally registered to vote. Nearly 12 million vote in Florida elections. Yet a scrutiny of registered voters in 2012 identified 207 *possible* noncitizens on the rolls, and only 39 of them had actually voted.[30]

Still, the nationwide Republican assault on voting continued unabated, aided significantly by the five-man conservative and partisan majority on the U.S. Supreme Court. In June 2013, in a suit brought by Shelby County, Alabama, the Roberts Court struck down a provision of the 1965 Voting Rights Act that required nine states and certain counties in other states, all with a history of discriminatory practices, to "preclear" any new voting restrictions with the U.S. Department of Justice or the D.C. Circuit Court of Appeals. Both the Mississippi and Texas legislatures enacted strict voter ID laws within twenty-four hours of the Supreme Court's decision. Before and after the ruling, legislators in thirty-three states introduced ninety restrictive bills, and by the end of the year, nine states enacted new restrictions on voting, with others pending throughout the country. North Carolina's harsh new law, challenged by the Department of Justice, required all voters to have a photo ID, cut down the early-voting period, eliminated same-day registration during early voting, and placed restrictions on which provisional ballots could be counted.[31]

These restrictive laws, passed largely by Republicans, aim directly at reducing minority and African American voting. Political scientists at the University of Massachusetts, Boston, analyzed laws enacted between 2006 and 2011 and found their "proposal and passage . . . highly partisan, strategic, and racialized." Legislatures with increased numbers of Republicans or in states with a newly elected Republican governor tended to enact restrictive measures. Strikingly, these states also had larger African American and noncitizen populations, and *higher minority and low-income turnout in 2008.* On *The Daily Show* (a satirical late-night television program), Don Yelton, a precinct chair in Buncombe County, North Carolina, succinctly revealed the motivation behind such legislation: if that state's new voter ID law "hurts a bunch of lazy blacks," then "so be it." Yelton candidly added that the new law "is going to kick the Democrats in the butt."[32]

The new "voter fraud" law in Texas is one of the most severe and went into effect the day early voting began for the state's November 5, 2013, elections. It requires Texans to show one of a limited number of government-issued photo IDs to vote. Acceptable IDs include expired gun licenses from out of state, but not social security cards and student IDs. The League of Women Voters has pointed out that the law creates excessive difficulties for women, since 34 percent of women voters nationally do not have an ID that carries their current name.

Elizabeth Pottinger of Tyler, Texas, was born in West Texas in 1917 and had lived and voted without a problem in East Texas for over thirty years. Since she no longer drives, her driver's license has expired, and local authorities have twice refused her attempt to register to vote. The second time they asked for a birth certificate and then would not accept that, either. Her daughter, Ann Finster, said that she had ordered a certified copy of her mother's birth certificate but was told that she also needed to bring marriage verification. Since Pottinger is over sixty-five (ninety-six, to be exact), she will be able to vote by mail, but to vote in person she needs to assemble multiple proofs of her identity. If she does decide to do that, a local cab company has offered to bring her and others who lack transport to the polls. As 2013 ended, the U.S. Department of Justice had once again brought suit against the Texas voter ID law.[33]

During 2014, Republicans in red states continued their campaign to disenfranchise groups that lean Democratic—African Americans, Hispanics, the young, the poor, many elderly—and it paid dividends in the midterm November elections. According to initial calculations by the Brennan Center for Justice, the margin of victory in several hotly contested races came very close to the probable margin of disenfranchisement. This pattern appeared in the elections for U.S. Senate in North Carolina, and for governor in Kansas and Florida; in Virginia, the state's strict new photo ID law contributed to Democratic Senator Mark Warner winning by just 12,000 votes.[34]

Political inequality is not going away; it is growing. Disenfranchisement continues. The brazen, anti-democratic war on millions of

Americans' "sacred" right to vote—a partisan, class, racial, and ethnic war on the most disadvantaged—constitutes a betrayal of what generations of Americans fought for, and many died for.

PRISONS AND FELONS

Nationally, an estimated 5.85 million Americans are denied the right to vote because of laws that prohibit voting by people with felony convictions. Felony disenfranchisement is an obstacle to participation in democratic life which is exacerbated by racial disparities in the criminal justice system, resulting in 1 of every 13 African Americans unable to vote.

THE SENTENCING PROJECT WEBSITE

Felony disenfranchisement is a legacy of the vicious treatment of freed African Americans after the Civil War, who became subject to arrest and sent to work camps, factories, and mines as convict labor on the flimsiest of excuses. Blacks also lost their right to vote if they committed what Southern states viewed as "Negro crimes," such as theft, arson, or obtaining money under false pretenses, while whites who committed "white crimes," including murder, did not lose their right to vote. In a 2003 history of felony disenfranchisement, Angela Behrens, Christopher Uggen, and Jeff Manza observed that in many Southern states, the percentage of nonwhite prison inmates nearly doubled between 1850 and 1870. "By restricting the voting rights of a disproportionately nonwhite population, felon disenfranchisement laws offered one method to avert 'the menace of negro domination.' " Although the remaining laws "are race neutral" on their face, the racial-containment strategies in their origin persist in what some scholars term "laissez-faire racism," in contrast to the earlier, explicit Jim Crow racism. In the twenty-first century, the authors found, a larger nonwhite prison population "significantly increases the odds that more restrictive felon disenfranchisement laws will be adopted."[35]

The United States maintains "the most restrictive [felon disenfranchisement] rules in the democratic world . . . and no state has ever completely abolished a felon disenfranchisement law." Most states instituted cumbersome methods of appeal by which former felons might regain full civil status. Kentucky imposes a lifetime denial of the vote and "one of the most burdensome" methods of appeal for restoration in the nation. In 2006, the state had the sixth-highest rate of disenfranchisement in the country and the highest rate of African Americans denied the vote: one out of every four black adults.[36]

Over the past two decades, there have been countervailing movements among the states, with some removing or liberalizing felon disfranchisement and others remaining rigidly punitive. Since the 2000 election fiasco, Florida's lifetime denial of the vote to former felons has added to the state's blemished reputation regarding elections. Nearly one-fourth of African Americans of voting age in Florida are denied the vote by the felon law. In 2007, the state moved to restore voting rights for felons who had served their sentences, but in 2011, Republican governor Rick Scott reversed those reforms and returned to a more stringent denial of the vote to former felons. A similar reversal took place in Iowa. Democratic governor Tom Vilsack, by executive order, reenfranchised former felons, and this action was upheld by the Iowa Supreme Court. But his successor, Republican Terry Branstad, restored felony disenfranchisement.

In 2006, Rhode Island voters approved a referendum amending the state constitution to allow former felons to register to vote after their release from prison. In 2013, Virginia governor Bob McDonnell, a Republican, issued an order for the automatic restoration of voting rights for nonviolent felons, but only on a person-to-person basis; the election of a new Democratic governor later that year offered hope for further liberalization. In Delaware, the legislature not only moved to restore voting rights to nonviolent offenders but also to institute same-day registration. Still, despite progress since the 1990s, as the editors of the *New York Times* put it, "barring offenders from the polls remains a pronounced and malignant problem in the South, . . . especially for blacks."[37]

DEFERRED MAINTENANCE AND INEQUALITY

In a candid exploration of "why our election system is failing," Heather K. Gerken suggested that "our election system suffers from the same problem that afflicts the nation's physical infrastructure:

deferred maintenance." Neglect and delay have led to collapsing bridges, bursting dams, sudden sinkholes, and washboard city streets. Likewise, the infrastructure of elections is failing because of too few voting machines, many obsolete machines, poorly trained poll workers, not enough polling places, and routine partisan interference. According to Gerken, localism and the decentralization of authority have created a national patchwork of administration that invites political parties to exploit systemic weaknesses. But partisan machinations are hardly the only reasons why voters of all racial, ethnic, and income groups encounter difficulties in casting a free and fair ballot.[38]

To make the point that partisan interference may not always be at the root of long lines of voters, Gerken deliberately examined Ohio's notorious conduct in the 2004 presidential election and the highly partisan behavior of Ohio's secretary of state, Kenneth Blackwell (who was also cochair of George W. Bush's reelection campaign in Ohio). She described Blackwell's brazen efforts at voter suppression by making both registration and voting more difficult, including discouraging voter-registration drives and even specifying the weight of paper to be used for registration forms. Criticism from members of his own party caused him to rescind the latter requirement. In 2006, when he ran for governor while still serving as secretary of state, he again tried to hinder voter-registration drives until stopped by a state court. Gerken cautiously concluded that "his actions created the appearance of political bias."[39]

Much more can be said (although not mentioned by Gerken) regarding Blackwell and the circumstances that led many Democrats to believe that the Ohio election was not just mismanaged, but "stolen." Before the 2004 election, Blackwell spent $100 million on electronic voting machines and, during the election, outsourced Ohio's vote count to a facility in Chattanooga, Tennessee, that also housed the servers for the Republican National Committee. In a 2003 message inviting 100 wealthy friends to a Republican fundraiser, Walter W. O'Dell, chief executive of Diebold, the company that made the machines, said that "I am committed to helping Ohio deliver its electoral vote to the president next year." Subsequently, Blackwell himself boasted of helping to "deliver" Ohio for President Bush's reelection. An investigation of the election, commissioned in 2007 by Ohio's new secretary of state, Democrat Jennifer Lee Brunner, found that "critical security failures were embedded throughout the state's voting systems." The December 2007 report by an independent consortium of companies found Ohio's vote count "vulnerable" and easily manipulated by "fairly simple techniques." As if all this were not enough, by 2007, in violation of federal election law, fifty-six of Ohio's eighty-eight counties had lost or destroyed all or part of their 2004 election records.[40]

Yet Gerken asserted that *deferred maintenance* must be taken into account. In Franklin County, Ohio (which includes Columbus, the state capital), people waited in line to vote for as long as five or six hours in 2004, and many left in frustration. The then director of the Franklin Board of Elections, Matt Damschroeder, a Republican, whom Gerken described as a well-respected "straight-shooter," claimed that his own mother waited in line for two hours. Further, Franklin's Board was bipartisan, and the real villain probably was not Damschroeder but a lack of funding for additional machines to prepare for the expected high voter turnout in 2004. Gerken did not insist on this explanation, but she lamented the inadequacy of infrastructure that fuels controversy and accusations of partisan mischief that may not be warranted.[41]

Gerken's *Democracy Index* objectively diagnoses problems, but she surely also knows that in 2004, long lines developed in Cleveland's black precincts because of too few voting machines. What her book does not consider is that inequality and class directly or indirectly influence decisions about election infrastructure, as they do for all manner of public facilities, from parks to roads to playgrounds. Underfunding—resulting in election snafus and challenges to voter legitimacy—are more likely to be experienced by racial and ethnic minorities and low-income voters.

Dirty Tricks
Deferred maintenance disproportionately affects vulnerable groups in the electorate, even members of the military on active duty. These same voters are also likely to be the target of "dirty tricks," which Richard Scher, in *Politics of Disenfranchisement*, calls "gaming the

system." In state and local elections, both Republicans and Democrats engage in underhanded ruses to keep the opposition's supporters from the polls, while Republicans on the national level seem to resort to them more often.

Dirty tricks have existed ever since there have been elections. Political scientist Richard Franklin Bensel's *The American Ballot Box in the Mid-Nineteenth Century* described not only the physical and spatial features of voting in eastern cities, but also the mayhem often attending elections as rival partisan gangs used fraud, violence, intimidation, bribery, and trickery to win elections. One such practice was known as "cooping," which involved locking up supporters in large rooms and keeping them there with food—and whiskey for all-night drinking—until the polls opened the next day. Less benignly, it meant gangs of ruffians confining opposing voters in sheds or cellars, handling them roughly, sometimes relieving them of their purses, and not releasing their victims until the election ended.[42]

In the twenty-first century, less-direct but often equally effective methods of "cooping" have become known as "caging." In 2008 in Virginia, fake Board of Elections fliers advised Republicans to vote on November 4 and Democrats to do so on November 5 (the election was held on the fourth). In Philadelphia, an anonymous flier circulated in low-income and African American neighborhoods erroneously telling voters they could be arrested at the polls if they had outstanding arrest warrants or unpaid parking tickets. Months earlier in Colorado, a letter was sent to out-of-state college students falsely warning them that they could not register to vote if their parents claimed them as dependents in another state.

In more recent examples of scams, in 2012 elderly voters in Florida, Virginia, and other states reportedly received phone calls advising them they could vote over the phone. African American and Latino voters claimed to have received calls informing them that car insurance and registration would be checked at the polls in order to vote. Clear Channel (a right-wing radio network) erected billboards in minority areas in Ohio and Wisconsin that warned "Voter Fraud Is a Felony." After protests, the billboards were removed.[43]

The trick that led to the term "caging" has been practiced for some time, but it gained notoriety in Florida in 2004. The Bush-Cheney reelection campaign sent thousands of registered letters marked "Do not forward" to voters' homes, principally to African Americans and college students, who tend to vote Democratic, but also to soldiers away at war and to the homeless. If the postal service returned mail to the sender because the recipients were no longer at the address used, those voters could get taken off the registration rolls. (The term caging, according to a Republican practitioner, derives from storing the returned letters on steel shelves or in files.) In 2012, a Tea Party–affiliated Florida organization, Tampa Vote Fair, updated the practice by both intimidating former felons into not voting and setting a "trap" for others who may not have had their franchise restored by encouraging them to vote, thus establishing grounds for claiming voter fraud.[44] Dirty tricks can happen to any voter, rich or poor, but more often chicanery targets the most vulnerable.

Bosses and Voters in the New Gilded Age

In the New Gilded Age, even many voters with good jobs who are not necessarily minority or low-income individuals experience constraints on their ability to express their political voice freely, as well as coercion to vote as their boss wants. In recent years, employers have increasingly exploited their position of power to sway the votes of both blue-collar and white-collar workers. Corporate bosses defend these efforts as attempts to persuade, but critics see the unequal relationship of employer and employee as intimidation.

The attempt to control the votes of Americans in dependent circumstances reaches back deep into the nation's history. Tenant farmers and others in rural communities often followed the lead of local landowners, creditors, or merchants. Lawyers who acted as debt collectors stood at the polls, in the interest of their creditor employers, and watched how debtors voted. In the early and mid-nineteenth century, foremen sometimes marched factory workers to the polls. Well into the twentieth century, large-scale businesses told their employees that if they voted the wrong way (usually meaning if they did not vote for a Republican), they might lose their jobs because of the economic consequences of electing the wrong candidates or party.

Since the 2010 decision of the U.S. Supreme Court's conservative bloc in *Citizens United*, corporate executives have revived the practice. That decision, which exponentially increased the power of money in elections, contained another, less-recognized feature that injected more inequality into elections. *Citizens United* struck down laws banning employers from discussing political opinions with employees. Thus the 2012 presidential campaign began to resemble those of the First Gilded Age in the nineteenth century, when the Republican Party's corporate allies launched widespread efforts to influence the voting of their employees. Across the country, letters, fliers, emails, and "information packets" went out from corporate offices to workers, often suggesting and sometimes explicitly recommending for whom they should vote.

Koch Industries, headed by brothers David and Charles Koch, reactionary billionaires and Tea Party supporters, sent out a packet to 30,000–50,000 employees of their Georgia Pacific subsidiary, containing materials identifying Republican candidates favored by the company and warning of the harmful economic consequences of Obama's reelection and the Affordable Care Act. Other CEOs echoed this theme of their businesses being damaged, with possible consequences resulting for employees through reduced paychecks or lost jobs. David Seigel, chief of Westgate Resorts, a time-share empire, informed his 7,000 employees that "if new taxes are levied on me, or my company, as our current president plans, I will have no choice but to reduce the size of this company." Arthur Allen, of ASG Software Solutions, said those who voted for Obama would have only themselves to blame if the company needed to undergo drastic changes. The 30,000 employees of Cintas, a uniform supply company (that obtains many federal contracts), received a letter from their CEO warning that health-care reform "amounts to the single largest tax on Americans and business in history" and that overregulation was "suffocating many companies."[45]

The U.S. Chamber of Commerce encouraged businesses to distribute political advice in paycheck envelopes, and in June 2012, presidential candidate Mitt Romney, in a conference call organized by a business lobby, urged executives to make "very clear to your employees what you believe is in the best interest of your enterprise and therefore their jobs." Since *Citizens United*, none of these activities are illegal, but labor union officials believe that suggestions about employees losing their jobs cross the line into intimidation and do, in fact, constitute a veiled threat to fire workers, which *is* illegal. Business groups counter that labor unions have long engaged in similar activities and also advise their members how to vote. But labor unions cannot fire a worker. Adam Skaggs, senior counsel at the liberal Brennan Center for Justice, argues that "there is an unavoidable power disparity between management and employees."[46]

The Business Industry Political Action Committee, a lobbying group originally organized in 1963, has stepped up its efforts over the years to realize its slogan, "Electing Business to Congress," and "to marshal the vast army of American workers" to support policies and candidates favored by their employers. A study commissioned by BIPAC found that "workers tend to trust bosses' recommendations." No doubt some do, but backlash may result, with other workers resenting the intrusion into their lives outside of their jobs, as well as the creation of a workplace where they feel as though they are under surveillance and inhibited from expressing views contrary to those of the company. Nevertheless, no American citizen should be intimidated into believing that they might lose their job if they do not follow their employer's wishes. Alexander Hamilton, one of the most conservative of the nation's founders, warned that "in the main, power over a man's support is power over his will."[47]

From the early republic through the nineteenth century and well into the twentieth century, at various times and places employers told their workers how to vote. With the rise of unions from the 1930s on, and during the Shared Prosperity era from the 1940s to the 1970s, bosses' interference in the workplace diminished. In the New Gilded Age of the "dollarocracy," weak unions, and rising inequality, political coercion is rising again and taking America back to the late nineteenth century.

THE FRACTURING
OF AMERICA

Strong metaphors of society were supplanted by weaker ones.
Imagined collectivities shrank; notions of structures and power
thinned out. Viewed by its acts of the mind, the last quarter of the
[twentieth] century was an era of disaggregation, an age of fracture.
DANIEL T. RODGERS, Age of Fracture

Pundits and social scientists have often doubted that Americans care about inequality of income and wealth—understandably, because citizens' attitudes toward inequality are complex and often contradictory. So are attitudes toward the rich. In a 2012 survey by the Pew Research Center, 46 percent said that most rich people "are wealthy because they know the right people or were born into wealthy families," yet 43 percent stated that the rich became so "mainly because of their own hard work, ambition, or education." A recent Gallup poll found that 54 percent said they believe income inequality is "an acceptable part of our economic system." On these grounds, the Pew researchers concluded that their findings indicated that "the issue of class conflict has captured a growing share of the national consciousness."[1]

Really? At one time the phrase "class conflict" contained Marxian overtones of the proletariat rising up against capitalists, and, at a minimum, suggested often-violent strikes, work stoppages, picketing, and militant unionism in pursuit of higher pay, better working conditions, and the right to negotiate with employers. It meant organized labor seriously confronting organized capital for its fair share of the fruits of its labor. Class conflict fed the industrial strife of the late nineteenth century, marked by huge and often violent strikes. Automobile and steel workers, coal miners, and other blue-collar laborers exuded class consciousness in the fierce sit-down strikes and battles to unionize in the Great Depression of the 1930s. Now the phrase, along with the much more common, politically useful, and content-empty phrase "class warfare," has come to mean anything from criticism of the rich to a demand for a tax higher than 15 percent on hedge-fund income—a suggestion that inflames plutocrats even when proposed by billionaire Warren Buffet. In the Pew Research Center report, "class conflict" is so diluted that it refers merely to an opinion diffusely spread through the American populace. Meanwhile, the term "class warfare" has become embedded in contemporary Republican rhetoric as a way to deflect criticism of tax breaks for corporations and the wealthy and for any other advantage conferred on the "haves."

That the shibboleth of class warfare actually intimidates many Democrats reflects not just a centrist caution (to put it kindly) but also ignorance of Americans' attitudes toward inequality. In fairness, researchers have found a pervasive ambivalence in public opinion, what political scientist Larry M. Bartels called a "failure to connect the dots." In an influential 2008 book, Bartels concluded that while "considerable concern about inequality [exists] among ordinary Americans," it coexists with "a good deal of ignorance and misconnection between values, beliefs, and policy preferences [that prevail] among people who pay relatively little attention to politics and public affairs, and a good deal of politically motivated misperception among better-informed people."[2] Recent studies, however, describe a public intensely attuned to inequality of income and wealth and its consequences. Yet poll findings regarding inequality may rise and fall, depending on events and how questions are asked. Inequality nevertheless persists as a debilitating American fracture that rends the social fabric.

AMERICANS *DO* CARE ABOUT INEQUALITY

Americans have always cared about inequality, but their concern has awakened during eras when disparities in income have grown and intensifies when they perceive that extreme inequality is blocking opportunity. The present is one of those times, as poll after poll since the onset of the latest recession (and note that Bartels' book was published in 2008) has shown rising levels of disapproval with both inequality and the unfairness of the economic system. In a January 2014 Pew / *USA Today* poll, 65 percent said they thought inequality had grown in the past ten years, a view "shared by majorities across nearly all groups," including 61 percent of Republicans. Sharp partisan differences have emerged over how much government should do to redress inequality, but a majority of Republicans favor at least some governmental action to reduce poverty. By a margin of 63 to 36 percent, Americans are of the opinion that the country's economic system unfairly favors the wealthy.[3]

"Yet, amidst these skeptical views," the Pew Research Center report adds, "most Americans continue to believe that opportunity exists for those who make the effort." Thus the Pew analysis follows a conventional formula of positing an opposition between inequality and a persisting belief in opportunity—a faith that might be regarded as part of the bedrock of American secular religion.

But as Leslie McCall has argued in a recent, path-breaking book, Americans care about income inequality because "they view it as an indicator of unfairly restricted economic opportunities," and when they see opportunity being blocked by inequality, "it intensifies their opposition to it." McCall's analysis of decades of survey data led her to conclude that "a substantial share of Americans . . . have long desired less inequality, and sometimes much less." Many become more critical of inequality when recessions turn into recoveries that are "perceived as benefiting the rich at the expense of the rest of Americans." And she determined, after a systematic inquiry into the media's coverage of inequality, that it has been no apologist either of rising inequality or for those McCall describes as "the undeserving rich." Rather, media reports on inequality have sharpened critical awareness.[4]

In an early 2009 poll specifically addressing inequality and opportunity, 71 percent agreed that "greater economic inequality means that it is more difficult for those at the bottom of the income ladder to move up the ladder." Near-consensus has prevailed—97 percent in that poll—that everyone should have equal opportunity to get ahead. These results testify to the persistence of Americans' belief in opportunity, despite the reality of the United States now having *less upward mobility* than other advanced nations (see chapter 2). But while most Americans "do indeed have deep faith in the American Dream and in the rewarding of hard work and skill," political scientists Benjamin I. Page and Lawrence R. Jacobs caution that "we should not automatically assume that this tranquilizes the public against caring about inequality."[5]

THE FOUNDERS CARED ABOUT INEQUALITY

From its beginning in an anticolonial revolution, what made the new United States *exceptional* was its lack of extremes of wealth and poverty, at least among its white European population. Alexis de Tocqueville, a French aristocrat who visited the United States in 1831–1832, wrote one of the earliest and classic analyses of what made the nascent republic so different from European countries. He published his observations in *Democracy in America*, commenting that nothing in the United States struck him "more forcibly than the general equality of conditions. . . . The more I advanced in the study of American society, the more I perceived that the equality of condition is the fundamental fact from which all others seem to be derived, and the central point at which all my observations constantly terminated."

The American Revolutionary/founding generation valued what de Tocqueville later observed, and they expected it to continue. They were not "democrats" in the modern sense, or egalitarians disposed to erase social distinctions; nor were they unrealistic about the inevitability of inequality. They accepted slavery, as well as limits on who should be regarded as citizens and as members of the polity.

James Madison, the Father of the Constitution, recognized the reality of social distinctions during the ratification debates in the well-known "Federalist Paper Number 10," where he described the causes of "faction" and "party," which he thought of as great evils. The causes were "sown in the nature of man," he wrote, in "different opinions" concerning religion, government, and society, as well as in the struggle for "preeminence and power. . . . But the most common and durable source of factions has been the various and unequal distribution of property."

These words are often quoted either to justify the existence of inequality or simply to genuflect to its inevitability. But doing so ignores Madison's resolute rejection of political inequality, which he tied inextricably to combating extremes of wealth and poverty. True, the clash of different interests was (and is) unavoidable, but in a newspaper essay published in 1792, Madison offered remedies to combat "the evil of parties" (which today might translate roughly into the much-abused pejorative "special interests").[6]

1. By establishing political equality among all.

2. By withholding unnecessary opportunities from a few, to increase the inequality of property, by an immoderate, and especially an unmerited accumulation of riches.

3. By the silent operation of the laws, which, without violating the rights of property, reduce extreme wealth towards a state of mediocrity, and raise extreme indigence toward a state of comfort [ponder that last phrase for a moment].

4. By abstaining from measures which operate differently on different interests, and particularly such as favor one interest at the expence [sic] of another.

5. By making one party a check on the other, so far as the existence of parties cannot be prevented, nor their views accommodated. If this is not the language of reason, it is that of republicanism.

Thus Madison deemed it possible to prevent an "immoderate, and especially an unmerited accumulation of riches" and to reduce extreme wealth "without violating the laws of property." If this seems radical—Madison assumed that in the normal course of events, laws would "reduce extreme wealth toward a state of mediocrity, and raise extreme indigence toward a state of comfort"—he later expressed even more startling views on suffrage.

During 1821, as Madison prepared his notes to publish his *Records of Debates in the Federal Convention of 1787*, he confided "his more mature view" that "the right of suffrage is a fundamental Article in Republican Constitutions." Restricting the right to vote to "freeholders" (owners of land)—a policy Madison once accepted—he now rejected as obviously wrong. "It violates the vital principle of free Govt. that those who are bound by laws, ought to have a voice in making them."

After examining several possibilities as to how voting might be restricted, Madison concluded: "Under every view of the subject, it seems *indispensable* that the Mass of Citizens not be without a voice, in making the laws which they are to obey, & in chusing the Magistrates, who are to administer them, and if the only alternative be an equal & universal right of suffrage for each branch of the Govt. and a confinement of the entire right to a part of the Citizens, it is better that those having the greater interest at stake namely that of property & persons both, should be deprived of half their share in the Govt. than that those having the lesser interest, that of personal rights only, should be deprived of the whole."[7]

To be clear, Madison was not recommending restrictions on any class of persons—though he and the other framers of the U.S. Constitution gave no thought that the right to vote might be given to women, African Americans, or Native Americans (and he and other founders were not enthusiastic about the lowest order of white men voting, either). Rather, he preferred in theory that if anyone should be deprived of the vote, let it be the wealthy elite and not the great mass of "middling," or ordinary, citizens.

Madison's preference that "the Mass of Citizens" possess the franchise was an issue that divided the framers of the Constitution. But his and others founders' inclusive vision contrasts sharply with the reality of political voice in the twenty-first century (see chapter 6). Low-income citizens, marginalized minorities, the elderly poor, and others are blocked or hindered in their exercise of political voice. Money rules the political as well as the economic realm, and ordinary citizens do not have the resources to compete with billionaires and powerful corporations. In the simple matter of voting, the affluent enjoy less-obstructed access to the polls on election days, while low-income citizens encounter obstacles, and the very rich possess an inordinate political voice.

In 2003—well before the economic collapse of 2008, before Occupy Wall Street, and before recent attention to inequality—the American Political Science Association appointed a Task Force on Inequality and American Democracy. In its published report, the APSA committee stated:

> Generations of Americans have worked to equalize citizen voice across lines of income, race, and gender. Today, however, the voices of American citizens are raised and heard unequally. The privileged participate more than others and are increasingly well organized to press their demands on government. Public officials, in turn, are much more responsive to the privileged than to average citizens and the less affluent.

"The exercise of political voice," members of the committee declared elsewhere, "goes to the heart of democracy."[8]

PUBLIC OPINION

The founders of the American republic viewed public opinion as an indispensable correlate to the system of checks and balances written into the Constitution. As James Madison wrote in 1791, "public opinion sets bounds to every government, and is the real sovereign in every one." In his 1796 "Farewell Address," George Washington declared: "Promote then, as an object of primary importance, institutions for the general diffusion of knowledge. In proportion as the structure of a government gives force to public opinion, it is essential that public opinion be enlightened." Thomas Jefferson's startling remark about newspapers is well known: "Were it left to me to decide whether we should have a government without newspapers, or newspapers without government, I should not hesitate to prefer the latter." Newspapers informed the enlightened citizenry treasured by Jefferson, and *an enlightened public opinion* helped maintain a society free of gross concentrations of power or wealth.

In the twenty-first-century United States, public opinion matters very little, either in the routine functioning of government or on substantial matters of public policy. In recent decades, members of Congress have grown obsessively dependent on contributors to their reelection campaigns, which are largely corporate interests working through political action committees. Thus there has been "a steady increase in response to the affluent" that is not matched by politicians' attentiveness to the preferences of the less well-off. Political campaigns have grown astronomically expensive. Politicians need huge campaign war-chests to get reelected; and they respond to the activist millionaires and billionaires, PACs, lobbyists, and special interests that give them money.[9]

Meanwhile, interest groups, lobbyists, and "astroturf pressure groups" (corporate-funded organizations posturing as grassroots citizens) labor constantly to manufacture public opinion. While the correspondence between what majorities of Americans want and what legislators do has been episodic and never very close, the disconnect has never been greater. A recent study of "who gets what, when, and how" reached conclusions confirming what most average citizens believe to be true: economic elites and organized business groups "have far more independent impact upon policy change than the preferences of average citizens." Political scientists Martin Gilens and Benjamin I. Page find that the preferences of average Americans are implemented only when they happen to coincide with those of elites. But when "a majority of citizens disagrees with economic elites or with organized interests, they generally lose." Indeed, the preferences of average Americans "appear to have essentially zero . . . impact upon policy change."[10]

Majorities of Americans want their government to do more to lessen unemployment, create jobs, and reduce inequality. While "a measurable divide" on governmental interventions exists between Democrats and Republicans, even conservative scholars find a "broader consensus" in the general public regarding the responsibilities of government. "People in the United States want their government to do things. . . . A conservatism that more or less advocates leaving people on their own (libertarianism) is a very tough sell to the public."[11]

Page and Jacobs likewise found that "seven out of ten of all Americans, including large majorities of Republicans and of the affluent, told us that they would *not* like to live in a society in which government does nothing except provide national defense and police protection so that people would be left alone to earn whatever they could. . . . The idea of government-guaranteed food, clothing, and shelter has been favored by large majorities of Americans since at least 1964, and is embraced across lines of class, race, and party." Moreover, despite the antitax fervor whipped up by the Tea Party, majorities of all Americans, including Republicans and the affluent, express a willingness to pay more in taxes for the purposes of supporting early-childhood education in kindergarten and nursery school and ensuring a good education for all Americans.[12]

But Congress consistently disregards public opinion on major issues. Even before the 2000 presidential election—in which Al Gore, the winner of the popular vote, went down to defeat first in the Electoral College and then by a Supreme Court decision—"solid majorities of Americans" (73% or 86%, in different polls) favored abolishing the Electoral College and electing the president by popular vote.[13] In 2001 and 2003, when Congress passed the Bush administration's tax cuts disproportionately favoring the wealthy ("large, regressive cuts in income and estate taxes"), polls showed that firm majorities of Americans preferred to retain those taxes and use the money from them to bolster Social Security and Medicare or reduce the budget deficit. In 2003, a Harris poll found 65 percent describing that year's tax cuts favoring the wealthy as "unfair."[14]

Before Barack Obama took office and the subsequent passage of the Affordable Care and Patient Protection Act, about two-thirds of all Americans, including a majority of high-income earners and nearly half of all Republicans, favored "national health insurance, financed by tax money, that would pay for most forms of health care." A majority (54%) even favored "a national health plan, financed by taxpayers, in which all Americans would get their insurance from a single government plan."[15] When President Obama and a Democratic Congress took on health-care reform, a single-payer system and an extension of Medicare benefits were taken off the table from the start, in deference to lobbyists from the insurance and drug industries. Then the proposed act went through a messy Congressional process that resulted in a jury-rigged plan closer to that favored by conservative think tanks.

Public opinion also matters little when it comes to the enactment of modest gun-control legislation. In April 2013, just four months after the horrific massacre at an elementary school in Newtown, Connecticut, the U.S. Senate voted down a bipartisan compromise bill requiring background checks for gun purchases on the Internet and at gun shows. While fifty-four Senators voted for the measure, sixty votes were needed to break the Senate filibuster and allow the bill to pass. Polls showed 86 percent or more of the public in favor of the proposed bill, but the gun manufacturers' lobbyists and militant gun-ownership groups prevailed. Although the mass shooting in Newtown produced only a modest increase in public support for other control measures, 65 percent believed ownership of assault weapons makes the country more dangerous, and 56 percent favored banning bullets designed to explode or penetrate bulletproof vests.[16]

A March 2013 Gallup poll showed that 72 percent of Americans, including a majority of Republicans, would support a major, federally financed infrastructure-repair program to create 1 million jobs. When the question omitted mention of government spending, those favoring a program similar to the New Deal's Works Progress Administration rose to 77 percent. Similar majorities favored a federal jobs-creation law designed to produce more than a million new jobs (72% and 75%, respectively, with and without government spending mentioned).[17] The U.S. House of Representatives has not considered such measures.

Public opinion does not function as an informal check on government, as the framers of the Constitution once expected. But the founders were realistic enough to know that public opinion could be manipulated, and they would perhaps not be surprised at the extent to which "political leaders, organized interest groups, large corporations, or others can manipulate the opinions of ordinary citizens."[18] In 1791, scarcely three years into George Washington's first administration, Secretary of State Thomas Jefferson recoiled from the economic program promoted by Treasury Secretary Alexander Hamilton and approved by the president. Jefferson and his ally in Congress, James Madison, established a newspaper in Philadelphia (then the nation's capitol) to counter the influence of an existing pro-administration paper.

The degree to which public opinion is *informed* rather than *manipulated* today seems to be an open question. Many citizens get information from what the great early-twentieth-century political analyst Walter Lippmann termed the "pseudo-environment." Too many disheartening polls reveal high levels of public ignorance and misinformation regarding both key issues and the simple mechanics of how the government functions. When that circumstance is combined with the great disparity of resources available to ordinary citizens compared with those exercised by the top 10 percent and 5 percent working through the corporate–financial–political elite axis, the result is even more likely to be manipulation rather than information.[19]

Proposals to raise the federal minimum wage from its current $7.25 an hour are another example of an issue with strong public support that has encountered obstinate political resistance in Congress. Nationally, more than two-thirds of Americans approve of raising the minimum wage to $10.10 an hour. In a January 2014 Pew Research Center poll, 73 percent overall were in favor of the raise. Even in the very red and anti-Obama state of Kentucky, 61 percent favored raising the minimum wage, with support highest in the economically depressed counties of eastern Kentucky that have voted Republican in recent elections.[20]

Most studies of the economic impact of raising the minimum wage have found that it will not cause significant job loss and will boost the economy (see chapter 4). But the Employment Policies Institute, "a widely quoted research center" in Washington, D.C., argues otherwise. (This organization should not be confused with the Economic Policy Institute, a liberal think tank also based in Washington, D.C.) The Employment Policies Institute churns out "academic" reports warning that a higher minimum wage will cost workers jobs and increase poverty. This nonprofit "institute" is run by a public-relations firm headed by Richard B. Berman, an advertising executive whose clients come from corporate America. Berman and Company, located in an office building four blocks from the White House, occupies the same floor as the so-called institute and seems indistinguishable from it. Berman's firm represents restaurant chains that have been in the vanguard of opposition to a higher minimum wage.[21]

Think-tank studies from the political Right or Left probably do not matter much in Appalachian counties where decent-paying coal jobs have been disappearing. All their residents need to do for *information* is to look around and talk to family, friends, or neighbors.

Members of Congress might be more sympathetic to public opinion and the plight of minimum-wage workers if they themselves had experienced poverty or economic insecurity; instead, they are far from it. By early 2014, the House of Representatives—"the people's house"—reached a milestone. Over half of its members were millionaires; the median net worth of Congressional representatives had risen to $1.5 million. Their wealth distanced them from ordinary Americans, as did their backgrounds. As Nicholas Carnes has shown in *White-Collar Government: The Hidden Role of Class in Economic Policy Making,* "people from what we might call the *working class* are rare in American political institutions, especially compared to their numbers in the nation as a whole." Members of Congress, state legislators, and city councilors are likely to come from better-off white-collar families and have a college degree. Carnes found that voting by class in Congress has been "remarkably stable since World War II." The consequences have been unfavorable to working-class Americans, while "business regulations are more relaxed, tax policies are more generous to the rich, social safety-net programs are stingier, and protections for workers weaker."[22]

White-collar government usually results in more inequality. But state legislatures that contain working-class representatives tend to enact progressive legislation, such as more spending on social safety nets and higher taxes on corporations. Local governments are even more diverse and the same pattern emerges: "Where workers govern in greater numbers, income inequality is less severe."[23]

THE CONSTITUTIONAL STACKED DECK

Any discussion of inequality cannot avoid mentioning features of the Constitution that do not treat all Americans equally in their capacity as political beings. Created in the eighteenth century as a pragmatic compromise to promote national development, in the twenty-first century it presents barriers to the lessening of economic inequality and its social ills.

The U.S. Senate, a primary locus of inequality, is one of the most undemocratic upper chambers in any federal system. The delegates to the 1787 Constitutional Convention hotly debated granting each state two seats in the Senate. Tradition has it that this feature resulted from a compromise between the big and small states, but in recent years historians have instead attributed it to demands by Southern states for greater security for their "peculiar institution." Slavery, though never mentioned in the Constitution, enjoyed other protections and advantages as well, such as the provision giving the slave states additional representation in the House, equal to three-fifths of their slave population.

In 1789, population differences among the states were not very large, about twenty to one, but in 2010 the ratio between the most- and least-populous states had become sixty-six to one. California, teeming with 38 million residents, contains as many people as the twenty-two least-populous states put together. A vote in Wyoming, coming in last with only half a million people, is worth sixty-six times that of a Californian. All federal systems have some degree of unequal representation, but as the eminent political scientist Robert Dahl put it, "the degree of unequal representation in the U.S. Senate is by far the most extreme." And this bias in the framework of government presently tips the scales toward conservative reactions and inequality.[24]

The Senate's undemocratic structure carries over in diluted but significant fashion to the Electoral College, with each state entitled to "a number of electors equal to the whole number of Senators and Representatives" from that state. The Electoral College itself has been a source of controversy and undemocratic outcomes, since the presidency has been won in the Electoral College by a candidate with the minority of popular votes eighteen times from 1824 to 2000—one out of three elections (although several involved third-party candidates).[25]

The overrepresentation of rural, low-population states, together with the rise of partisan polarization in Congress, has created something of a procedural monster: the filibuster, which is nowhere to be found in the Constitution. Before 1975, if a Senator wished to delay (or derail) a vote on a bill, that person needed to be present and engage in a marathon of incessant speechifying, a tableau immortalized in the 1939 Frank Capra film, *Mr. Smith Goes to Washington*. At that time, a two-thirds vote was needed to end a filibuster. But after 1975, with the threshold for calling a halt to this tactic lowered to three-fifths, the Senate made it easier to launch a filibuster. Any Senator could initiate one without needing to take to the floor to talk at length; the rules change replaced the "talking filibuster" with a "virtual filibuster." A senator does not even need to be present to initiate a filibuster, and the three-fifths vote requirement (sixty out of a hundred senators) can keep a law from being enacted, even though a majority (albeit short of sixty) may favor the bill. With sixty votes now usually required to enact important laws, the Senate has become dysfunctional, and the United States grows more unequal as progressive legislation is blocked. Since the Constitution is very specific about when supermajorities are required—for example, the ratification of treaties—the framers clearly did not intend for them to become a routine part of the legislative process.[26]

The ascent of the filibuster over the past three decades reflects the increase of polarization in America (see chapter 6), and this legislative device both parallels and drives the growth of inequality. From 1920 to 1970 filibusters averaged about one a year. They began to uptick in the 1970s, with Democrats and Republicans (even more so) increasingly invoking them in the 1980s. From the 1990s on filibusters actual and threatened (and obstructionist points of order) have skyrocketed. During President Obama's first term Republican filibusters broke all records, well over two hundred. Hundreds of bill that have passed the House, many with bipartisan support, have died in the Senate.[27] Most of the policy infrastructure that has nurtured inequality of income and wealth, meanwhile, remains in place.

The nationalists who wrote the Constitution had witnessed firsthand "the dangerous consequences of minority obstruction" during the drafting of the Articles of Confederation (1781–1787), when unanimous consent of all the states was needed to do business. Alexander Hamilton, no fan of democracy, nevertheless called a minority's "negative [effect] upon the majority (which is always the case where more than a [simple] majority is required for a decision)" not a "remedy" but a "poison." "If a pertinacious minority can control the opinion of a majority, respecting the best mode of conducting it, the majority, in order that something may be done, must conform to the views of the minority, and thus the sense of the smaller number will overrule that of the greater, and give it a tone to national proceeding. Hence, tedious delays, continual negotiation, and intrigue; contemptible compromises of the public good."[28] Perhaps this seems familiar to observers of the U.S. Congress in the twenty-first century.

The "trivialization" of the filibuster in recent decades for merely "partisan and parochial uses" has done real harm to democracy and society's well-being. The authors of a full-scale study of what was once "a procedural weapon of last resort" maintain that it now "is used in ways that most people would argue are contrary to the nation's welfare. . . . The fit between a policy outcome on a filibustered measure and the popular will is often merely coincidental." In terms of perpetuating inequality, the origin of the term seems appropriate: from the Dutch *vrijbuiter* ("freebooter") and French and Spanish words originally meaning "robber," "looter," and "pirate."[29]

Small states—most of them heavily Republican—use the U.S. Senate filibuster more often and to their material advantage. In 2008–2010, as the federal government spent billions in stimulus grants to respond to the financial crisis, a disproportionate share went to small states. The top five per capita recipients were states with just one House member. As noted in chapter 3, the states of the Old Confederacy receive far more in federal benefits than they pay in taxes, setting up an exchange between red-state takers and blue-state givers. Nine out of the top ten states that receive more in federal benefits than are paid in federal taxes are small, mostly red states.[30]

Over the past four decades, filibusters have maintained or increased income inequality: in 1978 by epically defeating a critical labor-reform bill strengthening unions (despite a Congress full of Democrats); by preventing action on raising the federal minimum wage over a number of years; by blocking the Clinton administration's proposed health-care reform in the 1990s; and, in 2009–2010, by taking single-payer health care off the table, preventing the expansion of Medicare, diluting the Affordable Care Act, and weakening regulation of the financial industry. The small-state weapon of the filibuster in the federal system sabotages representative government and promotes inequality.[31]

THE DECLINE OF "THE COMMONS"

In a brilliant essay, Jonathan Rowe, a contributing editor at *Washington Monthly* and *Yes!* magazines, described "the Commons" as "the wealth of nature and society that precedes both the market and the state. The rivers, the oceans, and atmosphere; the sidewalks and public spaces; the vast array of languages and species; the processes of democracy; the accumulated store of knowledge—these and more make up the foundation of human well-being and, indeed, of life itself." Although Rowe focused mostly on the "expropriation" of resources, he also pointed to a consequence of the enclosure, or privatization, of "the assets we own" by corporations and the rich: "No less important, the social glue begins to crack." The "we" disappears. "The fact that rich and poor can stroll together in Boston's Common or New York's Central Park is significant both literally and metaphorically."[32]

The contemporary extreme of inequality is dissolving the social glue. The poor become walled off in both physical and emotional ghettos. The very rich—the plutocrats—insulate themselves from contact with their fellow citizens and find more in common with the very wealthy in other countries. Indeed, those for whom price is no object abhor mingling with those beneath them, who consist of practically everyone else. Rowe tells of Norbetto Foretti, head of a company that builds yachts for the superrich, who explains why this upper echelon likes the privacy of their floating mansions. "Rich people can go to a beautiful hotel and pay $3,000 a night for a suite," Foretti said. "The trouble is, when you go down the elevator, you are in the lobby with people who paid twenty times less. My clients don't like that."

Increasingly, the superrich are avoiding ordinary Americans by leaving the country. Their departures have increased since 2008, when the Internal Revenue Service clamped down on tax evasion through moving one's assets overseas. Although small numbers of individuals had been exiting before then, from 2008 to 2009 that figure rose from 231 to 743. American expatriates increased even more after the 2010 Foreign Account Compliance Act and the UBS scandal that opened Swiss bank accounts to greater IRS scrutiny. Fears of further obligatory income disclosures on tax forms and more-stringent filing requirements—not a rise in taxes—resulted in exoduses of 1,534 of the wealthy in 2010; 1,781 in 2011; 932 in 2012; and a record 2,999 in 2013. Not all of those who are giving up their U.S. passports are superrich; some are responding to "onerous financial reporting and tax-filing requirements" recently imposed by the IRS. Yet the growing numbers of those leaving reinforce Chrystia Freeland's point in *Plutocrats* that the über-rich have more in common with the wealthy in other countries than with their fellow citizens and, for some these days, their former fellow citizens. International banks like Credit Suisse, Freeland noted, pay close attention to "the difference between the world's rising middle class, which remains rooted in and defined by nationality, and the increasingly shared and global character of people at the very top."[33]

Within the United States, withdrawal from public into private space increasingly takes the form of gated communities. These enclaves were already on the rise in the 1970s, when satirist Edwin Newman lampooned advertising that appealed to home seekers with "exciting living concepts (a bold concept and landmark for our times, where the facilities created a total concept of leisure and an ambience that would become synonymous with my way of life and an integral part of my exciting lifestyle)."[34]

By 2007, an estimated 4 million people (and perhaps as many as 8 million) lived in approximately 30,000 of these private enclaves, which have controlled entrances and their own security systems. Some gated communities emphasize recreational activities (notably golf), while the more expensive and secluded are "prestige" habitats. Although boosters and developers trumpet the blessings of "genuine mutual community, the means they use are sometimes far less communal than controlling." Edward J. Blakely and Mary Gail Snyder, the authors of *Fortress America: Gated Communities in the United States*, concluded that these living spaces (and some do look like fortresses) reflect the fact that "America is an increasingly unequal place." Blakely and Snyder commented that the residents of gated enclaves are engaged in a form of "civic secession."[35]

In their retreat from wider civic ties, these withdrawers tend to concentrate their loyalties on their circumscribed "common-interest community," an umbrella term covering "planned single-family home developments, gated and walled communities, condominiums, and housing complexes, all under the aegis of a homeowners' association." Society beyond is on its own. For the self-removed, "we're *not* in this together."[36]

In the hills above San Diego, California, sits the affluent town of Rancho Santa Fe (population around 3,100), where the estimated median income approaches $170,000. California has endured a historic drought for three years now, but the lawns, landscaping, putting greens, and horse pastures of Rancho Santa Fe have not thirsted for sprinkling and irrigation water. In September 2014, the town earned the distinction of being the state's "biggest water hog," with each household using 584 gallons a day, nearly five times the average for coastal Southern California. During the preceding year, the district's use fell 1.5 percent, compared with 10.3 percent statewide. (To be fair, Rancho Santa Fe had cut its use by 20 percent since the last drought in 2007.) Ironically, shortly after a *New York Times* story drew unwanted national attention to Rancho Santa Fe, new numbers from the State Water Resources Control Board showed the enclave had dropped to third place in California water consumption, behind Palm Springs and a wealthy area above Anaheim. In general, upscale compounds in Los Angeles typically used more water and cut back less during droughts, according to a study by researchers at the University of California, Los Angeles. High-income households ignored fines and increased water bills, while in low-income neighborhoods in East Los Angeles, residents used fewer than 50 gallons per day. Poorer people using less water may not necessarily be more public-minded than richer people using excessive amounts, but the contrast fits with findings that the more wealth families accumulate, in general the less concern they have for others.[37]

Increasingly, the affluent can buy not just extra water in a drought but a range of special services unavailable to those without resources. The Affordable Care Act has helped to accelerate the rise of "boutique doctors" or "concierge medicine" (the latter term applying to the viewpoint of physicians). By paying a yearly fee, ranging from lows of around $1,500 to $25,000 or more, patients can escape crowded waiting rooms, and days or weeks of delay for an appointment, with same-day access available by phone. In Louisville, Kentucky, Dr. Robert Ellis used to have 8,000 patients, spending very little time with each one. Now he has just 600, and he says that people who are busy or chronically ill benefit the most from paying his yearly fee. (Of course, they are also affluent.) Concierge medicine is growing fast, rising by 25 percent between 2012 and 2013, with 4,400 physicians classified as boutique doctors. They are happy to be avoiding third-party insurers and paperwork, and their patients enjoy immediate access, while critics wonder what will happen to everyone else.[38]

For Harvard University philosopher Michael J. Sandel, concierge medicine is one symptom of a broader pattern that has changed the United States from having a "market economy" to a country that is a "market society." "We live in a time when almost everything can be bought and sold"—even places in line. Motorists in some cities can pay to drive solo in fast lanes restricted to high-occupancy vehicles; lobbyists use line-standing companies, who hire homeless people to wait in line overnight on Capitol Hill, to get them into a Senate or House hearing room; amusement parks sell passes to allow customers to jump the queue, and first-class and business-class air travelers have long been able to board before everyone else. Sandel also mentions the number of private guards, now consisting of twice the number of public police officers, hired by security firms in the United States and Britain, a reflection in part of the rise in gated living spaces.

One wonders what Sandel would think of recently launched enterprises in San Francisco that use apps to auction off public parking spaces—"Monkey Parking"—and make reservations at popular upscale restaurants and then sell them at premium prices to bidders, who go to the restaurant under a false name. This sophisticated form of scalping only benefits those who can afford it and has spread across the country to the East Coast.

In a society where practically everything is for sale, inequality deepens, and "life is harder for those of modest means." Sandel adds that the commodification of everything corrodes values and social relations, since "a price on the good things in life can corrupt them." He does not begrudge the ability of the rich to purchase expensive toys like yachts and sports cars, "but as money comes to buy more and more—political influence, good medical care, a home in a safe neighborhood rather than a crime-ridden one, access to elite schools rather than failing ones—the distribution of income and wealth looms larger and larger."[39]

As money continues to buy almost *everything*, equal opportunity declines and inequality rises. A market society acts as a powerful solvent to "social glue," that is, Americans' sense of their imagined community. The public interest and a feeling of community diminish, and values become distorted, in a society defined by who can buy what, where the wealthy purchase ever more privileges—like those enjoyed by an aristocracy—unavailable to the great majority of Americans.

CONCLUSION: CONSIDERING THE UNDESERVING, POOR AND RICH

Contemporary forms of organized politics have their origin in the struggle against capitalism and the particular tyranny of money. And surely in the United States today it is the tyranny of money that most clearly invites resistance: property/power rather than power itself. But it is the common argument that without property/power, power itself is too dangerous. State officials will be tyrants, we are told, whenever their power is not balanced by the power of money. It follows, then, that capitalists will be tyrants whenever wealth is not balanced by a strong government.

MICHAEL WALZER, *Spheres of Justice*

The fiftieth anniversary of President Lyndon B. Johnson's declaration of a War on Poverty sparked a debate on the effectiveness of federal programs in reducing poverty. Conservatives, like U.S. Representative Paul D. Ryan (R-WI), believe that the persistence of the poverty rate at around 15 percent of the population means that government programs not only have not worked but have prevented that rate from falling. This critique serves the political purpose of forcing proponents of the governmental safety net to expend their energy defending it rather than working for fundamental reform. Meanwhile, the most vehement critics of antipoverty and redistributive programs advance the interests of the wealthy and powerful ("property/ power") in public policy without hesitation, much less compunction.

ANTIPOVERTY PROGRAMS: EFFECTIVE?

Supporters of antipoverty efforts point out that LBJ's "war" reduced those afflicted by poverty from 19 percent of the population in 1964 to about 11 percent by the mid-1970s. They add that the rate would have been much higher without public assistance, and that the U.S. Census Bureau's ongoing (and arbitrary) measure of what is poverty leaves out benefits from programs that help the poor, such as SNAP and the Earned Income Tax Credit, with the latter program alone reducing the number of people living in poverty by about 5.5 million people.[1]

Those in Congress who argue that antipoverty programs are ineffective engage in a self-fulfilling prophecy by cutting programs that *do* make a difference. The real debate should not be about the effectiveness of public assistance, but instead center on the fact that the government's poverty index remains too low. Historian Michael B. Katz has described the haphazard way in which this measure came into being in 1963 (and was regarded as insufficient by the official who originally devised it) and then was revised—but not updated— through the years, instead resting "on unrealistic assumptions about the relationship of food to income." Economist Angus Deaton lamented the U.S. government's failure since 1963 to recalculate the poverty line; had that been done, the "poverty rate would have risen *more rapidly* than actually happened." Deaton described the American poverty line as *"absolute."* But in a wealthy country like the United States, he adds, "it is very hard to justify anything other than a *relative* poverty line. And a relative poverty line means that, compared with 1963, both the level and the rate of growth of poverty are being understated."[2]

The term "poverty" itself, as David A. Shipler observed in *The Working Poor*, is unsatisfying because it "is not a category that can be delineated by the government's dollar limits on annual income. In real life, it is an unmarked area along a continuum, a broader region of hardship than the society usually recognizes. More people than those officially designated as 'poor' are, in fact, weighted down with the troubles associated with poverty."[3] Thus the arbitrary line between poor and nonpoor underestimates what low-income people need to get by.

Moreover, the increase in inequality since the 1970s—with the flow of income shifting upward, and stagnant or declining wages dominating elsewhere—is partly responsible for keeping the "official" rate at about 15 percent, with one out of five American children living in poverty. This flow of income to the top has made the United States the most unequal in wealth and income among twenty-seven peer countries. At the same time, the United States has one of the weakest safety nets among developed nations. Pope Francis recognized that government programs to alleviate poverty, while meeting "certain urgent needs, should be considered merely temporary responses"; temporary, perhaps, but in Francis's view, absolutely necessary. The American safety net needs to be stronger, not weaker, and a recalculation of the poverty line is long overdue. Janet Gornick, a professor of political science and sociology at the City University of New York, recommends that the United States emulate European countries, which use a relative poverty line that measures distance from the median income in a country. This defines poverty in relation to the standard of living in that country.

Gornick, as director of the Luxembourg Income Study Center, has examined poverty extensively across developed nations and observes that in comparison with Europe, the United States relies on programs "targeted on the poor, such as TANF [Temporary Assistance for Needy Families], SSI [Supplemental Security Income], Food Stamps, and Medicaid." But in many European countries, "social policy provisions have a universal structure. So the rich, the middle class, and the poor are in the same programs." This creates popular as well as political support. For this reason, she opposes removing the rich from those eligible for Social Security benefits, because "that would break the universality. . . . I don't think Bill Gates needs a Social Security check, but we need him to be in the Social Security program."[4]

An extension of public welfare can also be a "growth strategy" that may stabilize the financial system. Monica Prasad, a Northwestern University professor of sociology, maintains that expanding the availability of public welfare will lessen the demand for credit and "reduce financial volatility." "A more developed [and more inclusive] welfare state will reduce the appetite for mortgage and credit that is built into the American political economy." It will also pave the way for economic growth, because "as demand for finance lessens, rewards in the financial sector will lessen, and other, more productive and less bubble-inclined sectors will attract resources and skilled workers. For the United States, poverty reduction is a growth strategy." More universal social policies accord with Pope Francis's call that the poor "be fully a part of society" and for "the creation of a new mindset which thinks in terms of community and the priority of the life of all over the appropriation of goods by a few."[5]

But programs to combat poverty over the short term struggle to come into being against a powerful minority in American politics who remain convinced that many, if not most, of the poor are undeserving. They hold this conviction not for economic or pragmatic reasons, but on cultural and political grounds.

THE UNDESERVING POOR

In *The Undeserving Poor*, Katz commented: "For more than two hundred years, one theme has run through the American response to poverty. It is the idea that some poor people are undeserving of help because they brought their poverty on themselves."[6] The conviction among the minority believing that any poor do not deserve help goes beyond the misguided notion that government aid—namely, help from the rest of us who can afford it—creates a dependence on government among the poor that perpetuates poverty. They also make a moral judgment on the poor, regardless of whether those in poverty are working or not. While strong majorities of Americans favor government programs to help relieve poverty, even among the "undeserving," in the echo chambers of Tea Party Republicans and Fox News there is no empathy—and much disdain—for the poor themselves and animus against a government disposed to help.

Critics who scorn those dependent on government aid believe that the needy are "moochers" who are lazy and cheat by accepting government benefits when they could work. Ironically, they are correct about cheating—by one particular group. According to the research of Kathryn Edin and Laura Lein, many impoverished "single" mothers do cheat by hiding the fact that they are working or making money in an underground economy; and they lie about the help they get from family, friends, and even the fathers of their children to whom they may or (most likely) may not be married. They do this not because they are born cheats, but because living solely on government benefits or minimum wages is unsustainable. So they adopt "survival strategies" and cycle between being wage reliant or welfare reliant, using both whenever possible.[7] And when these women do work, they are likely to earn about eighty cents on the dollar compared with what men earn in the same jobs.

Those eager to judge the poor as immoral need to be reminded about the changed structure of employment and the elimination of good-paying jobs for those with little education, along with a minimum wage that has lagged behind inflation. Their misplaced moralism leads to what Sasha Abramsky calls the "sticks" used against those seen as the undeserving poor, such as "requiring applicants for a host of assistance programs to undergo regular drug checks and fingerprinting." Abramsky adds that this provision falls disproportionately "on blue-collar workers, because—with certain professions, such as airline pilots or police officers, being the exception—the higher up the pay scale one goes, the less likely it is that an employer will make you pee in a cup before being hired on."[8]

THE UNDESERVING RICH

Just who is required to pee in a cup tells a great deal about the double standard applied to rich and poor and most of the rest of us. The United States of Inequality is pervaded by class-based double standards, illustrated by the differential application of the term "moral hazard" (taking risks and not bearing the consequences) during and after the Great Recession. The many low-income people who bought homes they could not afford when the housing bubble was in effect received little help after it burst and became scapegoats for conservative talking heads. But little was said about moral hazard in the case of financial institutions that recklessly and fraudulently enticed inexperienced home buyers into high-risk mortgages. The large banks that "securitized"—that is, sold a huge number of subprime residential mortgages to the government-sponsored mortgage enterprises Freddie Mac and Fannie Mae or to large investors (hedge funds, etc.)—had already been paid when the housing market collapsed. The financial institutions that bore heavy responsibility for the crisis received a taxpayer-funded $165 billion bailout that saved them, and their executives promptly rewarded themselves with millions in bonuses.[9] Henry Paulson, as George W. Bush's treasury secretary, and Timothy Geithner, while he was Obama's treasury secretary, typified government officials from or allied with Wall Street. They blithely attached no conditions to the federal bailout provisions, while providing generously low interest rates, thus mirroring the pliant corporate boards of directors that allow CEOs to determine their own compensation.

In recent years, Americans have become well aware of how white-collar crime committed by billionaires occupies a different legal system from the rest of us. Barbara Ehrenreich has commented: "Steal $400—you get four years in prison. Steal $400 million—you get a platinum parachute." While Ehrenreich's figure of $400 million is impressive, it could even have been much higher. The Lehman Brothers' executives who nearly collapsed the world economy in 2008 "ran up a $700 *billion* tab engaging in almost indescribably reckless and antisocial behaviors, borrowing on a grand scale to create and sell" dangerous financial products.[10]

The financial crisis of 2008 unleashed a groundswell of outrage, calling for reform of Wall Street practices that put the entire economy at risk. In July 2010, President Obama signed into law the Dodd-Frank Wall Street Reform and Consumer Protection Act. Since then, little evidence has surfaced to indicate that Wall Street has changed its ways. In 2012, Sheila Bair, who served as head of the Federal Deposit Insurance Corporation from 2006 to 2011 and did everything she could to rein in the reckless behavior of large banks, responded to the ongoing "greed, shortsightedness, and misbehavior" by asking "should we be surprised?" (Obama kept Bair, a moderate Republican initially appointed by President George W. Bush, in office for her competence and passion for protecting Main Street.) Our financial system, remarked Bair, continues to exist in a rapacious culture infecting even the best institutions, one "that reflects a craven desire for personal profit that overrides any understanding or care about harm to others. . . . Small wonder that no one on Wall Street has learned a lesson given the hand slaps they received for the subprime crisis."[11]

To be clear, many of the very rich—the 1 percent—are productive citizens. A sizeable number of them work long hours, more (on average) than the 99 percent. They are a heterogeneous slice of people across America, in a variety of occupations, and while most are Republicans, many hold diverse social and political views. The "undeserving rich," as described by Leslie McCall, are those who Americans see as prospering while others are engulfed in economic turmoil, and particularly those who are perceived as enriching themselves by blocking opportunity for others. *Blocking opportunity* are the key words here.[12]

But why not expand that understanding of the undeserving rich to include those who cheat, game the system, break the law, or legally/illegally bribe public officials to gain or increase their wealth? A portion of the poor (and some thieves who are not so poor) manipulate the welfare system to their advantage, but they do not leave economic distress for millions in their wake, as did the undeserving rich who committed financial fraud and brought on the Great Recession. If someone gets caught illegally accepting food stamps or other welfare benefits, they usually are punished. But in the aftermath of the 2008 recession and bank bailouts, *none* of the high-ranking Wall Street financial executives who were involved went to jail "for any of the systemic crimes that wiped out 40 percent of the world's wealth." "Even now," wrote journalist Matt Taibbi in a book that appeared in early 2014, "after JPMorgan Chase agreed to a settlement of $13 billion for a variety of offenses and the financial press threw up its arms over the government's supposedly aggressive approach to regulating Wall Street, the basic principle held true. Nobody went to jail. Not one person." CEOs of the firms that collapsed—Richard Fuld of Lehman Brothers (see chapter 4), Jimmy Cayne of Bear Stearns, Stan O'Neal of Merrill Lynch, and Chuck Prince of Citigroup—all walked away not only free, but rich.[13]

Judge Jed S. Rakoff of the Federal District Court in Manhattan was among those wondering why no high-level executives had been prosecuted. Through his rulings in a series of high-profile cases, Judge Rakoff, who had experience as both a defense attorney and a prosecutor, had already established himself as a critic of slaps on the wrist for financial malfeasance. In 2011, he gained national attention when he rejected a settlement between Citigroup and the Securities and Exchange Commission because it did not require the company to admit wrongdoing, calling the $285 million penalty levied on the firm "pocket change." With regard to Wall Street's role in the events of 2008, Rakoff carefully repeated several times that he neither possessed inside information nor had an opinion regarding anyone's guilt. But he did refer to the Financial Crisis Inquiry Report that used "variants of the word 'fraud' no fewer than 157 times in describing what led to the crisis."

In a long, thoughtful essay in the *New York Review of Books*, Rakoff considered multiple reasons why no prosecutions had been brought against those involved, but he was scathing in regard to U.S. Attorney General Eric Holder's comment that such actions "will have a negative impact on the national economy, perhaps even the world economy." This excuse, Rakoff said, is "frankly [disturbing to a federal judge] in what it says about the [Justice] Department's apparent disregard for equality under the law." Holder's rationale was irrelevant, the judge said, with regard to the prosecution of individuals. Rakoff disagreed with the trend in recent decades of the government prosecuting companies instead of individuals and suggested that "the future deterrent value of successfully prosecuting individuals far outweighs the prophylactic benefits of imposing internal compliance measures [on firms] that are often little more than window dressing."[14]

Two months earlier, prominent establishment figure William C. Dudley, president of the New York Federal Reserve Bank, gave a speech on potential solutions to the "too big to fail" problem and called attention to a prevailing culture in banking and finance of an "apparent lack of respect for law, regulation, and the public trust." He found alarming "evidence of deep-seated cultural and ethical failures at many large financial institutions." Dudley's words amounted to polite and restrained references to what a *New York Times* reporter bluntly called "money laundering, market rigging, tax dodging, selling faulty financial products, trampling homeowner rights, and rampant risk taking—these are some of the sins that big banks have committed in recent years."[15]

Any candid reports on these activities universally acknowledge that regulators and the U.S. Justice Department lack either the will or the mechanisms to prevent such abuses from continuing. Indeed, a 2014 report by the Justice Department's inspector general indicated that the federal government's interest in prosecuting mortgage fraud was negligible between fiscal years 2009 and 2011. In fact, wrote the *New York Times*' Matt Apuzzo in an article about this report, the Obama administration "made the crime its lowest priority and has closed hundreds of cases after little or no investigation." Ted Kaufman, a senator (D-DE) during the years covered by the report, unsuccessfully urged the Justice Department to prosecute mortgage fraud. He commented that the government's inaction "fits a pattern that is scary for democracy, that there really are two levels of justice in this country, one for the people with power and money and one for everyone else."[16]

Jeff Connaughton, a Washington insider who was Kaufman's chief of staff and a former lobbyist turned reformer, explained in a recent book why no punishment ensued: "Money is the basis of almost all relationships in D.C. And, in a nutshell, this is why our political campaign system and D.C.'s mushrooming Permanent Class—who alternate between government jobs and lawyering, influence peddling and finance—mean Wall Street always wins."[17] That the financial industry "always wins" may be hyperbole, but no one disputes that its influence over Congress, the executive branch, and the Supreme Court has enlarged in recent decades, even as its role in the economy has changed. Historically, big banks provided capital for important, job-creating sectors of the economy: transportation, manufacturing, scientific research, technology.

Now, however, Wall Street's role in financing entrepreneurial business is a small part of what it does, as John Cassidy pointed out in a provocative 2010 *New Yorker* essay, "What Good Is Wall Street?" "Most people on Wall Street," wrote Cassidy, "aren't finding the next Apple or promoting a green rival to Exxon. They are buying and selling securities that are tied to existing firms and capital projects, or to something less concrete, such as the price of a stock or the level of an exchange rate." The revenue of many big banks now comes from trading rather than corporate finance, an activity that critics have said amounts to "rents" that do not deliver "economic value." At the same time, compensation for work in the financial sector has risen to dizzying heights. Bright Ivy League graduates are flocking to Wall Street because, within a short time, they can be earning more than a brain surgeon with years of experience and be rewarded for working in an industry, Cassidy noted, that for the most part "doesn't design, build, or sell a single tangible thing."[18]

As their earnings grow, many of those recruits catch the competitive fever of "the Street" and become addicted to making more than the next guy, according to former derivatives trader Sam Polk. Wealth addiction, Polk discovered as he made his millions, can become insatiable. More importantly for politics and society, all of that money buys government. In 2008, the financial industry had given generously to presidential candidate Obama, but by 2012, after the Dodd-Frank Act and remarks about "fat cats" by President Obama, Wall Street opened its coffers wide for the Republican presidential candidate, Mitt Romney, and spent more than ever before on lobbying and campaign contributions. In the 2014 election cycle, banks and financial services spent well over a record $1 billion to influence Washington, and they began to reap the payoff by the end of the year (see below).[19]

Wall Street's ability to get what it wants from government also owes much to the Capitol's "revolving door." Attorney General Eric Holder and Lanny A. Breuer, assistant attorney general of the Criminal Division, both worked as partners at the huge, prestigious legal-defense firm of Covington & Burling. The firm's clients included the four largest U.S. banks—JPMorgan Chase, Bank of America, Citigroup, and Wells Fargo & Co—along with dozens of other banks and financial institutions. In moving to the Department of Justice, Holder and Breuer were now responsible for prosecuting banks instead of defending them. On their watch the DOJ pursued a policy of penalizing firms, not individuals, because of concern for "collateral consequences," or, harm to the whole economy.[20]

During January 2013, the public television show *Frontline* broadcast "Untouchables," a documentary examining Breuer's failure to use available tools to prosecute individual criminal behavior. This followed on the heels of the DOJ's decision the previous month not to indict any members of the international London bank HSBC for laundering drug money and helping finance terrorists. Instead, the bank, an accomplice of Mexican drug cartels and Islamic jihadists, paid penalties of almost $2 billion. "Too big to fail" had morphed into "too big to jail," even for collaborating with murderers and sociopaths. Soon after the *Frontline* exposé, Breuer resigned from the DOJ and quickly cashed in on his government "service." He returned to Covington & Burling (now expanding internationally) for an initial compensation of $400 million a year.[21]

The question here remains, should not those who accumulate wealth by favors, fraud, bribery, influence, or *crime*, be counted among the cohort regarded as the undeserving rich?

In a survey conducted in 2012 by Labaton Sucharow, a whistleblower law firm, 26 percent of the bankers in the United States and the United Kingdom said they had observed or had first-hand knowledge of wrongdoing; 25 percent said they believed they needed to engage in unethical or illegal behavior in order to succeed in finance; 30 percent felt pressured to commit such actions; and only 41 percent reported that members of their company had "definitely not" engaged in illegal or unethical behavior.[22]

Banks and other financial firms do not need to engage in illegal actions to make money, however. Successful, large-scale rent seeking (see chapter 4) can result in millions flowing into a firm's coffers at consumers' or taxpayers' expense. A recent episode involving Goldman Sachs illustrates the point. Goldman Sachs profited handsomely from the economic collapse of 2007–2008 by betting against the securities it had promoted and sold to clients. In 2009, Goldman and other Wall Street firms that had been bailed out by billions of dollars in taxpayers' money responded to a backlash of negative publicity by reducing somewhat the huge bonuses paid to their executives, but by 2010 those bonuses rebounded to Midas-level treasure. In 2012, Goldman Sachs CEO Lloyd Blankfein received $21 million in compensation, and the next year the firm's bonus pool climbed to $26.7

billion, the largest since 2007. The close ties between Goldman Sachs and the administrations of presidents Bush and Obama have been evident for some time. Henry Paulson served as CEO of Goldman, and Timothy Geithner was a protégé of Robert Rubin, a longtime Goldman Sachs executive. The firm contributed heavily to Senator Obama's 2008 presidential campaign, and around 15 to 20 high-level members of Obama's first administration had worked directly or indirectly for Goldman Sachs.[23]

A 2013 *New York Times* investigative report revealed that in 2010, Goldman Sachs bought the aluminum storage company Metro International Trade Services, along with twenty-seven industrial warehouses in Detroit, for $500 million. Goldman then exploited pricing regulations determined by the London Metal Exchange, owned by a Hong Kong company run by executives of big banks. Goldman charged rent for storing the aluminum in its newly acquired warehouses, except it was not "storing" the aluminum but holding it off the market. This chicanery poured money into Goldman's coffers and those of allied investors by upping the cost of aluminum cans, electronics, automobiles, siding for houses, and other products. The tenth of a cent thereby added to the price of an aluminum can seems tiny, but Americans use 90 billion aluminum cans every year. For all products manufactured with aluminum, the estimated cost to consumers is $5 billion a year.

In Detroit, forklift operators at Goldman Sachs's warehouses moved 1,500-pound bars of the metal among the various storage buildings, "a merry-go-round of metal," one former driver called it. This tactic (reminiscent of oil tankers making U-turns from port to port during the alleged energy shortages of 1973 and 1979) delayed the delivery of aluminum from what had been six weeks to sixteen months. Goldman then profited by raising the cost of delivery and supply, even when the overall price of aluminum in the metals market fell after 2010.[24]

Aluminum is just part of how financial firms capture basic commodities markets and infrastructure. Goldman Sachs, JPMorgan Chase, and Morgan Stanley "own oil tankers, run airports, and control huge quantities of coal, natural gas, heating oil, electric power, and precious metals. They likewise can now be found exerting direct control over a whole galaxy of raw materials crucial to world industry and to society in general, including everything from food products to metals like zinc, copper, tin, [and] nickel."[25]

Their running up the tab in these markets is entirely legal, thanks to the Financial Services Modernization Act of 1999 that allowed banks to merge with industry. The Federal Reserve spurred Wall Street to even greater commodities seizures by ruling that banks taking control of "nonfinancial businesses" could "reasonably be expected to produce benefits to the public." Such was the rationale for the Securities and Exchange Commission allowing JPMorgan Chase, Goldman Sachs, and Black Rock (a large money-management firm) to buy up 80 percent of the copper on the market and sequester it in warehouses.[26]

Thus, under cover of friendly legislation and regulations, Wall Street firms are able to engage in economic machinations that are the antithesis of free-market capitalism and reap "rents" unrelated to productive economic activity. Lord Adair Turner, a businessman, academic, and self-described technocrat, headed Britain's regulatory agency overseeing financial services from 2001 to 2013. Perhaps something like Goldman Sachs's aluminum shuffle was what Turner had in mind in 2009 when he commented that much of what happened in the financial centers of London and New York was "socially useless activity."[27]

The concentration of industrial market power in the financial sector also results from a thirty-five-year wave of *deregulation* that has permitted the formation of cartels and monopolies reminiscent of the First Gilded Age in the late nineteenth century. During the 1960s and 1970s, Congress, newly created federal regulatory agencies, and the courts limited the ability of corporate America to endanger workers' safety and health or despoil the environment and, in general, protected the economic rights of ordinary citizens. But beginning in the Carter administration and gathering speed during the Reagan years, Republicans as well as Democrats responded to a business offensive against regulatory agencies that was both ideological and political, as well as to corporate money poured into political campaigns and lobbying. What law professor Thomas O. McGarity calls a laissez-faire revival "contributed to the growing disparities of wealth and well-being that became painfully obvious during the last decade."[28]

The argument here is that wealth accumulated by individuals under cover of laws and deregulations that cheat everyone else is undeserved. People whose income is inflated by illegal actions (such as mortgage fraud) get away with it because there is one kind of unjust "justice" for them and another kind for everyone else; some of the former are not only undeserving, but have committed crimes. Surely criminals who get off scot free are undeserving.

The term "scot free" originally referred not to getting away with breaking the law, but to avoiding taxes. "Scot" comes from the Norse term "skot," meaning tax due from a tenant, and in England from the twelfth to the eighteenth centuries, "scot" (and "lot") applied to taxes due. Those who were exempt (usually the privileged) were "scot free." The term nowadays can loosely be applied to sixty large corporations that, under the chaotic and rigged U.S. corporate-tax code, offshored $166 billion in profits in 2012, shielding more than 40 percent of their revenues from federal taxes. Google, "one of the world's biggest tax avoiders," did get off scot free. But other companies trumped that by paying nothing on their corporate federal income tax returns and instead getting tax refunds, such as General Electric (to the tune of $3 billion), Boeing, Verizon, Kraft Foods, and Dow Chemicals.[29]

When Steve Jobs, cofounder and CEO of Apple, died in 2011, the world mourned a creative entrepreneur taken far too young. But Apple, which Jobs made into the world's most profitable technology company, also excelled at avoiding billions of dollars in federal taxes, as well as taxes in California and twenty-one other states. Although Apple's headquarters are in California, by setting up a small office in Reno, Nevada, Apple avoids California's corporate 8.84 percent tax rate. By creating subsidiaries in low-tax countries like Ireland, the Netherlands, Luxembourg, and the British Virgin Islands, Apple has avoided billions in taxes that might otherwise go into the U.S. Treasury. Jobs's net worth when he died was estimated at over $8 billion.[30]

These corporations and their lavishly compensated executives perhaps might be said not to deserve the protection of the U.S. armed forces should an unfriendly government decide to nationalize their resources; nor deserve the nation's use of military might to maintain their access to resources such as Middle Eastern oil; nor deserve actions by the Federal Reserve and the U.S. Treasury Department to provide billions in taxpayer money for bailouts; nor deserve the government's financing of scientific research from which they derive benefits. Such corporations and executives may be said not to deserve all these things (and more), but they expect them, and they get them.[31]

Excessively compensated CEOs of firms that have floundered, have laid off thousands of employees, and have received taxpayer bailouts (see chapter 4) also qualify as undeserving rich. Many Americans intensely resent the accumulation of wealth by these nabobs at the expense of both everyone else and the public good. But hostility to the undeserving rich does not move the political class to action and bring about remedial policy. Not even the actions of those who commit crimes seem to result in penalties that might deter such behavior—let alone sustained political backlash toward them— though the social costs are enormous.

The author of a standard textbook on white-collar crime commented on the relative disparity in the injury done to society by street thugs versus white-collar criminals:[32]

> To most people, the muggers, murderers, and drug dealers they might encounter on a dark city street are the heart of the crime problem. But the damage such criminals do is dwarfed by the respectable criminals who wear white collars and work for our most powerful organizations. The annual losses from antitrust violations—just one of a long list of major white-collar crimes— are estimated to be ten times greater than the annual losses from all the crimes reported to the police. The toll of injuries and deaths from white-collar crime is even more shocking. The asbestos industry's cover-up of the dangers of its products has probably cost almost as many lives as all the murders in the United States for an entire decade.

The undeserving rich include many who are not members of the criminal elite. Some do not break laws, however, merely because laws have been written in their favor or loopholes have been created by deregulation and special exemptions. These are wealthy and (mostly) powerful men whose corporations and lobbyists have captured the government. The plutocracy's hold over national and many state governments does not appear to be threatened, while exogenous forces in twenty-first-century capitalism seemingly reinforce politically generated policies that maintain and deepen inequality.

PLUTOCRACY ON THE MARCH, DEMOCRACY TRAMPLED UNDERFOOT

In early 2014, Thomas Piketty, the French economist who, with Emmanuel Saez, has done so much to raise awareness of the growth of inequality in income and wealth, published *Capital in the Twenty-First Century* (the English version came out in March, and the original appeared in France a few months earlier). Piketty argues that the global advance of inequality is perhaps all but inevitable—*unless.* He has assembled impressive evidence to show that until political action is taken by governments, income and wealth disparity will not stabilize and diminish, as American economic orthodoxy had it; instead, inequality will inexorably increase. The eventual result is likely to be an oligarchy of inherited wealth and privilege that will dominate global society. Piketty doubts that politicians have the will to reverse the forces creating inequality, and there is good reason to share his pessimism.[33]

Piketty largely attributes the enormous burgeoning of income inequality to the phenomenal increase in wage disparity, with ordinary workers getting less income from their production while top managers, who have "the power to set their own remuneration," reap unprecedented earnings. Spectacular salaries and other compensations at the "summit of the wage hierarchy," he asserts, are the principal cause of rising inequality in the United States. Capital in the twenty-first century is creating wealth for the owners of capital and assets at a rapid pace (especially in Europe), and what is emerging is "a new patrimonial capitalism." Eventually, the United States, too, will be ruled by oligarchies of family dynasties of inherited wealth.[34]

Although Piketty puts far less weight on technological change, other social scientists who forecast continuing socioeconomic stratification point to the digital revolution as destroying middle-class jobs while expanding low-income occupations and creating far fewer highly skilled and highly paid positions. Those who see digital technology as "driving an unprecedented reallocation of wealth and income" also predict that such forces will continue to foster inequality, even as technology creates "bounty for society and wealth for innovators" In a similar vein, economist Angus Deaton argues that the growth of inequality has accompanied progress in material well-being, both among and within nations. "Inequality is often a *consequence* of progress," but it can result in improvement as well as harm to people around the globe.[35]

But progress, as Deaton knows well, doesn't just *happen* entirely on its own. Globalization, technological change, progress, or "history" are concepts that invoke what Karl Marx referred to when he observed: "Man makes history, but not under conditions of his own choosing." Whatever causal agency attributed to what, for the sake of argument, can be called "impersonal forces," political decisions and policies have exacerbated inequality, and the United States, ranking among the most developed and putatively democratic nations, has done the least to reverse the growing inequality of income and wealth.

An accumulation of *policy* choices over several decades laid the groundwork for a political economy creating enormous disparities of income and wealth in the United States, not exogenous forces like globalization or technological change, though the latter have played a role. Ruinous asymmetrical governmental policies have influenced how those forces have taken effect. International comparisons demonstrate this again and again. There is nothing inevitable about inequality. A generation ago, economists accepted Simon Kuznets's theory that growth in the inequality of income and wealth would later plateau and stabilize, as if the economy of a society were self-regulating. Piketty has succeeded in putting Kuznets's prediction into the context of the period of shared prosperity from the 1940s to the 1970s, an era that Piketty and other economists describe as an anomaly.

Piketty deserves credit for making clear that the discipline of economics—absent politics or political economy—cannot, by itself, explain galloping inequality. He declares that "the history of the distribution of wealth has always been deeply political" and "is shaped by the way economic, social, and political actors view what is just and what is not." But Piketty, as some critics have observed, does not say enough about the policies of a plutocratic government, the weakening of unions, the shrinkage of progressive taxes on income, the steady decline of how much corporations pay in taxes, and the loosening of government regulations across the board that allow enormous profits to accrue to the drug, technology, and financial sectors of the economy, among others.[36] Add to that the rise of an aggressive, corporate-financed antigovernmental movement and the promotion of a free-market ideology that is little understood by the rank and file who embrace it (and is set aside by the financial and corporate elite when profitable). The reactionary Right aims not only to keep the infrastructure of rent-seeking and privilege in place so income will still flow to the top, but also to reverse the health, financial, and regulatory reforms President Obama and the Democrats have managed to obtain against fierce Republican opposition.[37] These right-wingers would reverse the social policies of the New Deal and the Progressive Era if they could.

Many analysts of America's rising inequality lament its existence on both practical and moral grounds, but they believe that the correlations—such as those discussed in this book—do not provide definitive proof of the "deleterious effects of inequality." Inequality rises, and as it does unions decline, life expectancy for low-income people is reduced, social mobility atrophies, wages for the bottom 50 percent go down, the middle class shrinks, the children of the affluent swamp elite universities and colleges, residential segregation by income expands, and on and on. But certitude in these matters, some say, is elusive.

Skeptics maintain their doubts in such areas as health and life expectancy, yet the indicators of a shorter and unhealthier life pile up in any accounting of probable causes: poverty and stress; low levels of education; lack of health insurance; nonavailability of healthy food; food insecurity; not enough work and not enough income; smoking;

obesity and lack of exercise; job loss; absence of social services in low-income localities; teenage births. In short, a stultifying web of inequality. Yet caring professionals devoted to helping society's afflicted sometimes warn that "it is hard to prove causality with the available information," and that aggregate data do not necessarily translate into individual behavior, a statistical red flag known as the "ecological fallacy."[38]

A long time ago, as a graduate student in history, I tried to learn statistics—unsuccessfully. (I became very knowledgeable about the first chapters of statistics texts, but beyond those . . .) I took comfort in the axiom that "There are lies, damned lies, and statistics." I did understand the logic of the ecological fallacy that bedevils reform-minded social scientists concerned about inequality. I grasped all too well, as the skeptics do, that *a correlation is not a cause*, and this was ingrained in my would-be historian's mind. But I am convinced, along with Richard Wilkinson and Kate Pickett in *The Spirit Level*, that the concatenation of multiple correlations associated with inequality can hardly be by chance. The American public, and their elected representatives, should also be persuaded by this. Imprinted in my memory, too, were the words of Charles Beard, a once-influential historian who got some things wrong, many things right, and shook up history writing in the early twentieth century. When it came to causes, Beard said, "we don't need to know everything to know *why*."

The plutocracy's capture of government in the United States has made the political economy of the New Gilded Age a poker game with a stacked deck that deals out royal flushes and full houses to the corporate elite and an enabling political class, while everyone else gets hands with broken straights. Middle-class America declines; low-income families—the working poor—struggle to get by; and the poor, well, they mostly stay poor or become worse off.

Rising inequality of income and wealth could be halted—and even reversed—by a government committed to full employment, and by corrective measures to diminish the rampant inequities affecting all the areas of life that have been described in the preceding pages. Given the present state of political dysfunction and the war being waged by reactionary plutocrats to destroy the remaining unions, keep wages low, undermine economic security for tens of millions of Americans by transferring risk and accountability away from prospering corporations and onto individuals and families, eliminate corporate taxes completely and allow giant oligopolies unregulated freedom in economic life, and generally enhance the power of the elites, it seems unrealistic indeed to hope for more than an incremental approach to the long list of needed reforms. Given the continual proliferation of inequality and its protean ability to take new guises, I have inevitably missed some dimensions. But what I have brought together in this book demonstrates inequality's breathtaking scope and how it affects almost all Americans' lives, except for the superrich.

Inequality does not merely maintain or increase poverty. It degrades the quality of life of society as a whole—not just the dwindling middle class, but those above it, and especially those below. All people are diminished by it. A society's civic health declines when most of its citizens believe that their economic, political, and judicial systems are tilted against them. Fairness requires the application of universal norms, ones where Warren Buffet's secretary would pay less income tax than he does. Fairness requires that there is one system of justice and that everyone plays by the same rules. Inequality will always exist, but in a fair society its sting lessens, and the poor have access to opportunities to change their lot.

The concept of the undeserving poor now serves as a political weapon in the arsenal of reactionary servants of the undeserving rich in the United States, and it distracts the country from how the rent-takers, the lawbreakers, and the unpunished enrich themselves and deepen inequality and its resultant social ills. Ironically, the cohort of the undeserving rich shares an important trait with the *imagined character* of the poor in the minds of reactionaries. The undeserving rich are *dependent* on the government for handouts in the form of a rigged tax system, corporate welfare, and favorable laws and regulations that increase their profits at the expense of the U.S. Treasury and add to the tax burden and social costs for everyone else. Should the media ever resurrect itself into responsible journalism, it might expose how these elites make their millions. When private-equity CEO Stephen Schwartzman complains that proposals to repeal the low tax-rate on carried interest remind him of the German invasion of Poland (he later apologized), a reporter might remind listeners/

readers that Schwartzman's fortune of over $10 billion could not exist without a biased tax system. When venture capitalist Tom Perkins (worth over $8 billion) suggests in a letter to the *Wall Street Journal* that criticism of the 1 percent compares with the Nazi's persecution of Jews, that only taxpayers should vote, and that the rich should have more votes, commentators might point out that the wealthy already possess inordinate political influence and that the United States is supposed to be a democratic republic, not the kind of corporate state Italy's fascist dictator Benito Mussolini once envisioned.[39]

Only the federal and state governments can restore fairness to a tax code that creates a Schwartzman and a Perkins and ensure that the wealthy and corporations pay their fair share. The social costs of a lightly taxed—or untaxed—plutocracy have been accumulating for decades, visible in the nation's crumbling infrastructure and the underfunding of public education at every level. Only the federal and state governments can make social-welfare programs less targeted only on the poor and more inclusive of other classes, with universality as an ultimate goal. States that raise revenue by disproportionately burdening the poor and near-poor through sales taxes while reducing or eliminating progressive income and corporate taxes need to end this inequity on practical as well as moral grounds. These states (mostly former members of the Confederacy), through regressive taxation, lower the standard of living and quality of life for all their citizens. Moreover, their public services would be worse off without the federal benefits paid to them that are well in excess of what these states contribute in tax dollars. State legislatures in all regions are cutting funds for education, especially higher education; reducing social mobility; and further squeezing the middle class. For-profit universities prey on veterans and low-income students and constitute exhibit one in the case establishing the breakdown of the American educational system. Or should that status be accorded instead to the 1,500 high school "drop-out factories"?

Only federal and state regulation can prevent the continuous expansion of the poverty industry and its predation on the poor. Information programs, sponsored by the government and private foundations, that educate and forewarn the predators' low-income victims could help. What will prevent the undermining and raiding of middle-class pensions, other than legislation and state regulation? Making the American educational system a cross-class meritocracy constitutes an enormous challenge, but universities are filled with smart and well-intentioned people who need to attack this problem, with help from a federal government that recently has contributed to increasing opportunity for low-income high school graduates, but also to disproportionately peopling the best institutions with the children of the affluent.

Raising the minimum wage will bump up the paychecks for those low-income workers making meager wages and lift millions of the poor and near-poor out of poverty and off of public assistance. Putting more cash into the hands of those millions will improve conditions for middle-class workers, whose pay has lagged far behind their increased productivity. In short, when the United States ceases to have one of the largest low-wage labor forces among developed nations, the salubrious effects will be experienced throughout the economy. More importantly, federal and state governments must commit themselves to a policy of full employment. The more people who are working, the fewer the unemployed; wages will rise, and a shared prosperity will reemerge.

The road ahead is steep. The nation's workforce—having undergone repeated shocks, offshoring, mergers, automation, deunionization, and the hard knocks of the Great Recession—has deteriorated. The labor-force participation rate of prime-working-age adults (those from age twenty-five to fifty-four) is now one of the lowest among comparable nations in the OECD, and it provides a depressing insight into the unavailability of good jobs and the damaging effects of a low-wage economy. In the 1960s, only about five out of a hundred men lacked a job at any one time. That ratio has tripled, to 16 percent, and the number of women who are out of the workforce has also risen. Many reasons cause men and women in that cohort not to work, according to a recent poll by the Kaiser Family Foundation, the *New York Times*, and CBS News. But among the 30 million Americans on the employment sidelines, many "are eager to find work and make large sacrifices to do so." Low-wage jobs paying $10 an hour, however, cannot improve their situation, much less restore their dignity after having lost better-paying jobs—and a sense of worth.[40]

More American women would reenter the workforce if they enjoyed the flexibility and support provided by some European governments, though, compared with men, not working tends to be more positive for many of them. The key for women with children is to balance family and work. A poll of prime-age nonworkers, and an extensive analysis of it by writers for the *New York Times*, made it clear that changes in society in the past several decades have contributed in multiple ways to the decline of the workforce. The fact remains that many who want to work and *would* work at decent jobs cannot. In early 1941, as World War II raged in Europe and the Pacific and the United States prepared for possible involvement in it, President Franklin D. Roosevelt delivered his "Four Freedoms" speech to Congress. Alongside freedom of speech and expression, freedom of worship, and freedom from fear, he listed "freedom from want," which, he made clear, meant economic security and "jobs for those who want them."

"Government" will not pursue full employment or other policies to promote economic security, however, without an outcry and action from millions of ordinary citizens. These Americans are getting plenty of advice about what to do—but they must listen to it.[41] It is past the time for what used to be an energetic, reforming middle class to awaken to what the nation has become. Minimum-wage workers staging walkouts and protests are showing more spirit and fight than most of those in the middle, who are better off. The task of books like this is to keep reminding the middle that they are getting screwed, especially by their elected representatives in Congress, whose overriding goal is to be reelected. A strong, progressive, populist voice, like that of Occupy Wall Street, needs to emerge, but it has to have specific goals that, one by one, will take apart the edifice of plutocratic government.

As the preceding chapters have shown, the consequences of inequality are multiple, and they interact with one another like hazardous chemicals. Few exist independently, while almost all merge with and reinforce one another, and thus produce further hardship for so many. Inequality in the twenty-first century is betraying the promise of America.

The mid-twentieth-century era of shared prosperity—economists call it the "Great Compression"—probably was an anomaly, as Thomas

Piketty has argued. But it resulted not from an act of God or from entirely natural forces beyond the control of government. Rather, the infrastructure underlying the growth of widespread economic security was created by government policies, strong labor unions, a high-wage labor market, investment in education (such as the G.I. bill), and the restraint of a business-corporate elite that was not obsessed with maximizing personal wealth, whatever the social costs. During the Great Compression, the financial industry did not rake in 25–30 percent of all business profits—Wall Street's share of the latter rose as high as 41 percent in the last decade. Nor had finance captured the U.S. Congress, a reality all too evident as these words are being written at the end of 2014.

At a time when Citigroup (which received $50 billion in taxpayer aid in 2009), in a bill written by its lobbyists, persuaded Congress to repeal a requirement of the Dodd-Frank law that limited the risk of derivatives trading, Walzer's words at the outset of this chapter ring true: "capitalists will be tyrants whenever wealth is not balanced by strong government." No such government balance counteracts capital in the twenty-first-century United States. Americans' government is no longer theirs; its strength empowers capital and Wall Street at the expense of Main Street. In the United States, a burgeoning plutocracy is *the thing* in the saddle. Pope Francis's 2013 critique of "the new idolatry of money and the dictatorship of an impersonal economy" echoed Walzer and stripped away the mirage of a protective, just state. "While the earnings of a minority are growing exponentially," Francis declared in *Evangelii Gaudium*, "so too is the gap separating the majority from the prosperity enjoyed by those happy few. This imbalance is the result of ideologies which defend the autonomy of the marketplace and financial speculation. Consequently, they reject the right of states, charged with vigilance for the common good, to exercise any form of control. A new tyranny is thus born, invisible and often virtual, which unilaterally and relentlessly imposes its own laws and rules."

NOTES

Introduction

1. *Inequality for All*, a film by Jacob Kornbluth, narrated by Robert B. Reich (2013), http://inequalityforall.com.

2. Richard Fry and Rakesh Kochhar, "America's Wealth Gap between Middle-Income and Upper-Income Families Is Widest on Record," Pew Research Center, December 17, 2014, www.pewresearch.org/fact-tank/2014/12/17/wealth-gap-upper-middle-income/.

3. Martin Gilens, *Affluence and Influence: Economic Inequality and Political Power in America* (Princeton, NJ: Princeton University Press, 2012), 1, 234.

4. "Focus on Inequality and Growth," OECD Directorate for Employment, Labour, and Social Affairs, December 2014, www.oecd.org/els/soc/Focus-Inequality-and-Growth-2014.pdf.

5. Benjamin I. Page and Lawrence R. Jacobs, *Class War? What Americans Really Think about Economic Inequality* (Chicago: University of Chicago Press, 2009), quotation 13.

6. Thomas Piketty's *Capital in the Twenty-First Century*, trans. Arthur Goldhammer (Cambridge, MA: Harvard University Press, 2014), has provoked debate about the inevitability of inequality. For examples of books proposing micro and macro remedies, see Dean Baker and Jared Bernstein, *Getting Back to Full Employment: A Better Bargain for Working People* (Washington, DC: Center for Economic and Policy Research, 2014), 6, www.cepr.net/documents/Getting-Back-to-Full-Employment_20131118.pdf; Joseph E. Stiglitz, *The Price of Inequality: How Today's Divided Society Endangers Our Future* (New York: W. W. Norton, 2013), 332–63; Sasha Abramsky, *The American Way of Poverty: How the Other Half Still Lives* (New York: Nation Books, 2013), 195–330; Robert Kuttner, *Debtors' Prison: The Politics of Austerity versus Possibility* (New York: Alfred A. Knopf, 2013), 272–95.

7. *Evangelii Gaudium*, Apostolic Exhortation of the Holy Father Francis, http://w2.vatican.va/content/francesco/en/apost_exhortations/documents/papa-francesco_esortazione-ap_20131124_evangelii-gaudium.html.

8. John Nichols and Robert W. McChesney, *Dollarocracy: How the Money and Media Election Complex Is Destroying America* (New York: Nation Books, 2013), quotation 3.

9. Michael E. Porter and Scott Stern, with Michael Green, "Findings of the Social Progress Index 2014," Social Progress Imperative, www.socialprogressimperative.org/data/spi/findings/.

10. Benedict Richard O'Gorman Anderson, *Imagined Communities: Reflections on the Origin and Spread of Nationalism* (New York: Verso, 1983; rev. ed. 1991), 6.

1. The Web of Inequality

Epigraph. *Evangelii Gaudium*, sections 53 and 202.

1. Robert B. Reich, *Beyond Outrage: What Has Gone Wrong with Our Economy and Our Democracy, and How to Fix It* (New York: Vintage Books, 2012), xii, 5–6.

2. "Crony Tigers, Divided Dragons," *Economist*, October 13, 2012, www.economist.com/node/21564408/.

3. Francesca Bastagli, David Coady, and Sanjeev Gupta, "Income Inequality and Fiscal Policy," International Monetary Fund Staff Discussion Note, June 28, 2012, www.imf.org/external/pubs/cat/longres.aspx?sk=26022.0/; Jacob S. Hacker and Paul Pierson, *Winner-Take-All Politics: How Washington Made the Rich Richer and Turned Its Back on the Middle Class* (New York: Simon & Schuster, 2010), 38–39.

4. Thomas Piketty and Emmanuel Saez, "The Evolution of Top Incomes: A Historical and International Perspective," *American Economic Review: Papers and Proceedings* 96, no. 2 (May 2006): 200–205; Emmanuel Saez, "Striking It Richer: The Evolution of Top Incomes in the United States (Updated with 2012 Preliminary Estimates)," September 3, 2013, 4, http://eml.berkeley.edu/~saez/saez-UStopincomes-2012.pdf; "Income Inequality," in Times Topics, *New York Times*, http://topics.nytimes.com (frequently updated); Chrystia Freeland, *Plutocrats: The Rise of the New Global Super-Rich and the Fall of Everyone Else* (New York: Penguin Press, 2012), 34; Annie Lowrey, "Incomes Flat in Recovery, but Not for the 1%," *New York Times*, February 15, 2013; Steven Rattner, "The Rich Get Even Richer," *New York Times*, May 25, 2012; Robert B. Reich, *Aftershock: The Next Economy and America's Future* (New York: Alfred A. Knopf, 2010), 6, 20; Annie Lowrey "The Rich Get Richer through the Recovery," *New York Times*, September 10, 2013; Emmanuel Saez and Gabriel Zucman, "Wealth Inequality in the United States since 1913," October 2014, http://gabriel-zucman.eu/files/SaezZucman2014Slides.pdf.

5. "Wealth Inequality in America," www.youtube.com/watch?v=l8HO8uqytYs/. Dan Ariely of Duke University, one of the researchers, described the results in "Americans Want to Live in a Much More Equal Country (They Just Don't Realize It)," *Atlantic*, August 2, 2012. The data appeared originally in Dave Gilson and Carolyn Perot, "It's the Inequality, Stupid," *Mother Jones*, March/April 2011, www.motherjones.com/politics/2011/02/income-inequality-in-america-chart-graph/.

6. Page and Jacobs, *Class War?*, 37–43; Alan Pyke, "Americans Have No Idea How Much Less They Make Than Their Companies' CEOs," *Think Progress*, September 24, 2014, http://thinkprogress.org/economy/2014/09/24/3571555/americans-underestimate-ceo-pay-gap/; Paul Krugman, "Our Invisible Rich," *New York Times*, September 28, 2014.

7. Robert Gebeloff and Shaila Dewan, "Measuring the Top 1% by Wealth, Not Income," *New York Times*, January 17, 2012, http://economix.blogs .nytimes.com/2012/01/17/measuring-the-top-1-by-wealth-not-income/; first quotation from Dave Boyer, "Obama to Use State of the Union as Opening Salvo in 2014 Midterms," *Washington Times*, January 26, 2014; second quotation from Nicholas D. Kristof, "Why Let the Rich Hoard All the Toys," *New York Times*, October 3, 2012; Sylvia A. Allegretto, "The State of Working America's Wealth, 2011," Economic Policy Institute Briefing Paper, http:// s1.epi.org/page/-/BriefingPaper292.pdf.

8. Susan Fleck, John Glaser, and Shawn Sprague, "The Compensation-Productivity Gap: A Visual Essay," *Monthly Labor Review*, January 2011, 61; OECD, *Divided We Stand: Why Inequality Keeps Rising* (OECD, 2011), 17–41, http://dx.doi.org/10.1787/9789264119536-en/.

9. Abramsky, *American Way of Poverty*, 9, quotation 6; Kathleen Short, "The Research Supplemental Poverty Measure, 2012," U.S. Census Bureau Current Population Reports, November 2013, www.census.gov/prod /2013pubs/p60-247.pdf; Zanny Minton Beddoes, "For Richer, for Poorer," *Economist*, October 13, 2012, www.economist.com/node/21564414/; Elise Gould and Hilary Wething, "U.S. Poverty Rates Higher, Safety Net Weaker Than in Peer Countries," Economic Policy Institute, July 24, 2012, www.epi.org /publication/ib339-us-poverty-higher-safety-net-weaker/; Peter Adamson, "Measuring Child Poverty," UNICEF Innocenti Research Centre Report Card 10, May 2012, www.unicef.ca/sites/default/files/imce_uploads/DISCOVER /OUR%20WORK/ADVOCACY/DOMESTIC/POLICY%20ADVOCACY /DOCS/unicefreportcard10-eng.pdf. On the rise of suburban poverty, see Elizabeth Kneebone and Alan Berube, *Confronting Suburban Poverty in America* (Washington, DC: Brookings Institution Press, 2013).

10. Elizabeth Kneebone, "The Growth and Spread of Concentrated Poverty, 2000 to 2008–2012," Brookings Institution, July 31, 2014, quotation 2, www .brookings.edu/research/interactives/2014/concentrated-poverty#/M10420.

11. Twenty-four percent blamed government welfare, but over 50 percent cited economic and environmental causes of poverty, such as lack of job opportunities (18%) and lack of education (13%). See Erin McClam, "Many Americans Blame 'Government Welfare' for Persistent Poverty, Poll Finds," NBC News, June 6, 2013, http://inplainsight.nbcnews.com/_news/2013/06/06 /18802216-many-americans-blame-government-welfare-for-persistent -poverty-polls-finds-v18802216/. On the success of government programs as well as the rise of extreme poverty, see Peter Edelman, *So Rich, So Poor: Why It's So Hard to End Poverty in America* (New York: New Press, 2012), 7–23, 26–28. On the near-poor, see David K. Shipler's magnificent book *The Working Poor: Invisible in America* (New York, Vintage, 2005; orig. pub. 2004).

12. On the IMF, see Eduardo Porter, "In New Tack, I.M.F. Aims at Income Inequality," *New York Times*, April 9, 2014. As the first signs of growing inequality emerged in the 1980s, the economics profession tended to ignore them. So did prestigious think tanks, because of the aversion of their corporate sponsors to studies of inequality. But some observers spotted the trend early, notably Thomas Byrne Edsall, then a *Washington Post* reporter and now professor of journalism at Columbia University and a frequent commentator in the *New York Times* on economics. His 1984 book, *The New Politics of Inequality* (New York: W. W. Norton), described how the policies of the Reagan administration were resulting in a shift of wealth upward in society. Edsall's book was recognized in Timothy Noah, *The Great Divergence: America's Growing Inequality Crisis and What We Can Do about It* (New York: Bloomsbury Press, 2012), 25, 26. See also Kevin Phillips, *The Politics of Rich and Poor: Wealth and the American Electorate in the Reagan Aftermath* (New York: Random House, 1990).

13. Paul Krugman, *The Conscience of a Liberal* (New York: W. W. Norton, 2007), 124–28. On the failure to prosecute Wall Street executives, see Matt Taibbi, *The Divide: American Injustice in the Age of the Wealth Gap* (New York: Spiegel & Grau, 2014).

14. Freeland, *Plutocrats*. Regarding offshoring, see Noah, *Great Divergence*, 106. Derek Curtis Bok earlier called attention to the impact of the rising pay of professionals in *The Cost of Talent: How Executives and Professionals Are Paid and How It Affects America* (New York: Free Press, 1993). At the risk of failing to mention other related and important books, see also Jeff Madrick, *The Age of Greed: The Triumph of Finance and the Decline of America, 1970 to the Present* (New York: Alfred A. Knopf, 2011); Claudia Goldin and Lawrence Katz, *The Race between Education and Technology* (Cambridge, MA: Belknap Press of Harvard University Press, 2008).

15. Erik Brynjolfsson and Andrew McAfee, "Why Workers Are Losing the War against Machines," *Atlantic*, October 26, 2011, http://theatlantic.com /business/archive/2011/10/why-workers-are-losing-the-war-against -machines/247278/; Nir Jaimovich and Henry Siu, "The Trend Is the Cycle: Job Polarization and Jobless Recoveries," March 31, 2012, http://faculty.arts .ubc.ca/hsiu/research/polar20120331.pdf; Brynjolfsson and McKee, *The Race against the Machine: How the Digital Revolution Is Accelerating Innovation, Driving Productivity, and Irreversibly Transforming Employment and the Economy* (Lexington, MA: Digital Frontier Press, 2011).

16. Enrico Moretti, *The New Geography of Jobs* (Boston: Houghton Mifflin Harcourt, 2012), 5, 6, 13, 14, 24.

17. "New York, New York, a Most Unequal Town," Inequality.org, July 12, 2012, http://inequality.org/york-york-unequal-town/; Joshua Freeman, "What

Happened to Working-Class New York?," *Nation*, May 6, 2013; Gene Balk, "Income Inequality: How Bad Is Seattle?," *Seattle Times*, January 17, 2014, http://blogs.seattletimes.com/fyi-guy/2014/01/17/income-inequality-how -bad-is-seattle/; John Nichols, "Seattle Swears in a Socialist," *Nation*, January 6, 2014; Erica Goode and Claire Cain Miller, "Backlash by the Bay: Tech Riches Alter a City," *New York Times*, November 24, 2013. On a similar situation in Chicago, see Megan Cottrell, "Second City or Dead Last? Income Apartheid in Chicago," Chicago Now, www.chicagonow.com/chicago -muckrakers/2011/02/second-city-or-dead-last-income-apartheid-in -chicago/. On the context of de Blasio's election, see Bob Master, "How the Zeitgeist Tracked Down Bill de Blasio," *Nation*, January 20, 2014. See also Alan Berube, "All Cities Are Not Created Unequal," Brookings Institution, February 20, 2014, www.brookings.edu/research/papers/2014/02/cities -unequal-berube/. Boston is a prime exemplar of a "brain hub." In 2007, one out of five individuals and families lived below the federal poverty line, and almost twice as many lived in "economic hardship." African Americans, Latinos, and Asians were much more likely to live in poverty, with a "significant number" of whites (about 12%) living below the poverty line. See Community Labor United, "Earnings, Poverty and Income Inequality in the City of Boston," August 26, 2008, http://massclu.org/sites/clud6 .prometheuslabor.com/files/Earnings,+Poverty,+and+Income+Inequality.pdf.

18. Alison Wolf, *The XX Factor: How the Rise of Working Women Has Created a Far Less Equal World* (New York: Crown, 2013), 206–28.

19. Dean Baker, *The End of Loser Liberalism: Making Markets Progressive* (Washington, DC: Center for Economic and Policy Research, 2011), 29–37, quotations 23, 30, 33, 36. Paralleling Baker's analysis, other economists point to "a two-decade household spending boom financed to a large extent by rising household debt." When the housing bubble burst, "the unsustainable increase in household leverage" and "inequality [became] a drag on demand growth that has held back recovery and led to slow employment growth." See Barry Z. Cynamon and Steven M. Fazzari, "Inequality, the Great Recession, and Slow Recovery," November 20, 2013, http://pages.wustl.edu/files/pages /imce/fazz/cyn-fazz_consinequ_130113.pdf. This research was sponsored by but does not reflect the views of the Federal Reserve Bank of St. Louis. See also Piketty, *Capital*, 315–21.

20. OECD, *Divided We Stand*, 24.

21. Stiglitz, *Price of Inequality*, 77; Moretti, *New Geography of Jobs*, 26; Judith Stein, *Pivotal Decade: How the United States Traded Factories for Finance in the Seventies* (New Haven, CT: Yale University Press, 2010); Kim Phillips-Fein, *Invisible Hands: The Making of the Conservative Movement from the New Deal to Reagan* (New York: W. W. Norton, 2009). On the insidious

effects of free trade and globalization removing any "democratically account-able institution capable of setting ground rules," see Robert Kuttner, "Don't Drink the Kool-Aid," in James Lardner and David A. Smith, eds., *Inequality Matters: The Growing Economic Divide in America and Its Poisonous Conse-quences* (New York: New Press, 2005), 230.

22. Jackie Calmes and Michael D. Shear, "Obama Says Income Gap Is Fraying the Social Fabric," *New York Times*, July 27, 2013.

23. For the transcript of the interview, see "Interview with President Obama," *New York Times*, July 27, 2013, www.nytimes.com/2013/07/28/us /politics/interview-with-president-obama.html?pagewanted=all/; Becky Pettit, *Invisible Men: Mass Incarceration and the Myth of Black Progress* (New York: Russell Sage Foundation, 2012).

24. Sam Roberts, "How Prisoners Make Us Look Good," *New York Times*, October 27, 2012; Stiglitz, *Price of Inequality*, 19; Michelle Alexander, *The New Jim Crow: Mass Incarceration in the Age of Colorblindness* (Jackson, TN: New Press, 2010). On the post-Emancipation South, see Douglas A. Blackmon, *Slavery by Another Name* (New York: Doubleday, 2008).

25. Vesla M. Weaver, "Unhappy Harmony: Accounting for Black Mass Incarceration in a 'Postracial' America," in Frederick C. Harris and Robert C. Lieberman, eds., *Beyond Discrimination: Racial Inequality in a Postracist Era* (New York: Russell Sage Foundation, 2013), 248–50; Jason Stanley and Weaver, "Is the United States a 'Racial Democracy'?," *New York Times*, January 12, 2014, http://opinionator.blogs.nytimes.com/2014/01/12/is-the -united-states-a-racial-democracy/; David T. Courtwright, *No Right Turn: Conservative Politics in a Liberal America* (Cambridge, MA: Harvard Univer-sity Press, 2010), 168.

26. Devah Pager, Bruce Western, and Bart Bonikowski, "Discrimination in a Low-Wage Labor Market: A Field Experiment," *American Sociological Review* 74 (October 2009): 777–99; Julia Story, "What Type of Jobs Are Off Limits to Felons?," eHow, www.ehow.com/print/info_8680107_types_jobs _off_limits_Felons.html; Melinda Tuhus, "To Help Ex-Felons Work, New Haven 'Bans the Box,'" *In These Times*, July 22, 2009, http://inthesetimes .com/working/entry/4641/to_help_ex-felons_work_new_haven_bans_the_box /; quotation from Kai Wright, "Boxed In," *Nation*, November 25, 2013, 22.

27. "Remarks by the President on Economic Mobility," Washington, D.C., December 4, 2013, www.whitehouse.gov/the-press-office/2013/12/04 /remarks-president-economic-mobility/.

28. Jim Tankersley and Scott Clement, "Among American Workers, Poll Finds Unprecedented Anxiety about Jobs, Economy," *Washington Post*, November 25, 2013. Hedrick Smith reported on a Metropolitan Life Insurance Company survey in 2007, before the economic meltdown, that found a

rampant sense of insecurity, with two-thirds saying they had not achieved "the American Dream of home ownership and solid economic life." See Smith, *Who Stole the American Dream?* (New York: Random House, 2012), 89–90. Heidi Shierholz, "Finding Low Unemployment in All the Wrong Places," Economic Policy Institute, January 10, 2014, www.epi.org/publication /finding-unemployment-wrong-places/; Kevin Phillips, "Numbers Racket: Why the Economy Is Worse Than We Know," *Harper's Magazine*, May 2008; Paul Krugman, "The Fear Economy," *New York Times*, December 26, 2013; Rebecca Riffkin, "Americans' Satisfaction with Job Security at New High," Gallup Economy, August 20, 2014, www.gallup.com/poll/175190/americans -satisfaction-job-security-new-high.aspx. Dean Baker and Jared Bernstein observe that the history of the United States "supports the notion that, when labor markets are tight, the benefits of growth are more likely to flow to the majority of working people. Conversely, when there's slack in the job market . . . working families fall behind." See Baker and Bernstein, *Getting Back to Full Employment*, 6.

29. *Report on the Economic Well-Being of U.S. Households in 2013* (Washington, DC: Board of Governors, Federal Reserve System, July 2014), www .federalreserve.gov/econresdata/2013-report-economic-well-being-us -households-201407.pdf. U.S. Financial Diaries released a preliminary report on household economic insecurity underscoring the Federal Reserve findings. USFD's survey of 235 low- and moderate-income households in five states over the course of a year found a "surprising amount of volatility of incomes from month to month." See "Live Today: USFD Announces Early Findings," U.S. Financial Diaries, December 3, 2014, www.usfinancialdiaries.org/blog /2014/12/3/live-today-usfd-announces-early-findings/.

30. Kuttner, *Debtors' Prison*, 44.

31. William D. Cohan, "How Quantitative Easing Contributed to the Nation's Inequality Problem," *New York Times*, October 22, 2014.

2. The Myth of Opportunity

1. Joseph E. Stiglitz, "Equal Opportunity, Our National Myth," *New York Times*, February 17, 2013; Timothy Noah, "The Mobility Myth," *New Republic*, March 1, 2012; Larry M. Bartels, *Unequal Democracy: The Political Economy of the New Gilded Age* (Princeton, NJ: Princeton University Press, 2008), 16; Dan Andrews and Andrew Leigh, "More Inequality, Less Social Mobility," *Applied Economics Letters* 16 (2009).

2. "Pursuing the American Dream: Economic Mobility across Generations," Pew Charitable Trusts Research & Analysis, July 9, 2012, www.pewtrusts.org /en/research-and-analysis/reports/0001/01/01/pursuing-the-american-dream.

3. Miles Corak, "Income Inequality: Equality of Opportunity, and

Intergenerational Mobility," *Journal of Economic Perspectives* 27, no. 3 (Summer 2013), 98; second quotation from "Like Father, Not Like Son," *Economist*, October 13, 2012, www.economist.com/node/21564417/. A study of intergenerational mobility across areas of the United States found significant correlations—but not necessarily causal ones—with "income inequality, economic and racial residential segregation, measures of K–12 school quality, . . . social capital indices, and measures of family structure (such as the fraction of single parents in an area). In particular, areas with a smaller middle class had lower rates of upward mobility." Social capital and family structure are especially strong predictors of upward mobility. See Equality of Opportunity Project, "Summary of Project Findings," July 2013, http://obs.rc.fas.harvard .edu/chetty/website/IGE/Executive%20Summary.pdf.

4. Corak, "Income Inequality," 98–99.

5. Noah, *Great Divergence*, 28–43, quotations 28–29.

6. Alan Krueger, "Rock and Roll, Economics, and Rebuilding the Middle Class," June 12, 2013, www.whitehouse.gov/blog/2013/06/12/rock-and-roll -economics-and-rebuilding-middle-class/.

7. Miles Corak, "The Economics of the Great Gatsby Curve: A Picture Is Worth a Thousand Words," January 18, 2012, http://milescorak.com/2012/01 /18/the-economics-of-the-great-gatsby-curve-a-picture-is-worth-a-thousand -words/; Noah, *Great Divergence*, 35, 36; Samuel Bowles, Herbert Gintis, and Melissa Osborne Groves, eds., *Unequal Chances: Family Background and Economic Success* (New York: Russell Sage Foundation, 2005).

8. Stephanie Simon, "High School Graduation Rate Up Sharply, but Red Flags Abound," Reuters, February 25, 2013, www.reuters.com/article/2013 /02/25/us-highschool-idUSBRE91O0JY20130225/; Cameron Brenchley, "High School Graduation Rate at Highest Level in Three Decades," Home Room, www.ed.gov/blog/2013/01/high-school-graduation-rate-at-highest -level-in-three-decades/; Robert Balfanz, John M. Bridgeland, Mary Bruce, and Joanna Hornig Fox, *Building a Grad Nation: Progress and Challenge in Ending the High School Dropout Epidemic: Annual Update, 2013* (Washington, DC: Civic Enterprises, Everyone Graduates Center at the Johns Hopkins University School of Education, America's Promise Alliance, and the Alliance for Excellent Education, 2013), www.americaspromise.org/building -gradnation-report/.

9. Susan Aud, William Hussar, Michael Planty, Thomas Snyder, Kevin Bianco, Mary Ann Fox, Lauren Frolich, Jana Kemp, and Lauren Drake, *The Condition of Education 2010*, NCES 2010-028 (Washington, DC: National Center for Education Statistics, Institute of Education Sciences, U.S. Department of Education, 2010), iii–vi, viii, xi–xii; Grace Chen, "Paupers and Princes: Economic Inequality at Public Schools," *Public School Review*, June 9, 2010,

www.publicschoolreview.com/articles/229/. See also Peter W. Cookson Jr., *Class Rules: Exposing Inequality in American High Schools* (New York: Teachers College Press, 2013).

10. Nicole Hannah-Jones, "Segregation Now . . . ," *Atlantic*, April 16, 2014, www.theatlantic.com/features/archive/2014/04/segregation-now/359813/.

11. Suzanne Mettler, *Degrees of Inequality: How the Politics of Higher Education Sabotaged the American Dream* (New York: Basic Books, 2014), 23, quotation 8; Paul Tough, "Am I Supposed to Be Here? Am I Good Enough?," *New York Times Magazine*, May 18, 2014. On how the social atmosphere of elite universities causes low-income students to falter or leave, see Elizabeth A. Armstrong and Laura T. Hamilton, *Paying for the Party: How College Maintains Inequality* (Cambridge, MA: Harvard University Press, 2013).

12. Sean F. Reardon, Rachel Baker, and Daniel Klasik, "Race, Income, and Enrollment Patterns in Highly Selective Colleges, 1982–2004," Center for Education Policy Analysis, Stanford University, August 3, 2012, 1, 2, 14, http://cepa.stanford.edu/sites/default/files/race%20income%20%26%20selective%20college%20enrollment%20august%203%202012.pdf.

13. Ibid., 1, 2. Several top private and public universities have launched efforts to enroll more middle-class and poor students; see David Leonhardt, "Top Colleges That Enroll Rich, Middle Class, and Poor," *New York Times*, September 8, 2014, www.nytimes.com/2014/09/09/upshot/top-colleges-that-enroll-rich-middle-class-and-poor.html?emc=eta1&abt=0002&abg=1/.

14. Catherine Rampell, "Why Tuition Has Skyrocketed at State Schools," *New York Times*, March 2, 2012, http://economix.blogs.nytimes.com/2012/03/02/why-tuition-has-skyrocketed-at-state-schools; Lynn O'Shaughnessy, "Why College Tuition Keeps Rising," CBSMoneyWatch, September, 25, 2012, www.cbsnews.com/news/why-college-tuition-keeps-rising/; Robert Gordon, "The Great Stagnation of American Education," *New York Times*, September 7, 2013, http://opinionator.blogs.nytimes.com/2013/09/07/the-great-stagnation-of-american-education/?_r=2#Opinionator%20/.

15. "Annual Report of the CFPB Student Loan Ombudsman," Consumer Financial Protection Bureau, October 16, 2014, http://files.consumerfinance.gov/f/201410_cfpb_report_annual-report-of-the-student-loan-ombudsman.pdf.

16. Sean F. Reardon, "No Rich Child Left Behind," *New York Times*, April 28, 2013, http://opinionator.blogs.nytimes.com/2013/04/28/no-rich-child-left-behind/. Economists Richard J. Murname and Greg J. Duncan found that from 1972 to 2006, high-income families increased the amount they spent on educational enrichment by 150 percent, while that of middle-income families grew by 57 percent. See also James Lardner, "What's the Problem?," in Lardner and Smith, *Inequality Matters*, 20. Ashlyn Aiko Nelson and Beth Gazley, "The Rise of School-Supporting Non-profits," *Education Finance and*

Policy 9, no. 4 (Fall 2014): 541, www.mitpressjournals.org/doi/abs/10.1162
/EDFP_a_00146?journalCode=edfp#.VG3yfvJATrc/; Motoko Rich, "Nation's
Wealthy Places Pour Private Money into Public Schools, Study Finds," *New
York Times*, October 21, 2014.

17. Rebecca Strauss, "Schooling Ourselves in an Unequal America,"
New York Times, June 16, 2013, http://opinionator.blogs.nytimes.com/2013
/06/16/schooling-ourselves-in-an-unequal-america/; Mettler, *Degrees of
Inequality*, 10.

18. Catherine Rampell, "Freebies for the Rich," *New York Times Magazine*,
September 29, 2013, 14–15; Ashley Spalding, "New Commitment to Need-
Based Financial Aid Critical in Context of Rising Tuition," Kentucky Center
for Economic Policy, February 25, 2014, http://kypolicy.org/new-commitment
-need-based-financial-aid-critical-context-rising-tuition/. For a different
view, despite the title, see Kelly Petty, "Merit-Based Financial Aid Puts
Low-Income Students at Disadvantage," IVN, http://ivn.us/2013/09/30/merit
-based-financial-aid-puts-low-income-students-at-disadvantage/.

19. Caroline M. Hoxby and Christopher Avery, "Low-Income High-
Achieving Students Miss Out on Attending Selective Colleges," Brookings
Papers on Economic Activity, Spring 2013, www.brookings.edu/about/projects
/bpea/latest-conference/2013-spring-selective-colleges-income-diversity
-hoxby/.

20. Ira Silver, letter to the editor, *New York Times*, March 18, 2013; second
quotation from Janet Belsky, letter to the editor, *New York Times*, March 17,
2013; Gordon, "Great Stagnation"; Jason DeParle, "For Poor, Leap to College
Often Ends in Hard Fall," *New York Times*, December 22, 2012. Tough (in "Am
I Supposed to Be Here?") addresses the complexities of low-income students
at elite public universities. In late 2014 Bloomberg Philanthropies formed a
coalition to enable more low-income high-performing high school students
to go to college; David Leonhardt, "A New Push to Get Low-Income Students
through College," *New York Times*, October 28, 2014, http://www.nytimes
.com/2014/10/28/upshot/a-new-push-to-get-low-income-students-through
-college.html?emc=eta1&abt=0002&abg=1/.

21. Carolin Hagelskamp, David Schleifer, and Christopher DiStasi,
"Profiting Higher Education? What Students, Alumni, and Employers Think
about For-Profit Colleges," research report by Public Agenda, with support
from the Kresge Foundation, February 2014, http://kresge.org/sites/default
/files/Edu-Library-ProfitingHigherEducation_PublicAgenda_2014.pdf;
Suzanne Mettler, "College, the Great Unleveller," *New York Times Sunday
Review*, March 1, 2014.

22. David J. Deming, Claudia Goldin, and Lawrence F. Katz, "The For-
Profit Postsecondary School Sector: Nimble Critters or Agile Predators?,"

Working Paper 17710, National Bureau of Economic Research, December 2011, www.nber.org/papers/w17710/; Mettler, *Degrees of Inequality*, 2.

23. Tamar Lewin, "Senate Committee Report on For-Profit Colleges," *New York Times*, July 29, 2012; Michael Stratford, "Senate Report Paints a Damning Portrait of For-Profit Higher Education," *Chronicle of Higher Education*, July 30, 2012; second quotation from Farrah Fazal, "For-Profit Colleges Investigation," KSDK, May 20, 2013, www.ksdk.com/news/article/381380/3/For-profit-colleges-investigation/. Suzanne Mettler agrees that the "problems of the for-profits are not limited to a few bad apples." See Mettler, *Degrees of Inequality*, 37.

24. Paul Fain, "Ky. Attorney General Jack Conway Battles For-Profits," *Inside Higher Ed*, November 3, 2011, https://www.insidehighered.com/news/2011/11/03/ky-attorney-general-jack-conway-battles-profits/; Tim Hsia and Gus Giacoman, "Making the G.I. Bill Work for Veterans," *New York Times*, September 6, 2012, http://atwar.blogs.nytimes.com/author/gus-giacoman/; Office of the Attorney General, "Attorney General Conway Files Suit against Spencerian College," press release, January 16, 2013, http://migration.kentucky.gov/newsroom/ag/spenceriansuit.htm.

25. Mettler, *Degrees of Inequality*, 1–3, 12, 163, 165, quotation 3.

26. Susie Madrak, "Is a For-Profit College Scandal the Real Reason Olympia Snowe Decided Not to Run?," *Crooks and Liars*, March 2, 2012, http://crooksandliars.com/susie-madrak/profit-college-scandal-real-reason-ol/; Bill Allison and Lindsay Young, "Did Lawsuit Factor in Olympia Snowe's Departure?," *Sunlight Foundation*, February 29, 2012, http://sunlightfoundation.com/blog/2012/02/29/snowe/.

27. Annie Lowrey, "Student Debt Slows Growth as Young Spend Less," *New York Times*, May 10, 2013. But see also David Leonhardt, "The Reality of Student Debt Is Different from the Clichés," *New York Times*, June 24, 2014; Beth Akers and Matthew M. Chingos, "Is a Student Loan Crisis on the Horizon?," Brookings Institution, June 2014, www.brookings.edu/research/reports/2014/06/24-student-loan-crisis-akers-chingos/.

28. Richard Pérez-Peña, "Federal Lawsuit Accuses For-Profit Schools of Fraud," *New York Times*, February 19, 2014; John Lauerman, "For-Profit Colleges Face a New Wave of State Investigations," *Bloomberg Businessweek*, January 29, 2014, www.businessweek.com/news/2014-01-29/for-profit-colleges-face-new-wave-of-coordinated-state-probes/. For a mixed defense of for-profits, see Eduardo Porter, "The Bane and Boon of For-Profit Colleges," *New York Times*, February 25, 2014.

29. Kevin Carey, "Corinthian Colleges Is Closing: Its Students May Be Better Off as a Result," *New York Times*, July 2, 1014.

30. Mettler, *Degrees of Inequality*, 163–87, quotations 177, 186, 187.

31. Egregious as these salaries might be, they pale in comparison to those raked in by for-profit CEOs. In 2009–2010, when the salaries of the highest-paid presidents of public universities averaged $860,000, the chief executives at for-profits made an average of $10.5 million, Robert Silberman of Strayer University hauled in $41.9 million, and Robert Knutson, retired CEO of Education Management Corporation, took in $132.4 million over seven years. See Mettler, *Degrees of Inequality*, 168–70.

32. Peter Schworm, "College Chiefs' Salaries Increase," *Boston Globe*, November 15, 2010; Tamar Lewin, "Three Dozen Private College Presidents Earned over $1 Million in 2010, Study Finds," *New York Times*, December 9, 2012; Blake Ellis, "Colleges Pay Presidents Millions While Raising Tuition," *CNN/Money*, http://money.cnn.com/2011/12/20/pf/college/presidents_pay/index.htm; "President Profiles," in Facts & Figures, *Chronicle of Higher Education*, http://chronicle.com/article/What-Public-College-Presidents/131912/, accessed March 22, 2014; Ellis, "Help for Homeless College Students," *CNN/Money*, http://money.cnn.com/2013/12/31/pf/homeless-college-students/index.html.

33. Benjamin Ginsberg, *The Fall of the Faculty: The Rise of the All-Administrative University and Why It Matters* (New York: Oxford University Press, 2011), 19, 26, 27, 33, quotation 2.

34. Andrew Erwin and Marjorie Wood, "The One Percent at State U," Institute for Policy Studies, May 21, 2014, www.ips-dc.org/one_percent_universities/; Ginsberg, "Administrators Ate My Tuition," *Washington Monthly*, September/October 2011, www.washingtonmonthly.com/magazine/septemberoctober_2011/features/administrators_ate_my_tuition031641.php.

35. Ginsberg, *Fall of the Faculty*, 76–77.

36. Harry Jaffe, "Ben Ladner's Years of Living Lavishly," *Washingtonian*, April 1, 2006, www.washingtonian.com/articles/people/ben-ladners-years-of-living-lavishly/.

37. Michael Janofsky, "Suspended College President Offers to Accept Lesser Pact," *New York Times*, September 24, 2005; Janofsky, "College Chief at American Agrees to Quit for Millions," *New York Times*, October 26, 2005.

38. "University of Florida Head to Keep Job Despite Remark," *New York Times*, January 28, 1998.

39. Barry Klein and Stephen Hegarty, "Lombardi Spending Is Being Studied," *St. Petersburg [FL] Times*, August 26, 1999; "Life after Lombardi," *New York Times*, August 26, 1999; Klein, "Lombardi's Presidency Ends," *New York Times*, October 30, 1999.

40. Nanette Asimov, "UC Chief Lays Out 'Draconian' Budget Plan," *San Francisco Chronicle*, July 11, 2009; Asimov, "SFGate: Execs Still Get Raises as UC Cuts Staffing Pay," *San Francisco Chronicle*, August 7, 2009; Jill Tucker and

Asimov, "Thousands March in Berkeley over UC Cuts," *San Francisco Chronicle*, September 25, 2009; Larry Gordon, "UC Chief Yudof Quits, Citing Health Reasons," *Los Angeles Times*, January 18, 2013.

41. Jennifer Schuessler, "Academy's Troubles Shadow Key Report," *New York Times*, June 11, 2013; Todd Wallack, "Leader of Cambridge's Prestigious Academy of Arts and Sciences Inflated Resume, Falsely Claiming Doctorate," *Boston Globe*, June 3, 2013; Wallack, "No Record of Academy Head's Doctoral Degree, *Boston Globe*, June 4, 2013. Soon after, it was revealed that in 2004, the board quietly slipped Berlowitz's name onto the list of the new members voted into the Academy that year, when she had merely been on the list of nominees.

42. Steve Street, Maria Maisto, Esther Merves, and Gary Rhoades, "Who Is Professor Staff and How Can This Person Teach So Many Classes?," Center for the Future of Higher Education, August 2012, http://feaweb.org/who-is -professor-staff-and-how-can-this-person-teach-so-many-classes; quotation from "The Just-in-Time Professor: A Staff Report Summarizing eForum Responses on the Working Conditions of Contingent Faculty in Higher Education," Democratic Staff, House Committee on Education and the Workforce, January 2014, 1, 2, http://democrats.edworkforce.house.gov/sites /democrats.edworkforce.house.gov/files/documents/1.24.14-AdjunctEforum Report.pdf. Estimates of the proportion of contingent faculty in the total amount of faculty members differ in the two reports.

43. Street et al., "Who Is Professor Staff"; Peter Schmidt, "Advocates for Adjunct Instructors Think Broadly in Search for Allies," *Chronicle of Higher Education*, November 18, 2013; Colleen Flaherty, "Making the Case for Adjuncts," *Inside Higher Ed*, January 9, 2013, https://www.insidehighered .com/news/2013/01/09/adjunct-leaders-consider-strategies-force-change/; Tamar Lewin, "Gap Widens at Colleges, Report Finds," *New York Times*, April 8, 2013.

44. Richard Moser, "Overuse and Abuse of Adjunct Faculty Members Threaten Core Academic Values," *Chronicle of Higher Education*, January 13, 2014. Eleven percent of part-time faculty hold doctoral degrees, compared with 18 percent of full-time faculty; the percentages holding master's degrees are virtually the same, 67 and 66 percent. See "Contingent Commitments: Bringing Part-Time Faculty into Focus: A Special Report from the Center for Community College Student Engagement," [2014], 4, www.ccsse.org/docs /PTF_Special_Report.pdf.

45. Daniel Kovalik, "Death of an Adjunct," *Pittsburgh Post-Gazette*, September 18, 2013; Colleen Flaherty, "Newspaper Column on 'Death of an Adjunct' Prompts Debate," *Inside Higher Ed*, September 19, 2013, https:// www.insidehighered.com/print/news/2013/09/19/newspaper-column-death

-adjunct-prompts-debate/; Claudio Sanchez, "The Sad Death of an Adjunct Professor Sparks a Labor Debate," NPR, September 22, 2013, http://npr.org /2013/09/22/224946206/adjunct-professor-dies-destitute-then-sparks -debate/. For a counter-narrative to Kovalik's, see "The Compelling Life Story of Margaret Mary Vojtko," Call Me "Miss"!, http://callmemiss.com/2013/09 /19/the-compelling-life-story-of-margaret-mary-vojtko/.

3. The Shrinking Middle Class

1. David Leonhardt and Kevin Quealy, "The American Middle Class Is No Longer the World's Richest," *New York Times*, April 22, 2014. The comparisons are based on income data from the Luxembourg Income Study database, analyzed by researchers from LIS, the *New York Times*, and outside academic economists. Workers in other countries are also working fewer hours and enjoying more leisure time than those in the United States. See Eduardo Porter, "U.S. Workers Losing Ground in Leisure Time, Too," *New York Times*, April 23, 2014.

2. "The Lost Decade of the Middle Class: Fewer, Poorer, Gloomier," Pew Research Social & Demographic Trends, August 22, 2012, www.pewsocial trends.org/2012/08/22/the-lost-decade-of-the-middle-class/; Ronald Brownstein, "Being in the Middle Class Means Worrying about Falling Behind," Allstate/National Journal Heartland Monitor poll, April 25, 2013, www.nationaljournal.com/next-economy/solutions-bank/being-in-the -middle-class-means-worrying-about-falling-behind-20130425/.

3. Charles W. Blow, "The Morose Middle Class," *New York Times*, April 26, 2013; Emerson quotation in Richard Wilkinson and Kate Pickett, *The Spirit Level: Why Greater Equality Makes Societies Stronger* (New York: Bloomsbury Press, 2010), 44.

4. Jeff Tietz, "The Sharp, Sudden Decline of America's Middle Class," *Rolling Stone*, June 25, 2012, www.rollingstone.com/culture/news/the-sharp -sudden-decline-of-americas-middle-class-20120622/.

5. David Madland and Keith Miller, "Latest Census Data Underscore How Important Unions Are for the Middle Class," Center for American Progress, September 17, 2013, www.americanprogressaction.org/issues/labor/news/2013 /09/17/74363/latest-census-data-underscore-how-important-unions-are-for -the-middle-class/; Binyamin Appelbaum, "Families' Net Worth Drops to Level of Early '90s, Fed Says," *New York Times*, June 11, 2012; Ylan Q. Mui, "Americans Saw Wealth Plummet 40 percent from 2007 to 2010, Federal Reserve Says," *Washington Post*, June 11, 2012. As middle-tier median income fell, its median wealth—assets minus debt—declined by 28 percent, from $128,582 to $93,150. The lower tier got hammered even worse, with its wealth going down by 45 percent, though from a much smaller base (from $18,421 to $10,151).

6. United States Census Bureau, "More Families with an Unemployed Parent, Census Bureau Reports," press release, August 27, 2013, www.census .gov/newsroom/press-releases/2013/cb13-149.html.

7. Emily Badger, "The Steady Decline of Homeownership for Everyone, Everywhere," Atlantic Cities, July 30, 2013, www.theatlanticcities.com/ housing/2013/07/steady-decline-homeonership-everyone-everywhere /6373/; Bob Adelmann, "Home Ownership Rates Continue to Fall; New Plans to Reflate Bubble," *New American*, August 1, 2013, http://thenewamerican .com/economy/markets/item/16165-home-ownership-rates-continue-to -fall-new-plans-to-reflate-are-underway/; William R. Emmons and Bryan J. Noeth, "Why Did Young Families Lose So Much Wealth during the Crisis? The Role of Home Ownership," *Federal Reserve Bank of St. Louis Review* 95, no. 1 (January/February 2013), 1, 2, 24, http://research.stlouisfed.org /publications/review/article/9600/.

8. Quotation from Rakesh Kochhar, Richard Fry, and Paul Taylor, "Wealth Gaps Rise to Record High between Whites, Blacks, Hispanics," Pew Research Social & Demographic Trends, July 26, 2011, 1, 2, www.pewsocialtrends.org /2011/07/26/wealth-gaps-rise-to-record-highs-between-whites-blacks -hispanics/. According to this report, "in 2005 the comparable shares had been 29% for blacks, 23% for Hispanics and 11% for whites." See also Thomas Shapiro, Tatjana Meschede, and Sam Osoro, "The Roots of the Widening Racial Wealth Gap: Explaining the Black-White Economic Divide," Research and Policy Brief, Institute on Assets & Social Policy, February 2013, http:// iasp.brandeis.edu/pdfs/Author/shapiro-thomas-m/racialwealthgapbrief.pdf; D'Vera Cohn, "The Middle Class Shrinks and Income Segregation Rises," Pew Research Social & Demographic Trends, August 2, 2012, www.pewsocial trends.org/2012/08/02/the-middle-class-shrinks-and-income-segregation -rises/. Regarding the trend to 2013, see Rakesh Kochhar and Richard Fry, "Wealth Inequality Has Widened along Racial, Ethnic Lines since End of Great Recession," Pew Research Center, December 12, 2014, www.pewresearch .org/fact-tank/2014/12/12/racial-wealth-gaps-great-recession/.

9. Thomas J. Sugrue, "A Dream Still Deferred," *New York Times*, March 26, 2011; Stiglitz, *Price of Inequality*, 87, 419; Shaila Dewan, "Discrimination in Housing against Nonwhites Persists Quietly, U.S. Study Finds," *New York Times*, June 12, 2013, B3 (New York edition). For background, see Sugrue, *The Origin of the Urban Crisis: Race and Inequality in Postwar Detroit* (Princeton, NJ: Princeton University Press, 1996). In another context, Sherrilyn A. Ifill, director-counsel of the N.A.A.C.P. Legal Defense and Education Fund, commented in "Race vs. Class: The False Dichotomy," *New York Times*, June 13, 2013: "Whether the name on our resume is Lakeisha or Leslie matters when we try to get job interviews."

10. Sean F. Reardon and Kendra Bischoff, "Growth in the Residential Segregation of Families by Income, 1970–2009," US 2010, November 2011, www.s4.brown.edu/us2010/Data/Report/report111111.pdf (full report); several other websites have abstracts of the report and commentary on it. See also "Equality of Opportunity Project," Summary of Project Findings, July 2013, http://obs.rc.fas.harvard.edu/chetty/website/IGE/Executive %20Summary.pdf. The number of middle- or mixed-income neighborhoods correspondingly declined from 54 percent to 48 percent.

11. Reardon and Bischoff, "Growth in Residential Segregation." See also Sabrina Tavernise, "Middle-Class Areas Shrink as Income Gap Grows, New Report Finds," *New York Times*, November 15, 2011.

12. Becky M. Nicolaides and Andrew Wiese, "Suburban Disequilibrium," *New York Times*, April 6, 2013.

13. "The Gilded City," *Nation*, May 6, 2013, 11–12.

14. Kuttner, *Debtors' Prison*, 21, 23; second quotation from Oya Celasun, "United States: How Inequality Affects Savings Behavior," iMFdirect, September 13, 2012, http://blog-imfdirect.imf.org/2012/09/13/united-states -how-inequality-affects-saving-behavior/.

15. Robert H. Frank, "Income Inequality Too Big to Ignore," *New York Times*, October 16, 2010.

16. Adam Seth Levine, Robert H. Frank, and Oege Dijk, "Expenditure Cascades," Social Science Research Network, September 13, 2010, http:// ssrn.com/abstract=1690612/.

17. Ibid., 4–5, 9; Robert H. Frank, *Luxury Fever: Why Money Fails to Satisfy in an Era of Excess* (New York: Free Press, 1999). See also Chrystia Freeland, "Keeping Up with the 1 Percent," Reuters, March 23, 2012, www.reuters.com /article/2012/03/23/us-column-freeland-idUSBRE82M13520120323/. The housing trend has continued; while families are smaller, houses are larger. The typical home in 2012 was about 50 percent larger than in 1973, while the typical family is 10 percent smaller and the typical number of household members is 15 percent less. The three-bedroom house has been the standard and constitutes 47 percent of the market, while four-bedroom or larger homes make up 26 percent, even among families without kids. This could change, as multigenerational families recently have proliferated. See Greg Toppo and Paul Overberg, "New Houses Still Getting Bigger," *USA Today*, June 8, 2013.

18. Levine et al., "Expenditure Cascades," 11–12.

19. On status being local, see Avner Offner, *The Challenge of Affluence: Self-Control and Well-Being in the United States and Britain since 1950* (Oxford: Oxford University Press, 2006), 280; for the Emerson quotation, see note 3 above.

20. Levine et al., "Expenditure Cascades," 16–17, 23.

21. Marianne Bertrand and Adair Morse, "Trickle-Down Consumption," NBER Working Paper No. 18883, National Bureau of Economic Research, March 2013, www.nber.org/papers/w18883/.

22. Heidi Shierholz, "Six Years after Its Beginning, the Great Recession's Shadow Looms over the Labor Market," Issue Brief, Economic Policy Institute, January 9, 2014, http://s2.epi.org/files/2014/six-years-after-start -of-great-recession.pdf; Paul Krugman, "War on the Unemployed," *New York Times*, June 30, 2013; Bureau of Labor Statistics, "Employment Situation Summary," Economic News Release, November 7, 2014, www.bls.gov/news .release/empsit.nr0.htm; Alan Kreuger, Alexandre Mas, and Xiaotong Niu, "The Evolution of Rotation Group Bias: Will the Real Unemployment Rate Please Stand Up," Princeton University, August 2014, www.princeton.edu /~amas/papers/RGB.August.pdf. During 2013, several states reduced unemployment benefits because Republicans believe that social programs lure people who are able to work into dependency. North Carolina, controlled by Republicans, cut its benefits, knowing it would lose $700 million in federal aid by doing so.

23. Offner, *Challenge of Affluence*, 292.

24. "Recessions Can Take up to Three Years Off Older Workers' Lives, but Medicare and Social Security Can Help," Wellesley College press release, September 17, 2012, www.wellesley.edu/news/wellesley_news/node/29842. The full text of the study was released by the National Bureau of Economic Research and is available at www.nber.org/papers/w18361?utm_campaign =ntw&utm_medium=email&utm_source=ntw.

25. Robert E. Scott, "Displaced Minority Workers Suffered 29.6 Percent Drop in Wages from the Growing Trade Deficit with China," Economic Policy Institute, October 10, 2013, www.epi.org/publication-minority-workers -suffered-29-6-percent-drop/.

26. Barry C. Lynn and Phillip Longman, "Who Broke America's Job Machine?," *Washington Monthly*, March/April 2010, www.washington monthly.com/features/2010/1003.lynn-longman.html.

27. Emerging economies were "generally more resilient," according to "Global Wage Report 2012/13: Wages and Equitable Growth," International Labour Organization, December 7, 2012, v, www.ilo.org/global/research /global-reports/global-wage-report/2012/lang-en/index.htm. See also Nelson D. Schwartz, "Payroll Data Shows a Lag in Wages, Not Just Hiring," *New York Times*, February 7, 2014.

28. Catherine Ruckelshaus and Sarah Leberstein, *Manufacturing Low Pay: Declining Wages in the Jobs That Built America's Middle Class*, National

Employment Law Project, November 2014, 3–4, 12–13, quotation 8, www
.nelp.org/page/-/Justice/2014/Manufacturing-Low-Pay-Declining-Wages
-Jobs-Built-Middle-Class.pdf?nocdn=1/.

29. David Leonhardt, "The Great Wage Slowdown of the 21st Century,"
New York Times, October 7, 2014, www.nytimes.com/2014/10/07/upshot
/the-great-wage-slowdown-of-the-21st-century.html?abt=0002&abg=1/.

30. Quotation from Lawrence Mishel and Alyssa Davis, "CEO Pay
Continues to Rise as Typical Workers Are Paid Less," Issue Brief, Economic
Policy Institute, June 12, 2014, http://s1.epi.org/files/2014/ceo-pay-continues
-to-rise.pdf. Economists technically define the "nonlabor share" as returns to
capital, profits, net interest, depreciation, and indirect taxes. See Fleck et al.,
"Compensation-Productivity Gap," 59, 60, 61; Gould and Wething, "U.S.
Poverty Rates Higher," 2. Erik Brynjolfsson and Andrew McAfee point out
that the supply of educated workers is increasing. See Brynjolfsson and
McAfee, "Why Workers Are Losing."

31. Annette Bernhardt, Ruth Milkman, Nik Theodore, Douglas Heckathorn,
Mirabel Auer, James DeFilippis, Ana Luz González, Victor Narro, Jason
Perelshteyen, Diana Polson, and Michal Spiller, "Broken Laws, Unprotected
Workers: Violations of Employment and Labor Laws in America's Cities,"
National Employment Law Project, 2009, www.nelp.org/page/-/brokenlaws
/BrokenLawsReport2009.pdf?nocdn=1/; Brady Meixell and Ross Eisenbrey, "An
Epidemic of Wage Theft Is Costing Workers Hundreds of Millions of Dollars a
Year," Issue Brief No. 385, Economic Policy Institute, September 11, 2014, http://
s3.epi.org/files/2014/wage-theft.pdf; Gordon Lafer, "The Legislative Attack on
American Wages and Labor Standards, 2011–2012," Briefing Paper, Economic
Policy Institute, October 31, 2013, www.epi.org/publication/attack-on-american
-labor-standards/; "Acting Responsibly? Federal Contractors Frequently Put
Workers' Lives and Livelihoods at Risk," Majority Committee Staff Report,
United States Senate, Health, Education, Labor, and Pensions Committee, Tom
Harkin, Chairman, December 11, 2013, 7–8, quotation 8, www.help.senate.gov
/imo/media/doc/Labor%20Law%20Violations%20by%20Contractors
%20Report.pdf. An indirect form of wage theft is growing, with businesses
requiring their employees, even low-wage workers, to sign noncompetition
agreements binding them to that employer for a set period of time. Managers
who sign these contracts switch jobs less and earn less money. See Mark J.
Garmaise, "Ties That Truly Bind: Non-competition Agreements, Executive
Compensation and Firm Investment," UCLA Anderson, http://personal
.anderson.ucla.edu/mark.garmaise/noncomp7.pdf.

32. Robert Hiltonsmith and Amy Traub, "Underwriting Executive Excess,"
Demos, September 24, 2013, www.demos.org/publication/underwriting
-executive-excess-0/.

33. "Poll: Majority in U.S. Approve of Labor Unions," UPI, August 30, 2013, www.upi.com/Business_News/2013/08/30/Poll-Majority-in-US-approve-of-labor-unions/UPI-21911377883684/. The high-water marks of union approval came in the 1950s, at 75 percent in 1953 and 1957, with approval remaining above 60 percent until the end of the 1960s.

34. Jake Rosenfeld, *What Unions No Longer Do* (Cambridge, MA: Harvard University Press, 2014), quotations 4, 5.

35. Subtracting unionized public-sector workers from the total, 35 percent of whom are unionized, would reduce the private-sector cohort to well under 10 percent.

36. On the difficulty of organizing unions in the United States, see Thomas Geoghegan, *Which Side Are You On? How to Be for Labor When It's Flat on Its Back* (New York: Farrar, Straus & Giroux, 1991); Andrew Glyn, *Capitalism Unleashed: Finance Globalization and Welfare* (New York: Oxford University Press, 2006). See also Kevin Drum, "Why Screwing Unions Screws the Entire Middle Class," *Mother Jones*, March/April 2011, www.motherjones.com /politics/2011/02/income-inequality-labor-union-decline/.

37. Hacker and Pierson, *Winner-Take-All Politics*, 116–49; Jeffrey M. Berry, *The New Liberalism: The Rising Power of Citizen Groups* (Washington, DC: Brookings Institution, 1999). On the fallacy that conservatives are "devoted to the unfettered working of the market," see Baker, *End of Loser Liberalism*, 2.

38. Journalism Project Staff, "Who Drove the Economic News (and Who Didn't)?," Pew Research Journalism Project, October 5, 2009, www.journalism .org/2009/10/05/who-drove-economic-news-and-who-didnt/; Noah, *Great Divergence*, 129.

39. Rosenfeld, *What Unions No Longer Do*, 101–30, quotations 183, 187.

40. David Madland and Keith Miller, "Middle Classes Are Stronger in States with Greater Union Membership," Centers for American Progress Action Fund, September 20, 2013, www.americanprogressaction.org/issues /labor/news/2013/09/20/74751/middle-classes-are-stronger-in-states-with -greater-union-membership-2/; Ross Eisenbrey and Colin Gordon, "As Unions Decline, Inequality Rises," Economic Policy Institute, June 6, 2012, www.epi .org/publication/unions-decline-inequality-rises/.

41. Lawrence Mishel, "Unions, Inequality, and Faltering Middle-Class Wages," Issue Brief, Economic Policy Institute, August 29, 2012, 9, www.epi .org/files/2012/ib342-unions-inequality-middle-class-wages.pdf; quotation from Mishel and Matthew Walters, "How Unions Help All Workers," Economic Policy Institute, August 26, 2003, www.epi.org/publication/briefingpapers _bp143/.

42. Ibid., 9, quotation 11; Eisenbrey and Gordon, "As Unions Decline." For the role of agribusiness and long-haul trucking in the decline of unions, see

Shane Hamilton, *Trucking Country: The Road to America's Wal-Mart Economy* (Princeton, NJ: Princeton University Press, 2008).

43. Eric Schlosser, *Fast Food Nation: The Dark Side of the All-American Meal* (Boston: Houghton Mifflin, 2001), 94–107, quotations 94–95, 98, 102. Schlosser provides an excellent brief history of franchising and the transfer of risk.

44. Jacob S. Hacker, *The Great Risk Shift: The Assault on American Jobs, Families, Health Care, and Retirement and How You Can Fight Back* (New York: Oxford University Press, 2006), ix.

45. "The Last Private Industry Pension Plans," January 3, 2013, *TED: The Economics Daily*, U.S. Bureau of Labor Statistics, www.bls.gov/opub/ted/2013 /ted_20130103.htm; David A. Smith and Heather McGhee, "Shredding the Retirement Contract," in Lardner and Smith, *Inequality Matters*, 78; James E. McWhinney, "The Demise of the Defined-Benefit Plan," Investopedia, www .investopedia.com/articles/retirement/06/demiseofdbplan.asp; Barbara A. Butrica, Howard A. Iams, Karen E. Smith, and Eric J. Toder, "The Disappearing Defined-Benefit Pension and Its Potential Impact on the Retirement Incomes of Baby Boomers," *Social Security Bulletin* 69, no. 3 (2009), www.ssa .gov/policy/docs/ssb/v69n3/v69n3p1.html.

46. Monique Morrissey and Natalie Sabadash, "Retirement Inequality: How the 401(k) Revolution Created a Few Big Winners and Many Losers," Economic Policy Institute, September 26, 2013, www.epi.org/publication/retirement -inequality-chartbook/. Not surprisingly, during the stock market tumble of 2008–2009, many older employees decided to delay retirement and took bridge jobs before completely retiring. One-time permanent retirements now "are the exception rather than the rule." While people take bridge jobs for many reasons, the movement away from defined benefits "has been a pivotal part of this change."

See Kevin E. Cahill, Michael D. Giandrea, and Joseph F. Quinn, "Reentering the Labor Force after Retirement," *Monthly Labor Review*, June 2011, www.bls.gov/opub/mlr/2011/06/art2full.pdf.

47. The account here is indebted to Kuttner, *Debtors' Prison*, 200–204, quotations 201; Ellen Schultz, *Retirement Heist: How Companies Plunder and Profit from the Nest Eggs of American Workers* (New York: Penguin Group, 2011). For a good account of the collapse of retirement security, see Smith, *Who Stole the American Dream*, 170–91.

48. "'De-risking' Pensions Could be Risky to Pensioners," Pension Rights Center, October 18, 2012, www.pensionrights.org/newsroom/releases/%E2 %80%9Cde-risking%E2%80%9D-pensions-could-be-risky-pensioners/; Jerry Geisel, "De-risking Program Slashes Size of GM Pension Plans," Business Insurance, February 25, 2013; Eileen Ambrose, "The Great Pension Sell-Off,"

AARP: The Magazine, June/July 2014, 29–31, quotation 30, www.business insurance.com/article/20130225/NEWS03/130229879/.

49. Morrissey and Sabadash, "Retirement Inequality."

50. Rick Lyman and Mary Williams Walsh, "Public Pension Tabs Multiply as States Defer Costs and Hard Choices," *New York Times*, February 24, 2014; "Public Pension Shortfalls Are Everyone's Problem," *BloombergView*, August 8, 2013, www.bloombergview.com/articles/2013-08-08/public-pension -shortfalls-are-everyone-s-problem/.

51. First quotation from Michael H. Granof, "A Misguided Pension Reform for Government," *Governing*, September 26, 2013, www.governing.com/blogs /view/col-state-local-government-misguided-pension-reform.html; second quotation from Erik Kain, "Why Defined-Benefit Plans Are Safer Investments for State Governments and Workers," *Forbes*, March 1, 2011, www.forbes.com /sites/erikkain/2011/03/01/why-defined-benefit-plans-are-safer-investments -for-state-governments-and-workers/.

52. "Traditional Pension Plans," Union Plus, http://retirement.unionplus .org/money-for-retirement/pension-plans.html.

53. Steven Greenhouse, "Tackling the Concerns of Independent Workers," *New York Times*, March 23, 2013.

54. Doyle McManus, "Poof Goes the Middle Class," *Los Angeles Times*, October 23, 2013; Tyler Cowen, *Average Is Over: Powering America beyond the Age of the Great Stagnation* (New York: Dutton, 2013). Steven Rattner, longtime executive on Wall Street and advisor in the Obama administration, is pessimistic about a manufacturing revival. See Rattner, "The Myth of Industrial Rebound," *New York Times Sunday Review*, January 26, 2014. See also Cowen, *The Great Stagnation: How America Ate All the Low-Hanging Fruit of Modern History, Got Sick, and Will (Eventually) Feel Better* (New York: Dutton, 2011).

55. Nelson D. Schwartz, "The Middle Class Is Steadily Eroding: Just Ask the Business World," *New York Times*, February 2, 2014; Cynamon and Fazzari, "Inequality," 21, 22, 26, 27.

4. Keeping the Rich (Filthy) Rich and the Poor (Dirt) Poor

Epigraph. Thorstein Veblen, *The Theory of the Leisure Class: An Economic Study of Institutions* (New York: Macmillan, 1899).

1. "Income Inequality Reaches Record and Threatens American Dream," Wall Street Selector, October 3, 2013, www.wallstreetsectorselector.com /investment-articles/editors-desk/2013/10/income-inequality-reaches -record-threatens-american-dream/; Saez, "Striking It Richer," 1, 2, 5; Richard Fry and Paul Taylor, "A Rise in Wealth for the Wealthy; Declines for the Lower 93%," Pew Research Social & Demographic Trends, April 23, 2013,

www.pewsocialtrends.org/2013/04/23/a-rise-in-wealth-for-the-wealthy declines-for-the-lower-93/.

2. Bartles, *Unequal Democracy*, 127–61; definition of rent seeking from Stiglitz, *Price of Inequality*, 39–40; William L. Riordon, *Plunkitt of Tammany Hall* (New York: E. P. Dutton, 1963), 3.

3. David Cay Johnston, "The Great Tax Shift," in Lardner and Smith, *Inequality Matters*, 169.

4. Hacker and Pierson, *Winner-Take-All Politics*, 116–17, 118. The story has been told many times of future Supreme Court justice Lewis Powell, then a major corporate lawyer, sounding the alarm in a now well-known memo to the business community, stating that "the American economic system is under attack." Powell advised corporate Americans to get organized and accumulate political power. See also Phillips-Fein, *Invisible Hands*.

5. Ibid., 121–34, quotation 134.

6. The first two sentences are paraphrased from Andrew Fieldhouse, "Rising Income Inequality and the Role of Shifting Market-Income Distribution, Tax Burdens, and Tax Rates," Issue Brief, Economic Policy Institute, June 14, 2013, 7, www.epi.org/publication/rising-income-inequality-role -shifting-market/. "The fact that the US has the least progressive tax system and the most inequality in 'market' incomes may not be an accident." See Stiglitz, *Price of Inequality*, xxxi–xxxii, xxxiii, 90, 91.

7. Hacker and Pierson, *Winner-Take-All Politics*, 194, 239–41.

8. "Makers and Takers," *Economist*, October 13, 2012, www.economist.com /node/21564407/. Eduardo Porter, "A Nation with Too Many Tax Breaks," *New York Times*, March 13, 2012. Porter made similar calculations that were based on data from the Brookings Institution Tax Policy Center, the Urban Institute, and the Center on Budget and Policy Priorities. Relevant here is Suzanne Mettler, *The Submerged State: How Invisible Government Policies Undermine American Democracy* (Chicago: University of Chicago Press, 2011).

9. Johnston, "Great Tax Shift," 173–74; Gabriel Winston, "What Is the Payroll Tax Cap?," eHow, www.ehow.com/about_7227506_payroll-tax-cap_.html. Johnston (174–75) also describes how the Alternative Minimum Tax functions in a similar fashion to burden the middle class and not the rich.

10. First two quotations from Fieldhouse, "Rising Income Inequality," 2, 10–11; Stiglitz, *Price of Inequality*, 208–10; Amy Feldman, "New Estate Tax Rules Call for New Planning Tactics," Reuters, February 26, 2013, www.reuters .com/article/2013/02/26/us-column-feldman-idUSBRE91P0NY20130226/; Paul Krugman, "Now That's Rich," *New York Times*, May 8, 2014.

11. Alan Sloane, "The Real Reason Corporate Tax Reform Is Going Nowhere Fast," *Washington Post*, April 11, 2013, www.washingtonpost.com/business /economy/the-real-reason-corporate-tax-reform-is-going-nowhere-fast/2013

/04/11/d5fc3202-a2db-11e2-9c03-6952ff305f35_story.html; Nelson D. Schwartz, "Recovery in U.S. Is Lifting Profits, but Not Adding Jobs," *New York Times,* March 3, 2013; George Lefebvre, *The French Revolution,* trans. R. R. Palmer (Princeton, NJ: Princeton University Press, 1947; orig. pub. 1939), 8–9.

12. Jacques Leslie, "The True Cost of Hidden Money: A Piketty Protégé's Theory and Tax Havens," *New York Times,* June 15, 2014; Niels Johannesen and Gabriel Zucman, "The End of Bank Secrecy? An Evaluation of the G20 Tax Haven Crackdown," *American Economic Journal: Economic Policy* 6, no. 1 (2014): 65–91, http://dx.doi.org/10.1257/pol.6.1.65. Although the latter discusses offshore "sham corporations" (89), its purpose is to show the ineffectiveness of G20 treaties to prevent tax evasion.

13. Robert S. McIntyre, Matthew Gardner, Rebecca J. Wilkins, and Richard Phillips, "Corporate Taxpayers & Corporate Tax Dodgers, 2008–10," Citizens for Tax Justice, November 2011, 1, 2, 3, www.ctj.org/corporatetaxdodgers /CorporateTaxDodgersReport.pdf; McIntyre quotation in David Kocieniewski, "Biggest Public Firms Paid Little U.S. Tax, Study Says," *New York Times,* November 3, 2011. One enormous loophole allows companies to finance building projects with bonds that are exempt from federal taxes, and these bonds are often structured to avoid state sales taxes and local property taxes. More than $65 billion of these bonds have been issued by federal, state, and local governments from 2003 to 2013. Among businesses aided this way were an Egyptian construction company intending to build a fertilizer plant in Iowa, and a Pakistani company wanting to build one in Indiana. See Mary Williams Walsh and Louise Story, "A Stealth Tax Subsidy for Business Faces New Scrutiny," *New York Times,* March 4, 2013.

14. Jia Lynn Yang, "*Post* Analysis of Dow 30 Firms Shows Declining Tax Burden as a Share of Profits," *Washington Post,* March 26, 2013; Daria Camron and Yang, "Tax Burden for the Dow 30 Drops," *Washington Post,* March 26, 2013, Jim Nunns, "How TPC Distributes the Corporate Income Tax," Tax Policy Center, September 13, 2012, 1, www.taxpolicycenter.org/publications /url.cfm?ID=412651/; "No Replacement for Corporate Taxes," *New York Times,* May 30, 2013. Corporations benefit—and public treasuries lose—when state and local governments compete by lowering their tax rates to induce businesses to locate in their domain, with that revenue loss compounded when the firms break their promise to stay and instead seek better tax breaks elsewhere. Louise Stor calculated that these subsidies amounted to at least $80 billion a year. See Stor, "As Corporations Seek Tax Deals, Governments Pay High Price," *New York Times,* December 1, 2012.

15. Peter Eavis, "Invasion of the Supersalaries," Sunday Business section, *New York Times,* April 13, 2014; quotation from Lawrence Mishel, "The CEO-to-Worker Compensation Ratio in 2012 of 273 Was Far above That of the Late

1990s and 14 Times the Ratio of 20:1 in 1965," Economic Policy Institute, September 24, 2013, www.epi.org/publication/the-ceo-to-worker -compensation-ratio-in-2012-of-273/. Regarding valid and probably (unnecessarily) exaggerated ratios, see Louis Jacobson, "Viral Facebook Post on CEO-Worker Pay Ratio Has Obscure Past," *PolitiFact.com*, October 10, 2011, www.politifact.com/truth-o-meter/statements/2011/oct/10/facebook-posts /viral-facebook-post-ceo-worker-pay-ratio-has-obscu/. Ratios in 2012, according to the AFL-CIO, were as follows: Canada 206:1, Germany 147:1, France 104:1, Australia 93:1, Sweden 89:1, United Kingdom 84:1, and Japan 67:1. See "CEO-to-Worker Pay Ratios around the World," AFL-CIO, www .aflcio.org/Corporate-Watch/Paywatch-Archive/CEO-Pay-and-You/CEO-to -Worker-Pay-Gap-in-the-United-States/Pay-Gaps-in-the-World./

16. Kevin Shih, Sam Pizzigati, Chuck Collins, and Sarah Anderson, "Executive Excess 2010: CEO Pay and the Great Recession," Institute for Policy Studies, September 1, 2010, 1, 3, 5, www.ips-dc.org/reports/executive_excess_2010. Joseph Stiglitz has the ratio of executive to worker pay going back to 273-to-1 after the recession, the EPI figure. See Stiglitz, *Price of Inequality*, 4.

17. Annie Lowrey, "Pay Still High at Bailed-Out Companies, Report Says," *New York Times*, January 26, 2013.

18. See, for example, Tad Dehaven, "Corporate Welfare in the Federal Budget," Cato Institute Policy Analysis, July 25, 2012, http://object.cato.org /sites/cato.org/files/pubs/pdf/PA703.pdf; David Callahan, "Where Cato Goes Wrong on Corporate Welfare," September 3, 2013, www.demos.org/blog/9/3 /13/where-cato-goes-wrong-corporate-welfare/. For a critique of Cato's ideologically driven treatment of data on a related topic, see Rick Ungar, "The Conservative Case for Welfare Reform Suffers Massive Blow via Cato Institute Study," *Forbes*, September 3, 2013, www.forbes.com/sites/rickungar/2013/09 /03/the-conservative-case-for-welfare-reform-suffers-massive-blow-via-cato -institute-study/.

19. Daniel Sullivan and Till von Wachten, "Mortality, Mass-Layoffs, and Career Outcomes: An Analysis Using Administrative Data," NBER Working Paper 13626, November 2009, www.nber.org/papers/w13626.pdf?new _window=1/.

20. Stiglitz, *Price of Inequality*, 98; Lawrence Mishel and Natalie Sabadash, "CEO Pay in 2012 Was Extraordinarily High Relative to Typical Workers and Other High Earners," Economic Policy Institute, June 26, 2013, www.epi.org /publication/ceo-pay-2012-extraordinarily-high/. On skimming, see Freeland, *Plutocrats*, 138–39. On tax rules benefiting CEOs, see Scott Klinger, Sam Pizzigati, Chuck Collins, and Sarah Anderson, "Executive Excess 2012: The CEO Hands in Uncle Sam's Pocket," Institute for Policy Studies, August 16, 2012, www.ips-dc.org/reports/executive_excess_2012/.

21. Scott Klinger, Sam Pizzigati, and Sarah Anderson, "Executive Excess 2013: Bailed Out, Booted, and Busted," Institute for Policy Studies, August 28, 2013, www.ips-dc.org/reports/executive-excess-2013/. Some resistance to soaring CEO pay has developed. See Gretchen Morgenson, "As Shareholders Say 'Enough Already,' Some Boards Are Starting to Listen," *New York Times*, April 7, 2012; but see also Susanne Craig, "At Banks, Board Pay Soars Amid Cutbacks," *New York Times*, March 31, 2013; Taibbi, *The Divide*, 143–96, quotation 143.

22. Scott Klinger and Sarah Anderson, "A Pension Deficit Disorder: The Massive CEO Retirement Funds and Underfunded Worker Pensions at Firms Pushing Social Security Cuts," Institute for Policy Studies, November 27, 2012, www.ips-dc.org/reports/pension-deficit-disorder/; Hacker and Pierson, *Winner-Take-All Politics*, 62–63; information on Fuld is easily available on the Internet. Some of those 5 and 1 percent executives of large companies have found another way to profit from their employees' retirement funds: switching to annual lump-sum payments to these pension accounts, thus getting to use the money meanwhile and keeping the amounts accrued by workers who leave for other jobs or are laid off before the end of the year. See "Making Retirements Less Secure," *New York Times*, February 14, 2014.

23. David Brooks, "Thurston Howell Romney," *New York Times*, September 17, 2012. Suzanne Mettler and John Sides commented that the deeper reality Mitt Romney "glossed over is that nearly all Americans have used government social policies at some point in their lives." See Mettler and Sides, "We Are the 96 Percent," *New York Times*, September 24, 2012.

24. Lucy Madison, "Fact-Checking Romney's '47 Percent' Comment," *CBS News*, www.cbsnews.com/8301-503544_162-57515033-503544/fact-checking -romneys-47-percent-comment/; Derek Thompson, "The 47%: Who They Are, Where They Live, How They Vote, and Why They Matter," *Atlantic*, September 18, 2012, www.theatlantic.com/business/archive/2012/09/the-47 -who-they-are-where-they-live-how-they-vote-and-why-they-matter/262506/.

25. "Makers and Takers"; Gould and Wething, "U.S. Poverty Rates Higher"; Beddoes, "For Richer, for Poorer." The same point is made by John Micklethwait and Adrian Wooldridge, *The Right Nation: Conservative Power in America* (New York: Penguin Press, 2004), 7.

26. Carl Davis, Kelly Davis, Matthew Gardner, Harley Heimovitz, Robert S. McIntyre, Richard Phillips, Alla Sapozhnikova, and Meg Wiehe, *Who Pays? A Distributional Analysis of the Tax Systems in All 50 States*, 4th ed. (Washington, DC: Institute on Taxation & Economic Policy, 2013), 1, 2.

27. Katherine S. Newman and Rourke L. O'Brien, *Taxing the Poor: Doing Damage to the Truly Disadvantaged* (Berkeley: University of California Press, 2011), xlii, 65, 66–67, 122, 123, 140, 148, quotations 65, 142.

28. Ibid., 140–48, quotation 148.

29. Jessica Silver-Greenberg, "Major Banks Aid in Payday Loans Banned by States," *New York Times*, February 12, 2013; Shipler, *Working Poor*, 13–26, quotation 21; Thomas B. Edsall, "Making Money Off the Poor," *New York Times*, September 17, 2013, http://opinionator.blogs.nytimes.com/category/thomas-b-edsall/. Edsall discusses research about the poor exploiting the poor.

30. "The State of Lending: Payday Loans," Center for Responsible Lending, September 10, 2013, www.responsiblelending.org/payday-lending/tools-resources/fast-facts.html.

31. Blake Ellis, "Big Banks to Stop Offering Payday-Like Loans," *CNN/Money*, January 21, 2014, http://money.cnn.com/2014/01/21/pf/bank-payday-loans/index.html; David Dayen, "Payday Lending: The Loans with 350% Interest and a Grip on America," March 23, 2014, *Guardian*, www.theguardian.com/money/2014/mar/23/payday-lending-interest-banks-advantage-congress/; Robert W. Snarr Jr., "No Cash 'til Payday: The Payday Lending Industry," Federal Reserve Bank of Philadelphia, www.philadelphiafed.org/bank-resources/publications/compliance-corner/2002/first-quarter/q1cc1_02.cfm. While banks are scarce in poor neighborhoods, post offices are not; hence a proposal has been made for the U.S. Postal Service to offer basic banking services, thus helping both the postal service and low-income families. See Dayen, "The Post Office Should Just Become a Bank: How Obama Can Save USPS and Ding Cash-Checking Joints," *New Republic*, January 28, 2014. Senator Elizabeth Warren (D-MA) has supported this proposal. See Mehrsa Baradaran, "Post Office Banks on the Poor," *New York Times*, February 7, 2014.

32. "Director Richard Cordray's Remarks at the Payday Field Hearing," Consumer Finance Protection Bureau, March 25, 2014, www.consumerfinance.gov/newsroom/director-richard-cordray-remarks-at-the-payday-field-hearing/.

33. Jessica Silver Greenburg, "Tougher Shields for Soldiers against Predatory Lenders," *New York Times*, September 26, 2014, http://dealbook.nytimes.com/2014/09/26/tougher-shield-for-soldiers-against-predatory-lenders/?_r=0/. The lenders are gaining ground in several states; see Michael Corkery, "States Ease Interest Rate Laws That Protected Poor Borrowers," *New York Times*, October 21, 2014, http://dealbook.nytimes.com/2014/10/21/states-ease-laws-that-protected-poor-borrowers/.

34. Alex H. Lexy, "Rein in Shady Tax Preparers," *New York Times*, April 7, 2014.

35. Gary Rivlin, *Broke, USA: From Pawnshops to Poverty, Inc.; How the Working Poor Became Big Business* (New York: Harper, 2010), 329; Jessica Silver-Greenberg and Michael Corkery, "In a Subprime Bubble for Used Cars, Borrowers Pay Sky-High Rates," *New York Times*, July 19, 2014; Michael Sallah,

Debbie Cenziper, and Steven Rich, "Left with Nothing," *Washington Post*, September 8, 2013 (this was one of a four-part series). Rivlin's superb book is required reading on this topic.

36. Rivlin, *Broke, USA*, 27–28. Predators that are somewhat off the radar are gambling casinos, which are increasing in numbers and spreading across the landscape. Many now are close to low-income neighborhoods, and recent studies have shown that poorer people are twice as likely to have gambling problems as the more affluent. "Living within ten miles of one or more casinos more than doubles the rate of problems from excessive gambling," according to Barbara Dafoe Whitehead, "Gaming the Poor," *New York Times*, June 21, 2014. Casino spokespersons claim that they bring economic benefits wherever they locate, but the question always is, benefits for whom? University of Buffalo researchers have studied this problem; Whitehead's article referred to their most recent research, which was published in the *Journal of Behavioral Addiction*, June 2013.

37. Wal-Mart Stores Inc., "Annual Report Pursuant to Section 13 or 15(d) of the Securities Exchange Act of 1934 for the Fiscal Year Ended January 31, 2014," United States Securities and Exchange Commission Form 10-K, March 2014, 3; Lawrence Mishel, "Declining Value of the Federal Minimum Wage Is a Major Factor Driving Inequality," Issue Brief, Economic Policy Institute, February 21, 2013, www.epi.org/publication/declining-federal-minimum -wage-inequality/; Steven Greenhouse, "Low-Wage Workers Are Finding Poverty Harder to Escape," *New York Times*, March 16, 2014; "Trickle-Up Economics," *Economist*, February 16, 2013; Annie Lowrey, "Raising Minimum Wage Would Ease Income Gap but Carries Political Risks," *New York Times*, February 13, 2013.

38. Eric Lipton, "Industry behind Anti–wage Hike Letter," *New York Times*, March 15, 2014; Dave Jamieson, "Most States Will Now Have a Higher Minimum Wage Than the One Set by Congress," *Huffington Post*, November 6, 2014, www.huffingtonpost.com/2014/11/05/minimum-wage-by-state_n _6110204.html.

39. Michael D. Shear, "After Push by Obama, Minimum-Wage Action Is Moving to the States," *New York Times*, April 2, 2014; quotation from Eduardo Porter, "Dwindling Tools to Raise Wages," *New York Times*, December 10, 2013; Arindrajat Dube, T. William Lester, and Michael Reich, "Minimum Wage Shocks, Employment Flows, and Labor Market Frictions," eScholarship, University of California, http://escholarship.org/uc/item/76p927ks; "The Case for a Higher Minimum Wage," *New York Times*, February 8, 2014; Michael Reich and Ken Jacobs, "All Economics Is Local," *New York Times*, March 22, 2014. For a contrary view, see David Neumark and William Wascher, "Minimum Wages and Low-Wage Workers: How Well Does Reality Match the

Rhetoric?," *Minnesota Law Review* 92 (2008): 1296–1316. In 2014, Michigan, Maryland, and Massachusetts raised their minimum wage, and New York is preparing to do so. See Shaila Dewan, "Mayors Put Focus on How to Raise Wages for Lowest Paid Workers in Cities," *New York Times*, June 22, 2014.

40. Jefferson Cowie, "The Future of Fair Labor," *New York Times*, June 24, 2013; "Wage Theft across the Board," *New York Times*, April 21, 2014. Cowie's important book is *Stayin' Alive: The 1970s and the Last Days of the Working Class* (New York: New Press, 2010).

41. Annie-Rose Strasser, "McDonalds Tells Workers to Budget by Getting a Second Job and Turning Off Their Heat," *ThinkProgress*, July 15, 2013, http://thinkprogress.org/economy/2013/07/15/2300321/mcdonalds-budget -low-wage/. Strasser notes that "for an uninsured person to independently buy health care, he or she must shell out *$215 a month*—just for an individual plan [italics added]."

42. Steven Greenhouse, "A Day's Strike Seeks to Raise Fast-Food Pay," *New York Times*, July 31, 2013.

43. "Restoring a Fair Work Week," Center for Popular Democracy, http://populardemocracy.org/campaign/restoring-fair-workweek/; Steven Greenhouse, "A Push to Give Steadier Shifts to Part-Timers," *New York Times*, July 15, 2014.

44. Sylvia Allegretto, Marc Doussard, Dave Graham-Squire, Ken Jacobs, Dan Thompson, and Jeremy Thompson, "Fast Food, Poverty Wages: The Public Cost of Low-Wage Jobs in the Fast-Food Industry," University of California, Berkeley, and University of Illinois at Urbana-Champaign, October 15, 2013, 1, http://laborcenter.berkeley.edu/publiccosts/fast_food_poverty _wages.pdf.

45. "Super-Sizing Public Costs: How Low Wages at Top Fast-Food Chains Leave Taxpayers Footing the Bill," National Employment Law Project, October 2013, www.nelp.org/page/-/rtmw/uploads/NELP-Super-Sizing-Public-Costs -Fast-Food-Report.pdf?nocdn-1/.

46. "The 12 Companies Paying Americans the Least," *24/7 Wall Street*, November 21, 2012, http://247wallst.com/special-report/2012/11/21/the-12 -companies-paying-americans-the-least/; Josh Bivens, "Inequality, Exhibit A: Walmart and the Wealth of American Families," July 17, 2012, Economic Policy Institute, www.epi.org/blog/inequality-exhibit-wal-mart-wealth-american/.

47. "The Low-Wage Drag on Our Economy: Wal-Mart's Low Wages and Their Effect on Taxpayers and Economic Growth," Democratic Staff, U.S. House Committee on Education and the Workforce, May 2013, 1, http://democrats.edworkforce.house.gov/sites/democrats.edworkforce.house.gov /files/documents/WalMartReport-May2013.pdf.

48. Ibid., 10–12.

49. Wal-Mart Stores Inc., "Annual Report"; Edelman, *So Rich, So Poor*, 53; quotation from David Cooper, "Raising the Federal Minimum Wage to $10.10 Would Lift Wages for Millions and Provide a Modest Economic Boost," December 19, 2012, Economic Policy Institute, www.epi.org/publication /raising-federal-minimum-wage-to-1010/.

50. On the company's culture, see Nelson Lichtenstein, *Retail Revolution: How Wal-Mart Created a Brave New World of Business* (New York: Metropolitan Books, 2009); Bethany Moreton, *To Serve God and Wal-Mart: The Making of Christian Free Enterprise* (Cambridge, MA: Harvard University Press, 2009).

51. Tate quotations in Nelson Lichtenstein, "Wal-Mart, John Tate, and Their Anti-union America," in Lichtenstein and Elizabeth Tandy Shermer, eds., *The Right and Labor in America: Politics, Ideology, and Imagination* (Philadelphia: University of Pennsylvania Press, 2013), 255, 274–75.

52. Ylan Q. Mui, "Wal-Mart Works with Unions Abroad, but Not at Home," *Washington Post*, June 7, 2012; Travis Waldron, "Walmart Allows Its Workers to Unionize in Other Countries, Just Not in the United States," June 8, 2011, *ThinkProgress*, http://thinkprogress.org/economy/2011/06/08/239411/walmart -unions-other-countries/. During 2013, in anticipation of Walmart entering the Washington, D.C., market, the city council passed a bill requiring big-box retailers to pay a minimum wage of $12.50 per hour. Walmart officials said they were "infuriated" and threatened to cancel coming into the city. The city's mayor vetoed the legislation, but the council voted to gradually raise the minimum wage from $8.25 an hour to $11.50 by 2016. See "Wal-Mart Opens D.C. Stores after Wage Fight," *Wall Street Journal*, December 4, 2013, http:// blogs.wsj.com/washwire/2013/12/04/wal-mart-opens-d-c-stores-after-wage -fight/. The city council voted unanimously in favor of the law, making it veto proof, and coordinated with lawmakers in nearby Maryland suburbs in Montgomery and Prince George's Counties. In June 2014, the Supreme Court of Canada finally ruled that Walmart had illegally closed their store in Quebec; the decision would not affect other stores attempting to unionize, but the 190 workers who lost jobs probably would be compensated.

5. Inequality, Life, and Quality of Life

Epigraph. Göran Therborn, *The Killing Fields of Inequality* (Cambridge: Polity, 2013); Alexis de Tocqueville, *Democracy in America*, 2 vols., trans. Henry Reeve (New York: J. & H. G. Langley, 1840).

1. Michael A. Fletcher, "Research Ties Economic Inequality to Gap in Life Expectancy," *Washington Post*, March 10, 2013, www.washingtonpost.com /business/economy/research-ties-economic-inequality-to-gap-in-life -expectancy/2013/03/10/c7a323c4-7094-11e2-8b8d-e0b59a1b8e2a_story.html. In 2014, *New York Times* reporter Annie Lowrey described a similar contrast

between two counties—prosperous Fairfax County, Virginia, and depressed McDowell County, West Virginia—where life expectancies are starkly different. McDowell County's life expectancies, she pointed out, are about the same as those in Iraq, and life expectancies for women has fallen by two years since 1985. See Lowrey, "Income Gap, Meet the Longevity Gap," *New York Times*, March 15, 2014.

2. S. M., "Your Money, Your Life," *Economist*, March 14, 2013, http:// economist.com/blogs/democracyinamerica/2013/03/wealth-inequality/; Therborn, in *Killing Fields of Inequality*, surveys the worldwide effects of inequality on life and health.

3. Steven H. Woolf and Laudan Aron, eds., "U.S. Health in International Perspective: Shorter Lives, Poorer Health (2013)," Institute of Medicine, www .iom.edu/Reports/2013/US-Health-in-International-Perspective-Shorter -Lives-Poorer-Health.aspx; Susan Dentzer, "America's Health Deficit: Dying from Policy Neglect," *Health Affairs* 32, no. 3 (March 2013), 446; Y. Ho, "Mortality under Age 50 Accounts for Much of the Fact that US Life Expectancy Lags That of Other High-Income Countries," *Health Affairs* 32, no. 3 (March 2013), 459. The fourteen-country comparison and more comes from Howard Steven Friedman, *The Measure of a Nation: How to Regain America's Competitive Edge and Boost Our Global Standing* (New York: Prometheus Books, 2012), 33–60.

4. Sabrina Tavernise, "For Americans under 50, Stark Findings on Health," *New York Times*, January 9, 2013.

5. Woolf and Aron, "U.S. Health in International Perspective"; Sarah Kliff, "Graph of the Day: The United States Has a Really High Infant Mortality Rate," *Washington Post*, January 9, 2013, www.washingtonpost.com/blogs /wonkblog/wp/2013/01/09/graph-of-the-day-the-united-states-has-a-really -high-infant-mortality-rate/; Abby Goodnough, "U.S. Infant Mortality Rate Fell Steadily From '05 to '11," *New York Times*, April 7, 2013.

6. Offner, *Challenge of Affluence*, 288. Life expectancy in the Borough of Manhattan in New York State has increased more than in any other county in the nation, for reasons only partly due to affluence. An educated population engaging in physical activity and healthy food choices, along with bans on smoking and trans fats, has led to a dramatic increase in longevity. The New York boroughs of Brooklyn, the Bronx, and Queens also were among the twelve counties nationally where life expectancy increased the most. See Sam Roberts, "Prosper and Live Long: Health-Minded Manhattan Leads in Increased Life Expectancy," *New York Times*, July 18, 2013.

7. Reich, *Aftershock*, 86.

8. Peter Wehrein, "Astounding Increase in Antidepressant Use by

Americans," Harvard Health Publications, October 20, 2011, www.health
.harvard.edu/blog/astounding-increase-in-antidepressant-use-by-americans
-201110203624/; "Anti-Depressant Use Up by a Quarter since Credit Crunch,"
Telegraph, December 30, 2011, www.telegraph.co.uk/health/healthnews
/8931793/Anti-depressant-use-up-by-a-quarter-since-credit-crunch.html;
quotation from Shadra Bruce, "Recession Depression Increases Use of
Antidepressant Meds," Mental Health News Organization, July 2, 2010,
www.mentalhealthnews.org/recession-depression-increases-use-of
-antidepressant-meds/841421/. Reports released by the Centers for Disease
Control and Prevention and the National Center for Health Statistics, as well
as articles in medical journals, generated extensive commentary.

9. Reich, *Aftershock*, 87.

10. Hope Yen, "Exclusive: Signs of Declining Economic Security," July 28,
2013, AP: The Big Story, http://bigstory.ap.org/article/exclusive-4-5-us-face
-near-poverty-no-work-0/.

11. Ibid.

12. Jason DeParle, Robert Gebeloff, and Sabrina Tavernise, "Older,
Suburban, and Struggling, 'Near Poor' Startle the Census," *New York Times*,
November 18, 2011; Lisa McGirr, "The New Suburban Poverty," *New York
Times*, March 19, 2012.

13. Brandon Roberts, Deborah Povich, and Mark Mather, "Low-Income
Working Families: The Growing Economic Gap," Working Poor Families
Project Policy Brief, Winter 2012–2013, 5, quotations, 2, 7, www.workingpoor
families.org/wp-content/uploads/2013/01/Winter-2012_2013-WPFP-Data
-Brief.pdf.

14. Ibid., 4.

15. "Missing Workers: The Missing Part of the Unemployment Story,"
Economic Indicators, Economic Policy Institute, November 7, 2014, www.epi
.org/publication/missing-workers/; Valerie Wilson, "Resilience of Black
Labor Force Participation," Economic Snapshot, Economic Policy Institute,
May 14, 2014, www.epi.org/publication/resilience-black-labor-force
-participation/; Rebecca J. Rosen, "Why Is the Black Unemployment Rate
So High?," *Atlantic*, June 12, 2014, www.theatlantic.com/business/archive
/2014/06/why-is-the-black-unemployment-rate-so-high/372667/.

16. Moises Velasquez-Manoff, "Status and Stress," *New York Times*, July 27,
2013, http://opinionator.blogs.nytimes.com/2013/07/27/status-and-stress/.

17. "Hunger & Poverty Fact Sheet," Feeding America, www.feedingamerica
.org/hunger-in-america/impact-of-hunger/hunger-and-poverty/hunger
-and-poverty-fact-sheet.html; "Food Security in the U.S.," U.S. Department of
Agriculture, Economic Research Service, www.ers.usda.gov/topics/food

-nutrition-assistance/food-security-in-the-us/key-statistics-graphics.aspx.

18. Kim Severson and Winnie Hu, "Cut in Food Stamps Forces Hard Choices on Poor," *New York Times*, November 7, 2013.

19. Sheryl Gay Stolberg, "On the Edge of Poverty, at the Center of a Debate on Food Stamps," *New York Times*, September 4, 2013.

20. Mark Bittman, "Welfare for the Wealthy," *New York Times*, June 4, 2013, http://opinionator.blogs.nytimes.com/2013/06/04/welfare-for-the-wealthy/.

21. Ron Nixon, "Billionaires Received U.S. Farm Subsidies, Report Finds," *New York Times*, November 7, 2013; quotation from Joseph E. Stiglitz, "Our Crazy Food Policy," *New York Times Sunday Review*, November 17, 2013. See also Ronald P. Formisano, *The Tea Party: A Brief History* (Baltimore: Johns Hopkins University Press, 2012), 92–93, 94–95, on members of Congress, including Tea Partyites, receiving subsidies.

22. Arthur Delaney, "Food Stamp Cuts Backed by Farm Subsidiary Beneficiaries," *Huffington Post*, May 23, 2013, www.huffingtonpost.com/2013/05/23/food-stamp-cuts_n_3324418.html; Trudy Lieberman, "The Real Hunger Games," *Nation*, October 14, 2013; Melissa Boteach, "Food for Thought: New Poverty Data Underscore Effectiveness of Nutrition Assistance as Congress Considers Cuts to Food Aid," Center for American Progress, November 6, 2013, www.americanprogress.org/issues/poverty/news/2013/11/06/78980/food-for-thought-new-poverty-data-underscore-effectiveness-of-nutrition-assistance-as-congress-considers-cuts-to-food-aid/.

23. "Hunger and Homelessness Survey: Executive Summary," United States Conference of Mayors, December 2012, http://usmayors.org/pressreleases/uploads/2012/1219-report-HH.pdf; Homelessness Research Institute, "The State of Homelessness in America 2013," National Alliance to End Homelessness, April 8, 2013, www.endhomelessness.org/library/entry/the-state-of-homelessness-2013/.

24. Kim Parker, "Yes, the Rich Are Different," Pew Research Social & Demographic Trends, August 27, 2012, www.pewsocialtrends.org/2012/08/27/yes-the-rich-are-different/.

25. "CDC Health Disparities and Inequalities Report—United States, 2011," *Morbidity and Mortality Weekly Report* 60, suppl. (January 14, 2011), www.cdc.gov/mmwr/pdf/other/su6001.pdf; "Hispanics and Social Security," Social Security Administration, www.socialsecurity.gov/people/hispanics/; "Health Disparities Experienced by Hispanics—United States," *Morbidity and Mortality Weekly Report* 53, no. 40 (October 15, 2004), www.cdc.gov/mmwr/preview/mmwrhtml/mm5340a1.htm. Ironically, Hispanics seem to enjoy a longer life expectancy. See Jim Lamare, "Latino Life Expectancy: The Hispanic Paradox," December 2, 2012, New America Media, http://newamericamedia.org/2012/12/latino-life-expectancy-exploring-the-hispanic-paradox.php.

26. "Health Disparities and Inequalities Report—United States, 2013," *Morbidity and Mortality Weekly Report* 62, no. 3, suppl. (November 22, 2013), 9, 15, 23, www.cdc.gov/mmwr/pdf/other/su6203.pdf.

27. Elisabeth Rosenthal, "The Soaring Cost of a Simple Breath," *New York Times*, October 12, 2013; Jordan Weissmann, "Census: Medical Expenses Put 10.6 Million Americans in Poverty," *Atlantic*, November 7, 2013, www.theatlantic.com/business/archive/2013/11/census-medical-expenses-put-106-million-americans-in-poverty/281256/.

28. Robin A. Cohen, Renee M. Gindi, Whitney K. Kirzinger, "Financial Burden of Medical Care: Early Release of Estimates from the National Health Interview Survey, January–June 2011," Centers for Disease Control, March 2012, www.cdc.gov/nchs/data/nhis/earlyrelease/financial_burden_of_medical_care_032012.pdf.

29. Elizabeth Rosenthal, "Patients' Costs Skyrocket: Specialists' Incomes Soar," *New York Times*, January 18, 2014; quotation from Robert Pearl, M.D, "The High Cost of American Health Care," *Forbes*, January 9, 2014, www.forbes.com/sites/robertpearl/2014/01/09/high-cost-of-american-health-care/.

30. Eduardo Porter, "Health Care's Overlooked Cost Factor," *New York Times*, June 12, 2013, B1, 2; Margaret Clapp, Michael A. Pie, and Phillip L. Zweig, "How a Cabal Keeps Generics Scarce," *New York Times*, September 2, 2013; Jayne O'Donnell and Laura Ungar, "Rural Hospitals in Critical Condition," *USA Today Weekend*, November 14–16, 2014. For a brilliant exposé of why American health-care costs are out of control, see Steven Brill, "Bitter Pill: Why Medical Bills Are Killing Us," *Time*, February 20, 2013. *Time* devoted the entire features section to this article by a single writer, the first time in the magazine's history.

31. Elizabeth Rosenthal, "Even Small Medical Advances Can Mean Big Jump in Bills," *New York Times*, April 5, 2014.

32. "Report," National Commission on Physician Payment Reform, March 4, 2013, http://physicianpaymentcommission.org/report/; quotation from H. Gilbert Welch, "Diagnosis: Insufficient Outrage," *New York Times*, July 4, 2013. For a now-classic analysis of how doctor-owned and profit-driven systems of health care are ratcheting up costs, see Atul Gawande, "The Cost Conundrum: What a Texas Town Can Teach Us about Health Care," *New Yorker*, June 1, 2009.

33. Wendell Potter, "Skyrocketing Salaries for Health Care CEOs," June 9, 2014, http://wendellpotter.com/2014/06/skyrocketing-salaries-for-health-insurance-ceos/; "Health Insurance CEO Pay Skyrockets in 2013," *Healthcare—NOW!* May 5, 2014, www.healthcare-now.org/health-insurance-ceo-pay-skyrockets-in-2013/.

34. Wendell Potter, *Deadly Spin: An Insurance Company Insider Speaks Out*

on How Corporate PR Is Killing Health Care and Deceiving Americans (New York: Bloomsbury Press, 2010). Excessive salaries and other abuses also result from lack of competition; see Leemore S. Dafney, "Are Health Insurance Markets Competitive?," *American Economic Review* 100, no. 4 (2010): 1399–1431.

35. S. Jay Olshansky et al., "Differences in Life Expectancy due to Race and Educational Differences Are Widening, and Many May Not Catch Up," *Health Affairs* 31, no. 8 (August 2012), 1805, 1806, 1807 (the differences among Hispanics noted in the previous paragraph are in this source, 1804). Sabrina Tavernise, in "Life Spans Shrink for Least-Educated Whites in the U.S.," *New York Times*, September 20, 2012, reported on the Olshansky article and other studies.

36. "Poverty, Single Mothers, and Mobility," Family Inequality, February 27, 2013, http://familyinequality.wordpress.com/2012/02/27/poverty-single -mothers-and-mobility/.

37. Awori J. Hayanga, "Residential Segregation and Lung Cancer Mortality in the United States," *JAMA Surgery* 148, no. 1 (January 2103): 37–42, http:// archsurg.jamanetwork.com/article.aspx?articleid=1558105/; Sabrina Tavernise, "Segregation Linked in Study with Lung Cancer Deaths," *New York Times*, January 16, 2013.

38. Punam Ohri-Vachaspati, Zeynep Isgor, Leah Rimkus, Lisa M. Powell, Dianne C. Baker, and Frank J. Chaloupka, "Child-Directed Marketing Inside and on the Exterior of Fast Food Restaurants," *American Journal of Preventive Medicine*, October 29, 2014, www.ajpmonline.org/article/S0749-3797 (14)00478-4/fulltext/; Jennifer L. Harris, Marlene B Schwartz, Megan LoDolce, Christina Munsell, Frances Fleming-Milici, James Elsey, Sai Liu, Maia Hyary, Renee Gross, Carol Hazen, and Cathryn Dembek, "Sugary Drink F.A.C.T.S. [Food Advertising to Children and Teens Score] 2014: Some Progress but Much Room for Improvement in Marketing to Youth," Rudd Center for Food Policy and Obesity, November 2014, 79–88, www.sugarydrinkfacts.org /resources/SugaryDrinkFACTS_Report.pdf. Quotation from Naa Oyo A. Kwate, "Racial Segregation and the Marketing of Health Inequality," in Harris and Lieberman, *Beyond Discrimination*, 318–19.

39. Paul Krugman, "Stranded by Sprawl," *New York Times*, July 28, 2013; William J. Wilson, *The Truly Disadvantaged: The Inner City, the Underclass, and Public Policy* (Chicago: University of Chicago Press, 1987).

40. Wilkinson and Pickett, *Spirit Level*.

41. Ibid., 33–45.

42. Ibid., 66–67, 287.

43. Ibid., 103–17. See also Offner, *Challenge of Affluence*, 299: "There is little doubt about the *costs* of inequality and insecurity; being low down the

scale of absolute income is associated with misery: with shorter lives, bad health, discrimination, poor education, incarceration, and many other detriments. GDP [gross domestic product] per head is a fiction; no one earns GDP per head."

44. John De Graaf, David Wann, and Thomas H. Naylor, *Affluenza: The All-Consuming Epidemic* (San Francisco: Berrett-Koehler, 2002), xii.

45. Clive Hamilton and Richard Dennis, *Affluenza: When Too Much Is Never Enough* (Crows Nest, NSW, Australia: Allen & Unwin, 2005), 3.

46. Thomas B. Edsall, "The Hidden Prosperity of the Poor," *New York Times*, January 20, 2013, http://opinionator.blogs.nytimes.com/2013/01/30 /the-hidden-prosperity-of-the-poor/?_r=0/; Harrington quotation in Shipler, *Working Poor*, 8.

47. Daniel Goleman, "Rich People Just Care Less," *Sunday New York Times*, October 6, 2013.

48. Stephen Bezruchka, "Inequality Kills," in David Cay Johnston, ed., *Divided: The Perils of Our Growing Inequality* (New York: New Press, 2014), 195. The IOM report in book form is National Research Council and Institute of Medicine, *U.S. Health in International Perspective: Shorter Lives, Poorer Health* (Washington, DC: National Academies Press, 2013).

49. Angus Deaton, *The Great Escape: Health, Wealth, and the Origins of Inequality* (Princeton, NJ: Princeton University Press, 2013), 7, 27.

6. Political Inequality

Epigraph. Kay Lehman Schlozman, Sidney Verba, and Henry E. Brady, *The Unheavenly Chorus: Unequal Political Voice and the Broken Promise of American Democracy* (Princeton, NJ: Princeton University Press, 2012), 26.

1. "Democracy Index 2012: Democracy at a Standstill," Economist Intelligence Unit, 2013, 1, http://pages.eiu.com/rs/eiu2/images/Democracy-Index -2012.pdf.

2. Charles M. Blow, "Empire at the End of Decadence," *New York Times*, February 18, 2011.

3. Nichols and McChesney, *Dollarocracy*, 61; Joe Soss and Lawrence R. Jacobs, "The Place of Inequality: Non-participation in the American Polity," *Political Science Quarterly* 124, no.1 (2009), quotation 124; Sabrina Tavernise, "Study Finds Big Spike in Poorest in the U.S.," *New York Times*, November 3, 2011. See also Theda Skocpol, *Diminished Democracy: From Membership to Management in American Civic Life* (Norman: University of Oklahoma Press, 2003). On unions increasing the voting turnout of low-income voters, see Rosenfeld, *What Unions No Longer Do*, 171–77.

4. Walter Dean Burnham, "Democracy in Peril: The American Turnout Problem and the Path to Plutocracy," Roosevelt Institute Working Paper No. 5,

December 1, 2010, 22–23; Richard J. Coley and Andrew Sum, "Fault Lines in Our Democracy: Civic Knowledge, Voting Behavior, and Civic Engagement in the United States," ETS Center for Research on Human Capital and Education, Educational Testing Service, April 2012, www.ets.org/s/research/19386 /rsc/pdf/18719_fault_lines_report.pdf.

5. Gilens, *Affluence and Influence*, 9; Bartels, *Unequal Democracy*, 267–75, quotation 275.

6. Benjamin I. Page, Larry M. Bartels, and Jason Seawright, "Democracy and the Policy Preferences of Wealthy Americans," *Perspectives on Politics* 11, no. 1 (March 2013), 54–55, quotation 54. This study was also published as Fay Lomas Cook, Benjamin I. Page, and Rachel L. Moskowitz, "Political Engagement of Wealthy Americans," *Political Science Quarterly* 129: 3 (Fall 2014), 381–98.

7. Chrystia Freeland, "Plutocrats vs. Populists," *New York Times*, November 1, 2013.

8. Page et al., "Democracy and Policy Preferences," 67–68.

9. Zephyr Teachout, *Corruption in America: From Ben Franklin's Snuff Box to Citizens United* (Cambridge, MA: Harvard University Press, 2014), 6, 9.

10. Nicholas Confessore, "Power Surge for Donors as Terrain Is Reshaped on Campaign Money," *New York Times*, April 2, 2014; quotation from "The Court Follows the Money," *New York Times*, April 2, 2014. For details of the *McCutcheon* decision, see *McCutcheon, et al. v. FEC, Case Summary*, Federal Election Commission, www.fec.gov/law/litigation/McCutcheon.shtml. For a history of campaign finance laws, see Kurt Hohenstein, *Coining Corruption: The Making of the American Campaign Finance System* (DeKalb: Northern Illinois University Press, 2007), which covers the pre–*Citizens United* period very well.

11. "Democracy Index 2012," 1; Hacker and Pierson, *Winner-Take-All Politics*, 148–49, 158–60, 239; Nolan McCarty, Keith T. Poole, and Howard Rosenthal, *Polarized America: The Dance of Ideology and Unequal Riches* (Cambridge, MA: MIT Press, 2006), 2, quotation 3. See also "Up and Out: Income Inequality and Political Polarization in the U.S.," Develop Economies, October 30, 2011, http:// developeconomies.com/uncategorized/up-and-out-income-inequality-and -political-polarization/. In contrast, Martin Gilens concluded that "gridlock may have both positive and negative impacts on the relationship between public preferences" and found that a unique set of circumstances in the early George W. Bush years resulted in high responsiveness to all income groups. See Gilens, *Affluence and Influence*, 193–233, quotation 211.

12. McCarty et al., *Polarized America*, 13, 14, 136–38.

13. For a fuller discussion of what determines voter turnout, see Friedman, *Measure of a Nation*, 139–42.

14. Richard K. Scher, *The Politics of Disenfranchisement: Why Is It So Hard to Vote in America?* (Armonk, NY: M. E. Sharpe, 2011), 4. See also Spencer Overton, *Stealing Democracy: The New Politics of Voter Suppression* (New York: W. W. Norton, 2006).

15. On the late nineteenth-century Midwest, notably Wisconsin, Michigan, Indiana, and Illinois, see Peter H. Argersinger, *Representation and Inequality in Late Nineteenth-Century America: The Politics of Apportionment* (New York: Cambridge University Press, 2012). In the states of the post-Reconstruction South, the dominance of the Democratic Party, champion of white supremacy, did not depend on apportionment schemes but rather on violence and Jim Crow laws to disenfranchise the great majority of the now-emancipated African Americans. The suppression of these newly freed people had its origins in virulent racism and created an inequality of race and class, while laws establishing poll taxes and literacy and other tests also reduced voting by poor whites.

16. Quotation from Chisun Lee, Brent Ferguson, and David Earley, "After *Citizens United*: The Story in the States," Brennan Center for Justice, October 9, 2014, www.brennancenter.org/publication/after-citizens-united-story -states, quotation from the introduction; Nicholas Confessore, "A National Strategy Funds State Political Monopolies," *New York Times*, January 11, 2014.

17. In their 2000 *Bush v. Gore* decision, the Rehnquist Supreme Court's five Republican justices awarded the presidency to George W. Bush on the basis of the equal-protection clause. The majority held that counting Florida's flawed ballots for Democratic candidate Al Gore (allowed by Florida law if the voters' intent was known) would dilute the votes of those with cleanly counted ballots. See Alan M. Dershowitz, *Supreme Injustice: How the High Court Highjacked Election 2000* (New York: Oxford University Press, 2001), 55–81, who noted that the five-man majority opinion was "limited to present circumstances." Are the voters in gerrymandered districts perhaps also entitled to equal protection against "dilution"?

18. Adam Liptak, in "Lost Votes, Problem Ballots, Long Waits? Flaws Are Widespread, Study Finds," *New York Times*, February 3, 2013, describes a study of the elections of 2008 and 2010 commissioned by the Pew Charitable Trusts. See also Heather K. Gerken, *The Democracy Index: Why Our Election System Is Failing and How to Fix It* (Princeton. NJ: Princeton University Press, 2009); "The Elections Performance Index 2012," Pew Charitable Trusts Research & Analysis, April 7, 2014, www.pewtrusts.org/en/research-and -analysis/reports/2014/04/07/the-elections-performance-index-2012/.

19. "The Republican Threat to Voting," *New York Times*, April 26, 2011; "Election 2012: Voting Laws Roundup," Brennan Center for Justice, October 11, 2012, www.brennancenter.org/analysis/election-2012-voting-laws-roundup/.

20. Scher, *Politics of Disenfranchisement*, 84–85; "Voting and Registration in the Election of November 2010—Detailed Tables," United States Census Bureau, October 2011, www.census.gov/hhes/www/socdemo/voting /publications/p20/2010/tables.html; quotation from Wendy R. Weiser and Lawrence Norden, "Voting Law Changes in 2012," Brennan Center for Justice, October 3, 2011, 19, 20, www.brennancenter.org/publication/voting-law -changes-2012/. An indirect form of disenfranchisement results from states awarding their electoral votes on a winner-take-all basis. Consequently, presidential candidates now campaign in a dozen or fewer "battleground" states that are competitive and ignore the vast majority of states that are now solidly Republican or Democratic. See Adam Liptak, "The Vanishing Battleground," *New York Times*, November 3, 2012.

21. Justin Levitt, "The Truth about Voter Fraud," Brennan Center for Justice, November 9, 2007, www.brennancenter.org/publication/truth-about -voter-fraud/; Richard L. Hansen, "A Détente before the Election," *New York Times*, August 5, 2012. See also Susanne Gamboa, "South Carolina Voter ID Trial: State Sen. Admits Law Couldn't Address His Examples of Voter Fraud," *Huffington Post*, August 27, 2012, www.huffingtonpost.com/2012/08/27/south -carolina-voter-id_n_1834299.html.

22. Ethan Bronner, "Voter ID Rules Fail Court Tests across the Country," *New York Times*, October 3, 2012; "Election 2012: Voting Laws Roundup"; Darryl Paulson, "How Florida Kept Blacks from Voting," *Tampa Bay Times*, October 17, 2013.

23. Weiser and Norden, "Voting Law Changes in 2012," 21–23, 28, 30. See also Scher, *Politics of Disfranchisement*, 102–3, on purges in Florida and other states. As one of thirty-two states that offer early voting, Florida now allows just eight days for it, well below the national average of nineteen days.

24. Paulson, "How Florida Kept Blacks from Voting"; Susan Saulny, "With Less Time for Voting, Black Churches Redouble Their Efforts," *New York Times*, October 28, 2012; Alex Seitz-Wald, "Fla. Republican: We Wanted to Suppress Black Votes," *Salon*, July 27, 2012, www.salon.com/2012/07/27/fla _republican_we_suppressed_black_votes/.

25. Quotation from Paulson, "How Florida Kept Blacks from Voting"; Michael C. Herron and Daniel A. Smith, "Congestion at the Polls: A Study of Florida Precincts in the 2012 General Election," Advancement Project, June 24, 2013, 1, 3, http://b.3cdn.net/advancement/f5d1203189ce2aabfc _14m6vzttt.pdf.

26. Jeremy W. Peters, "Waiting Times at Ballot Boxes Draw Scrutiny," *New York Times*, February 4, 2013; Ethan Bronner, "Long Lines, Demands for ID, and Provisional Ballots Mar Voting for Some," *New York Times*, November 6, 2012; Jason Cherkisjason, "Election Problems Included Confusion,

Intimidation, Untrained Poll Workers," *Huffington Post*, November 8, 2012, www.huffingtonpost.com/2012/11/08/election-problems-confusion -intimidation_n_2095384.html; Benjy Sarlin, "Poll: Democratic Demographics Faced Significantly Longer Voting Lines," November 8, 2012, http://news .yahoo.com/poll-democratic-demographics-faced-significantly-longer-voting -lines-114827684—politics.html (this latter citation is a report on an AFL-CIO poll conducted by Hart Research).

27. Herron and Smith, "Congestion at the Polls," 1, 3.

28. On the Tea Party–sponsored groups who have sent white "poll watchers" into black districts to challenge voters (based on shoddy checking of registration lists), see Stephanie Saul, "Looking, Very Closely, for Voter Fraud," *New York Times*, September 16, 2012; "Voter Harassment, circa 2012," *New York Times*, September 21, 2012. Americans for Prosperity, a group founded by the reactionary billionaires David and Charles Koch, assisted in this attempt to suppress black voting. On the connection between AFP, the Kochs, and the Tea Party, see Formisano, *Tea Party*, 26–27, 67–68.

29. Anna Chu, Joshua Field, and Charles Posner, "Florida's Worst Election Offenders: A County-by-County Analysis of the Florida Election Administration in the 2012 Election," Center for American Progress Action Fund, December 9, 2013, 4–6, 8, 26, www.americanprogressaction.org/issues/civil -liberties/report/2013/12/09/80605/floridas-worst-election-offenders/.

30. "States That Expanded Voting in 2013 and 2014," Brennan Center for Justice, July 1, 2014, www.brennancenter.org/states-expanded-voting-2013 -and-2014; "Voting Laws Roundup 2013," Brennan Center for Justice, December 19, 2013, www.brennancenter.org/analysis/election-2013-voting -laws-roundup/; Lizette Alvarez, "Florida Governor Backs Voting Changes," *New York Times*, January 17, 2013; "New Florida Voting Law," *WINK News*, May 21, 2013, www.winknews.com/Local-Florida/2013-05-21/New-Florida -voting-law#.Uq-uLq-x5lm.

31. "Voting Laws Roundup 2013"; Mark K. Matthews and Scott Powers, "Supreme Court Decision Lets Florida Change Voting Rules," *Orlando Sentinel*, June 25, 2013.

32. Keith G. Bentele and Erin E. O'Brien, "Jim Crow 2.0? Why States Consider and Adopt Restrictive Voter Access Policies," *Perspectives on Politics* 11 (December 2013), 1088–1116, quotation from the abstract; Joe Coscarelli, "Don Yelton, GOP Precinct Chair, Delivers Most Baldly Racist *Daily Show* Interview of All Time," *New York Magazine*, October 24, 2013, http://nymag.com/daily/intelligencer/2013/10/don-yelton-racist-daily-show -interview.html.

33. "Texas Voter ID Law Took Effect Yesterday," *Ms. Magazine*, October 22, 2013, www.msmagazine.com/news/uswirestory.asp?ID=14664/; Shaley

Sanders, "Women Say New Voter ID Law Makes It More Difficult for Them to Vote," KLTV, October 22, 2013, www.kltv.com/story/23758563/etx-woman -struggling-to-get-official-voter-id.

34. Wendy R. Weiser, "How Much of a Difference Did New Voting Restrictions Make in Yesterday's Close Races?," Brennan Center for Justice, November 5, 2014, www.brennancenter.org/print/12822/. On the cost of a photo ID constituting a new form of poll tax, see Richard Sobel, "The High Cost of 'Free' Photo Voter Identification Cards," Charles Hamilton Houston Institute for Race & Justice, Harvard Law School, June 2014, http://today.law.harvard.edu /wp-content/uploads/2014/06/FullReportVoterIDJune2014l.pdf.

35. Angela Behrens, Christopher Uggen, and Jeff Manza, "Ballot Manipulation and the 'Menace of Negro Domination': Racial Threat and Felon Disfranchisement in the United States, 1850–2002," *American Journal of Sociology* 109, no. 3 (November 2003): 559–605, quotations 596, 598.

36. Behrens et al., "Ballot Manipulation," 599; "Felony Disfranchisement," Sentencing Project, www.sentencingproject.org/template/page.cfm?id =133/; "Felony Disfranchisement in the Commonwealth of Kentucky," League of Women Voters of Kentucky, October 2006, 2–3, www.prisonpolicy .org/scans/lwvky/Felony_Dis_Report.pdf. See Scher, *Politics of Disfranchisement*, 52–56, for a thorough discussion.

37. "Disfranchisement News," Sentencing Project, December 12, 2012, www.sentencingproject.org/detail/news.cfm?news_id=1441/; Brentin Mock, "What Will Virginia's New Governor Do about Felony Disenfranchisement?," *Colorlines*, November 7, 2013, http://colorlines.com/archives/2013/11/will _virginias_felony_disenfranchisement_finally_go_away_under_new_governor .html; "Delaware," *Voting News*, http://thevotingnews.com/state/delaware/; "Restoring the Vote in Virginia," *New York Times*, June 1, 2013.

38. Gerken, *Democracy Index*, 11.

39. Ibid., 17, 85. See also Scher, *Politics of Disfranchisement*, 19.

40. Bob Fitrakris and Harvey Wasserman, "Ohio Secretary of State Confirms 2004 Election Could Have Been Stolen," Free Press, December 14, 2007, http://freepress.org/departments/display/19/2007/2920/; O'Dell and Blackwell quotation in "Vote Fraud 2004: How Ohio Was 'Delivered' to Bush," What Really Happened, http://whatreallyhappened.com/WRHARTICLES /2004votefraud_ohio.html. In January 2005, the Democratic members and staff of the U.S. House Judiciary Committee issued a report, boycotted by Republican members of the committee, detailing multiple election irregularities in Ohio in 2004. See Democratic Staff of the House Judiciary Committee, *What Went Wrong in Ohio: The Conyers Report on the 2004 Presidential Election* (Chicago: Academy Chicago Publishers, 2005).

41. Gerken, *Democracy Index*, 85–86.

42. Richard Franklin Bensel, *The American Ballot Box in the Mid-Nineteenth Century* (Cambridge: Cambridge University Press, 2004), 178–85.

43. Sam Stein, "As Election Nears, Dirty Tricks Grow More Common," *Huffington Post*, November 28, 2008, www.huffingtonpost.com/2008/10/28 /as-election-nears-dirty-t_n_138607.html; Richard L. Hasen, "Will Voter Suppression and Dirty Tricks Swing the Election?," *Salon*, October 22, 2012, www.salon.com/2012/10/22/will_voter_suppression_and_dirty_tricks_swing _the_election/; "Top 11 Republican Dirty Tricks . . . SO FAR," People for the American Way, October 31, 2012, http://blog.pfaw.org/content/top-11 -republican-dirty-tricks-so-far/.

44. Scher, *Politics of Disenfranchisement*, 103; Dahlia Lithwick, "Raging Caging: What the Heck Is Vote Caging and Why Should We Care?," *Slate*, May 31, 2007, www.slate.com/articles/news_and_politics/jurisprudence /2007/05/raging_caging.html. See also Jane Mayer, "Bullets," *New Yorker*, March 26, 2007; Brentin Mock, "Florida's Felonious Voting Trap," *Nation*, October 15, 2012.

45. Quotations from Steven Greenhouse, "Here's a Memo from the Boss: Vote This Way," *New York Times*, October 26, 2012; David A. Graham, "Can Your Boss Threaten to Fire You If You Don't Vote for Romney?," *Atlantic*, October 20, 2012, www.theatlantic.com/politics/archive/2012/10/can-your -boss-threaten-to-fire-you-if-you-dont-vote-for-romney/263709/.

46. Daniel Politi, "Hot Election 2012 Trend: Bosses Advising Employees How to Vote," *Slate*, October 27, 2012, www.slate.com/blogs/the_slatest /2012/10/27/employers_increasingly_telling_employees_workers_how_to _vote.html; quotations from Greenhouse, "Here's a Memo." In August 2012, hundreds of coal workers and family members appeared at a Romney rally at the Century Mine in Belleville, Ohio. Local news outlets carried reports of miners losing a day's pay and feeling coerced to attend. See Harry Bradford, "Murray Energy Miners Allege They Had to Give Up Pay to Attend 'Mandatory' Romney Rally," *Huffington Post*, August 28, 2012, www.huffingtonpost .com/2012/08/28/century=mine-romney-ohio-mandatory_n_1836674.html.

47. "Business Industry Political Action Committee," Center for Media and Democracy, www.sourcewatch.org/index.php?title=Business_Industry _Political_Action_Committee/; Ed Sealover, "Workers Tend to Trust Bosses' Voting Recommendations," *Denver Business Journal*, October 25, 2012, www .bizjournals.com/denver/blog/capitol_business/2012/10/workers-tend-to -trust-bosses-voting.html; quotation from Gordon Lafer, "Very Unwise for Employers to Tell Employees How to Vote," *The Hill*, October 25, 2012, http://thehill.com/blogs/congress-blog/economy-a-budget/264067-very -unwise-for-employers-to-tell-employees-how-to-vote/.

7. The Fracturing of America

Epigraph. Daniel T. Rodgers, *Age of Fracture* (Cambridge, MA: Belknap Press of Harvard University Press, 2011). 3.

1. Rich Morin, "Rising Share of Americans See Conflict between Rich and Poor," Pew Research Social & Demographic Trends, January 12, 2012, www.pewsocialtrends.org/files/2012/01/Rich-vs-Poor.pdf. See also the excellent commentary by Andrew Kohut, "Don't Mind the Gap," *New York Times*, January 26, 2012.

2. Bartels, *Unequal Democracy*, 4.

3. "Most See Inequality Growing, but Partisans Differ over Solutions," Pew Research Center for the People & the Press, January 23, 2014, www.people-press.org/2014/01/23/most-see-inequality-growing-but-partisans-differ-over-solutions. "Most Americans are aware of high and increasing inequality. Most are unhappy about it. Most favor a wide range of concrete, pragmatic government programs when their well-being is threatened or opportunity is blocked by forces beyond their control." See Page and Jacobs, *Class War?*, x.

4. Leslie McCall, *The Undeserving Rich: American Beliefs about Inequality, Opportunity, and Redistribution* (New York: Cambridge University Press, 2013), quotations 137, 8, 5, xiii.

5. Poll from 2009 reported in David Madland, "Americans Care about Economic Inequality," Center for American Progress, March 5, 2012, www.americanprogress.org/issues/economy/news/2012/03/05/11193/americans-care-about-economic-inequality/; Page and Jacobs, *Class War?*, 29.

6. Robert A. Dahl, *How Democratic Is the American Constitution?* New Haven, CT: Yale University Press, 2001), 33–34; Madison quotation for the *National Gazette*, [ca. January 23, 1792], in Robert A. Rutland, Thomas A. Mason, Robert J. Brugger, Jeanne K. Sisson, and Fredrika J. Teute, eds., *The Papers of James Madison*, vol. 14, *6 April 1791–16 March 1793* (Charlottesville: University Press of Virginia, 1983), 197.

7. Madison quotation [from his *Records of the Debates in the Federal Convention of 1787*, vol. 3, 452–55] in Dahl, *How Democratic*, 34, 35, 36.

8. Lawrence R. Jacobs and Theda Skocpol, "American Democracy in an Era of Rising Inequality," in Jacobs and Skocpol, eds., *Inequality and American Democracy: What We Know and What We Need to Learn* (New York: Russell Sage Foundation, 2005), 1; Task Force on Inequality and American Democracy, "American Democracy in an Age of Inequality," American Political Science Association, 2004, 1, www.apsanet.org/Files/Task%20Force%20Reports/taskforcereport.pdf; Schlozman et al., "Inequalities of Political Voice," in Jacobs and Skocpol, *Inequality and American Democracy*, 19.

9. Letter from Thomas Jefferson to Edward Carrington, January 16, 1787, *The Papers of Thomas Jefferson*, vol. 11, ed. Julian P. Boyd (Princeton, NJ:

Princeton University Press, 1955), 48–49; Gilens, *Affluence and Influence*, quotation 233. See also Robert G. Kaiser, *So Damn Much Money: The Triumph of Lobbying and the Corrosion of American Government* (New York: Alfred A. Knopf, 2009); Lawrence Lessig, *Republic, Lost: How Money Corrupts Congress—and a Plan to Stop It* (New York: Hachette Book Group, 2011).

10. Martin Gilens and Benjamin I. Page, "Testing Theories of American Politics: Elites, Interest Groups, and Average Citizens," *Perspectives on Politics* 12, no. 3 (September 2014) http://journals.cambridge.org/download.php?file =%2FPPS%2FPPS12_03%2FS1537592714001595a.pdf&code=d38098e991 df7d6e533e435a6523a1b7/, quotations 573, 575. A thoughtful essay on the pre-publication version of this paper appeared in John Cassidy, "Is America an Oligarchy?," *New Yorker*, April 18, 2014, www.newyorker.com/news/john -cassidy/is-america-an-oligarchy/. See also "The Public's Opinions on Congress: Q & A with Center Research Director Carmines," Center on Congress at Indiana University, March 14, 2011, http://congress.indiana.edu/the-public %E2%80%99s-opinions-congress-q-center-research-director-carmines/; continued in "The Public's Opinions on Congress: Q & A with Center Research Director Carmines," Center on Congress at Indiana University, April 4, 2012, http://congress.indiana.edu/the-public%E2%80%99s-opinions-congress-q -center-research-director-carmines-2/.

11. Joel D. Aberbach, "The Future of the American Right: Evidence and Questions from the Bush Years," in Aberbach and Gillian Peele, eds., *Crisis of Conservatism? The Republican Party, the Conservative Movement, and American Politics after Bush* (New York: Oxford University Press, 2011), quotations 61, 63. Though a "measurable divide" exists between partisans, it is one "often tempered by quite a bit of underlying agreement that it is important for the federal government to take responsibility for achieving different types of policy goals." See Aberbach, "Future of the American Right," 57.

12. Page and Jacobs, *Class War?*, 57, 60.

13. Schlozman et al., "Inequalities of Political Voice," 25–26.

14. Ibid., 24n9, 71. At the same time, however, the public was not well informed about the tax cuts, and 40 percent said they had not thought much about them. See Bartels, *Unequal Democracy*, 163, 165.

15. Page and Jacobs, *Class War?*, 65, 66–67.

16. In addition, 53 percent favored banning high-capacity ammunition clips. "After Newtown, Modest Change in Opinion about Gun Control," Pew Research Center for the People & the Press, December 20, 2012, www.people-press.org /2012/12/20/after-newtown-modest-change-in-opinion-about-gun-control/.

17. Jeffrey M. Jones, "Americans Widely Back Government Job Creation Proposals," Gallup Politics, March 20, 2013, www.gallup.com/poll/161438 /americans-widely-back-government-job-creation-proposals.aspx.

18. Schlozman et al., "Inequalities of Political Voice," 27.

19. For a discussion of Lippmann, see Michael Schudson, *The Good Citizen: A History of American Civic Life* (Cambridge, MA: Harvard University Press, 1998), 211–15. Lawrence R. Jacobs and Robert Y. Shapiro have argued that, more than ever, political leaders guide public opinion into preferred channels. They flip "the widespread image of politicians as 'pandering' to public opinion on its head. Public opinion is not propelling policy decisions. . . . Instead, politicians' own policy goals are increasingly driving major policy decisions." See Jacobs and Shapiro, *Politicians Don't Pander: Political Manipulation and the Loss of Democratic Responsiveness* (Chicago: University of Chicago Press, 2000), xv–xvi.

20. Emily Swanson, "Raising the Minimum Wage Is More Popular Than Capitalism," *Huffington Post*, February 6, 2014, www.huffingtonpost.com/2014/02/06/minimum-wage-poll_n_4733302.html; "Most See Inequality Growing"; Sam Youngman, "Kentuckians Favor Minimum Wage Hike," *Lexington Herald-Leader*, February 9, 2014.

21. Eric Lipton, "Fight over Minimum Wage Illustrates Web of Industry Ties," *New York Times*, February 9, 2014.

22. Eric Lipton, "Half of Congress Are Millionaires, Report Says," *New York Times*, January 10, 2014; Stephen Lurie, "Why It Matters That Politicians Have No Experience of Poverty," *Atlantic*, June 2, 2014, www.theatlantic.com/politics/archive/2014/06/why-it-matters-that-politicians-have-no-experience-of-poverty/371857/; Nicholas Carnes, *White-Collar Government: The Hidden Role of Class in Economic Policy* (Chicago: University of Chicago Press, 2013), 16, 25–58, 120–35, quotations 2, 48, 16.

23. Carnes, *White-Collar Government*, quotation 135.

24. Dahl, *How Democratic*, 53, 48–49, quotation 49.

25. Ibid., 81.

26. Thomas Geoghegan, "Mr. Smith Rewrites the Constitution," *New York Times*, January 11, 2010. Geoghegan, lawyer and author, points out that the framers of the Constitution required supermajorities only in a few special cases: ratifying treaties and constitutional amendments, overriding presidential vetoes, expelling members, and impeachments. The runaway filibuster also undermines Article I, Section 3 of the Constitution, giving the nation's vice president (as presiding officer) the deciding vote when senators are "equally divided." "The procedural filibuster effectively disfranchises the vice president, eliminating as it does one of the office's only two constitutional functions." Geoghegan also observes that although the House and Senate set their own rules, the constitution (Article I, Section 5) "mandates at least one rule of proceeding" for the Senate (and House): namely, that a majority shall constitute a quorum. While this provision recognized that travel in the

eighteenth century could be difficult, the rule was primarily intended to prevent a minority from walking out and blocking a majority vote. In "Federalist Paper No. 75," Alexander Hamilton made the case for not having a supermajority being necessary for a quorum: "All provisions which require more than a majority of any body to its resolutions have a direct tendency to embarrass the operations of government and an indirect one to subject the sense of the majority to that of the minority" (quoted in Geoghegan).

27. Garrett Epps, "How the Senate Filibuster Went Out-of-Control—and Who Can Rein It In," *Atlantic*, December 27, 2012, www.theatlantic.com /national/archive/2012/12/how-the-senate-filibuster-went-out-of-control -and-who-can-rein-it-in/266645/; Kevin Drum and Jaeah Lee, "3 Charts Explain Why Democrats Went Nuclear in the Filibuster," *Mother Jones*, November 22, 2013, www.motherjones.com/kevin-drum/2013/11/charts -explain-why-democrats-went-nuclear-filibuster/. In November 2013, the Senate's Democratic majority changed the filibuster rule to allow a simple majority to cut off debate on executive and judicial branch nominees, a change that does not apply to Supreme Court nominations or legislation. See Jeremy W. Peters, "In Landmark Vote, Senate Limits Use of the Filibuster," *New York Times*, November 21, 2013.

28. Hamilton quotation in Hacker and Pierson, *Winner-Take-All Politics*, 298–99.

29. Sarah A. Binder and Steven S. Smith, *Politics or Principle? Filibustering in the United States Senate* (Washington, DC: Brookings Institution Press, 1997), 3, quotations 115, 159.

30. Adam Liptak, "Big State, Small State," *New York Times*, March 3, 2013; Michael Moran, "Blue State, Red Face: Guess Who Benefits More from Your Taxes?," *Slate*, October 25, 2012, www.slate.com/blogs/the_reckoning/2012 /10/25/blue_state_red_face_guess_who_benefits_more_from_your_taxes.html.

31. Hacker and Pierson, *Winner-Take-All Politics*, 53, 128–34, 243, 268, 278–82.

32. Jonathan Rowe, "The Vanishing Commons," in Lardner and Smith, *Inequality Matters*, 51–52, 156. A classic essay by Garrett Hardin emphasized overpopulation and the depletion of common resources, including the earth itself. See Hardin, "The Tragedy of the Commons," *Science* 162 (December 1968), 1243–48.

33. Robert H. Frank, "Record Number of Americans Renouncing Citizenship," NBC News, February 11, 2014, www.nbcnews.com/business/economy /record-number-americans-renouncing-citizenship-n27381/; Freeland, *Plutocrats*, 58–59; quotation from Jonathan Tepper, "Why I'm Giving Up My Passport," *New York Times*, December 7, 2014.

34. Edwin Newman, *A Civil Tongue* (New York: Warner Books, 1976), 159–60.

35. Edward J. Blakely and Mary Gail Snyder, *Fortress America: Gated*

Communities in the United States (Washington, DC: Brookings Institution Press, 1997), 22, 24, 28, 71, quotation 27.

36. The definition comes from Paula A. Franzese and Steven Siegel, "Trust and Community: The Common Interest Community as Metaphor and Paradox," *Missouri Law Review* 72 (2007): 1111.

37. Ian Lovett, "Where Grass Is Greener, a Push to Share Drought's Burden," *New York Times*, November 29, 2014; Bettina Boxall, "Rancho Santa Fe Ranked as State's Largest Residential Water Hog," *Los Angeles Times*, December 2, 2014, www.latimes.com/local/california/la-me-water-rancho-20141202-story.html; Claire Trageser, "Rancho Santa Fe Residents No Longer Biggest Water Users in California," *KPBS News*, December 2, 2014, www.kpbs.org/news/2014/dec /02/rancho-santa-fe-no-longer-biggest-water-users-cali/. For a discussion of several studies of this syndrome, see Daisy Grewal, "How Wealth Reduces Compassion," *Scientific American*, April 10, 2012, www.scientificamerican.com /article/how-wealth-reduces-compassion/. Consider the impact of water usage on homes of 70,000–90,000 square feet, with as many as five swimming pools, in Los Angeles' superrich neighborhoods, as described by Peter Haldeman, "Battle of the Megamansions," *Sunday New York Times*, Sunday Styles section, December 7, 2014.

38. J. K. Wall, "Reform Could Create More 'Boutique Doctors,'" *Indianapolis Business Journal*, May 14, 2011, www.ibj.com/articles/27114-reform-could -create-more-boutique-doctors?v=preview/; Eric Flack, "Critics: Boutique Doctors Will Further Health Care Inequalities," WAVE News, November 25, 2013 (updated March 17, 2014), www.wave3.com/story/24064989/critics-fear -boutique-doctors/.

39. Michael J. Sandel, *What Money Can't Buy: The Moral Limits of Markets* (New York: Farrar, Straus and Giroux, 2012), 4, 5, 7, 10–11, 17, 21, quotations 11, 8. On the apps, see Andrew Leonard, "The 1 Percent's Loathsome Libertarian Scheme: Why We Despise the New Scalping Economy," *Salon*, July 11, 2014, www.salon.com/2014/07/11/the_1_percents_loathsome_libertarian_scheme _why_we_despise_the_new_scalping_economy/.

Conclusion: Considering the Undeserving, Poor and Rich

Epigraph. Michael Walzer, *Spheres of Justice: A Defense of Pluralism and Equality* (New York: Basic Books, 1983), 316.

1. Marsha J. Bailey and Sheldon Danziger, eds., *Legacies of the War on Poverty* (New York: Russell Sage Foundation, 2013); Annie Lowrey, "50 Years Later, War on Poverty Is a Mixed Bag," *New York Times*, January 4, 2014. The War on Poverty was based originally on "maximum feasible participation," dependent on the engagement of the poor and locally based solutions coming

from the bottom up, not top down. See Sasha Abramsky, "The Battle Hymn of the War on Poverty," *Nation*, February 3, 2014.

2. Arloc Sherman, "Why Isn't Poverty Falling? Weakening of Unemployment Insurance Is a Pivotal Factor," Center on Budget and Policy Priorities, October 7, 2013, www.cbpp.org/files/10-7-13pov.pdf; Michael B. Katz, *The Undeserving Poor: America's Enduring Confrontation with Poverty*, 2nd ed., revised (New York: Oxford University Press, 2013; orig. pub. 1989), 148–51, quotation 150; Deaton, *Great Escape*, 179–89, quotations 183, 184; Sheldon Danziger, "The Mismeasure of Poverty," *New York Times*, November 17, 2013. See also Abramsky, *American Way of Poverty*, 204–13.

3. Shipler, *Working Poor*, x–xi. Shipler continues: "Therefore, I use 'poor' not as a statistician would. I use it as imprecisely as it should be used, to suggest the lower stratum of economic attainment, with all its accompanying problems."

4. "Inequality: It Matters; an Interview with Janet Gornick," *Folio* [City University of New York], Winter 2013, http://lisdatacenter.org/wp-content /uploads/janet-bio/gornick-folio-2013.pdf. See also Janet Gornick, "Forty-Eighth Doctoral Commencement Address," May 24, 2012, Graduate Center, City University of New York, www.gc.cuny.edu/CUNY_GC/media/CUNY -Graduate-Center/PDF/Commencement/GORNICK_ADDRESS_2012.pdf. Her most recent book is Gornick and Markus Jäntii, eds., *Income Inequality: Economic Disparities and the Middle Class in Affluent Countries* (Stanford, CA: Stanford University Press, 2013).

5. Monica Prasad, *The Land of Too Much: American Abundance and the Paradox of Poverty* (Cambridge, MA: Harvard University Press, 2012), 262–63; *Evangelii Gaudium*, Sections 187, 188.

6. Katz, *Undeserving Poor*, x.

7. Kathryn Edin and Laura Lein, *Making Ends Meet: How Single Mothers Survive Welfare and Low-Wage Work* (New York: Russell Sage Foundation; 1997), 218–27; Stephanie Mencimer, "What If Everything You Knew about Poverty Was Wrong?," *Mother Jones*, March/April 2014. In most families (i.e., those with children) receiving food stamps, there is usually at least one adult with a job. In 615 U.S. cities and regions, the basic needs of families amount to at least twice the federal poverty line of $23,283.

8. Abramsky, *American Way of Poverty*, 135; Eduardo Porter, "Time to Try Compassion, Not Censure, for Families," *New York Times*, March 4, 2014.

9. Sheila Bair, *Bull by the Horns: Fighting to Save Main Street from Wall Street and Wall Street from Itself* (New York: Free Press, 2012), 355–60. In a recent development, the big banks are now rapidly selling mortgages to "servicers" (firms that collect mortgage payments), immersing homeowners in

a new round of "shoddy paperwork, [and] erroneous and wrongful evictions." William Erbey, the chairman of one of the largest of these companies, Ocwen, is also the chairman of Altisource Residential, which buys delinquent mortgages and foreclosed homes. See Jessica Silver-Greenberg and Michael Corkery, "Loan Complaints by Homeowners Rise Once More," *New York Times*, February 18, 2014. Freddie Mac is the Federal Home Loan Mortgage Corporation (FHLMC), and Fannie Mae is the Federal National Mortgage Association (FNMA).

10. Barbara Ehrenreich, "Earth to Wal-Mars," in Lardner and Smith, *Inequality Matters*, 43; second quotation from Taibbi, *The Divide*, 143.

11. Bair, *Bull by the Horns*, 362–63. According to Bair (218–19), Treasury Secretary Tim Geithner allied with Senate Republicans to weaken every provision of the Dodd-Frank Act. Wall Street's bingeing on credit-swap derivatives is often attributed to the 1999 repeal of the Depression-era Glass-Steagall Act, but the banks' reckless rush toward derivatives and "synthetic collateralized debt obligations" was well under way before then, and much of the Glass-Steagall Act was ineffective. See Gillian Tett, *Fool's Gold: How the Bold Dream of a Small Tribe at J.P. Morgan Was Corrupted by Wall Street Greed and Unleashed a Catastrophe* (New York: Free Press, 2009), 23–53. For a puncturing of financial jargon, see John Lanchester, *How to Speak Money: What the Money People Say—and What It Really Means* (New York: W. W. Norton, 2014).

12. Shaila Dewan and Robert Gebeloff, "One Percent, Many Variations," *New York Times*, January 15, 2012; McCall, *Undeserving Rich*, 8, 10–13, 137. Conservative economist Gregory Mankiw reminded critics of the 1 percent that they "often create extraordinary things." See Mankiw, "Yes, the Wealthy Can Be Deserving," *New York Times*, February 16, 2014.

13. Neal Irwin, "This Is a Complete List of Wall Street CEOs Prosecuted for Their Role in the Financial Crisis," *Washington Post*, September 12, 2013 [the list is empty], www.washingtonpost.com/blogs/wonkblog/wp/2013/09/12 /this-is-a-complete-list-of-Wall-Street-CEOs-prosecuted-for-their-role-in -the-financial-crisis/; quotation in Taibbi, *The Divide*, xix.

14. Adam Liptak, "Stern Words for Wall Street's Watchdogs, from a Judge," *New York Times*, December 16, 2013; Jed S. Rakoff, "The Financial Crisis: Why Have No High-Level Executives Been Prosecuted?," *New York Review of Books*, January 9, 2014. See also Glenn Greenwald, "The Untouchables: How the Obama Administration Protected Wall Street from Prosecutions," *Guardian*, January 23, 2013, www.theguardian.com/commentisfree/2013/jan /23/untouchables-wall-street-prosecutions-obama/. On the Holder memo regarding "collateral consequences" of letting white-collar criminals off the hook, see Taibbi, *The Divide*, 13–19.

15. William C. Dudley, "Ending Too Big to Fail," remarks at the Global Economy Policy Forum, New York City, November 7, 2013, www.newyorkfed .org/newsevents/speeches/2013/dud131107.html; Peter Eavis, "Regulators Size Up Wall Street, with Worry," *New York Times*, March 12, 2014. Even when a company itself—not particular individuals in it—pleads guilty to criminal wrongdoing, the firm emerges "largely unscathed." See Ben Protess and Jessica Silver-Greenberg, "Credit Suisse Pleads Guilt in Felony Case," *New York Times*, May 19, 2014.

16. Office of the Inspector General, "Audit of the Department of Justice's Efforts to Address Mortgage Fraud," U.S. Department of Justice, March 2014, www.justice.gov/oig/reports/2014/a1412.pdf; first quotation from Matt Apuzzo, "U.S. Criticized for Lack of Action on Mortgage Fraud," *New York Times*, March 13, 2014, http://dealbook.nytimes.com/2014/03/13/u-s-overstates -efforts-to-prosecute-mortgage-fraud-watchdog-says/?emc=eta1/; Kaufman quotation in Gretchen Morgenson, "A Fraud War That's Short on Combat," Sunday Business section, *New York Times*, March 16, 2014.

17. Jeff Connaughton, *The Payoff: Why Wall Street Always Wins* (Westport, CT: Prospecta Press, 2012), 11.

18. John Cassidy, "What Good Is Wall Street?," *New Yorker*, November 29, 2010; Thomas Phillippon, "Are Bankers Paid Too Much?," February 2, 2009, www.voxeu.org/article/are-bankers-paid-too-much/; Danielle Kucera and Christine Harper, "Traders' Smaller Bonuses Still Top Pay for Brain Surgeons, 4-Star Generals," January 13, 2011, *Bloomberg*, www.bloomberg.com/news /print/2011-01-13/traders-smaller-bonuses-still-top-pay-for-brain-surgeons -4-star-generals.html.

19. Sam Polk, "For the Love of Money," *New York Times*, January 18, 2014; Doug Weber and Russ Choma, "Wall Street's Steeply Increasing Republicanism," *OpenSecrets*, January 4, 2013, www.opensecrets.org/news/2013/01 /wall-street-republicans/; "Wall Street Money in Washington," Americans for Financial Reform, 2013–14 Election Cycle, December 11, 2014, http:// ourfinancialsecurity.org/blogs/wp-content/ourfinancialsecurity.org/uploads /2014/07/WallStreetMoneyDec2014.pdf.

20. Connaughton, *The Payoff*, 67–68; Taibbi, *The Divide*, 22–38, quotation 37.

21. Scot J. Paltrow, "Insight: Top Justice Officials Connected to Mortgage Banks," Reuters, January 20, 2012, www.reuters.com/article/2012/01/20/us -usa-holder-mortgage-idUSTRE80J0PH20120120/; Mary Bottari, "*Frontline* Gets Its Man: Lanny Breuer Leaves DOJ after Exposé," *PR Watch*, January 24, 2013, www.prwatch.org/print/11959/; "Too Big to Indict," *New York Times*, December 11, 2012; Ben Protess, "Once More through the Revolving Door for Justice's Breuer," *New York Times*, March 28, 2013.

22. "Wall Street Fleet Street Main Street: Corporate Integrity at a Cross-roads: United States & United Kingdom Financial Services Industry Survey," Labaton Sucharow, July 2012, http://labaton.com/en/about/press/upload /US-UK-Financial-Services-Industry-Survey.pdf. In November 2014, Swiss researchers at the University of Zurich released a corroborative study. See Kate Kelland, "Banking Culture Breeds Dishonesty, Scientific Study Finds," Reuters, November 19, 2014, www.reuters.com/article/2014/11/19/science-banking -honesty-idUSL6N0T91V120141119/.

23. "List of Goldman Sachs Employees in the White House," *Whiteout Press*, December 12, 2012, www.whiteoutpress.com/articles/q42012/list-of -goldman-sachs-employees-in-the-white-house/. In November 2014, a former employee of the New York Federal Reserve Bank revealed that a Goldman banker, who had worked for the Federal Reserve Bank of New York, enjoyed access to confidential information from the bank provided by an inside source at the bank. See Jessica Silver-Greenberg, Ben Protess, and Peter Eavis, "New Scrutiny of Goldman's Ties to the New York Fed after a Leak," *New York Times*, November 19, 2014.

24. David Kocieniewski, "A Shuffle of Aluminum, but to Banks, Pure Gold," *New York Times*, July 20, 2013; Joseph A. Palermo, "Goldman Sachs, JPMorgan Chase: Pulling an Enron with Commodities," *Huffington Post*, July 21, 2013, www.huffingtonpost.com/joseph-a-palermo/goldman-sachs-jp-morgan-c_b _3632901.html.

25. Quotation from Matt Taibbi, "The Vampire Squid Strikes Again: The Mega Banks' Most Devious Scam Yet," *Rolling Stone*, February 12, 2014. Senate Democrats recognized the risk to the entire U.S. economy from banks' and bank holding-companies' involvement with physical commodities. See Majority and Minority Staff Report, United States Senate, Permanent Subcommittee on Investigations, "Wall Street Bank Involvement with Physical Commodities," November 20 and 21, 2014, Hearing, https://www .documentcloud.org/documents/1363910-senate-report-on-wall-st-s-role -in-commodities.html; Nathaniel Popper and Peter Eavis, "Senate Report Finds Goldman and JPMorgan Can Influence Commodities," *New York Times*, November 19, 2014, http://dealbook.nytimes.com/2014/11/19/senate-report -criticizes-goldman-and-jpmorgan-over-their-roles-in-commodities-market /?_r=0.

26. Quotation from Palermo, "Goldman Sachs, JPMorgan Chase." For a detailed account of how government and corporate policy evolved, see Taibbi, "Vampire Squid Strikes Again."

27. Lord Adair Turner quotation in Cassidy, "What Good Is Wall Street?" In 2009, Turner proposed a multibillion-pound tax on banks as a way to curb extravagant bonuses. See Phillip Inman, "Financial Services Authority

chairman backs tax on 'socially useless' banks," *Guardian*, August 26, 2009, www.theguardian.com/business/2009/aug/27/fsa-bonus-city-banks-tax/. For Turner's later views, see Adair Turner, *Economics after the Crisis* (Cambridge, MA: MIT Press, 2012).

28. Thomas O. McGarity, "What Obama Left Out of His Inequality Speech: Regulation," *New York Times*, December 3, 2013, http://opinionator.blogs .nytimes.com/2013/12/08/what-obama-left-out-of-his-inequality-speech -regulation/?_php=true&_type=blogs&_r=0/. See also McGarity's *Freedom to Harm: The Lasting Legacy of the Laissez Faire Revival* (New Haven, CT: Yale University Press, 2013).

29. Scott Thurm and Kate Linebaugh, "More U.S. Profits Parked Abroad, Saving on Taxes," *Wall Street Journal*, March 10, 2013; quotation from Paul Buchheit, "16 Giant Corporations That Have Basically Stopped Paying Taxes— While Also Cutting Jobs!" AlterNet, March 18, 2013, www.alternet.org/print /corporate-accountability-and-workplace/16-giant-corporations-have -basically-stopped-paying-taxes/.

30. Charles Duhigg and David Kocieniewski, "How Apple Sidesteps Billions in Taxes," *New York Times*, April 28, 2012. In September 2014, the European Commission released a public version of a report accusing Ireland of giving Apple illegal tax breaks. See European Commission, "State aid SA.38373 (2014/C) (ex 2014/NN) (ex 2014/CP)—Ireland: Alleged Aid to Apple," June 6, 2014, http://ec.europa.eu/competition/state_aid/cases /253200/253200_1582634_87_2.pdf.

31. The points in this paragraph were raised by Robert Scheer, "If Corporations Don't Pay Taxes, Why Should You?," *Nation*, March 12, 2013, www.thenation.com/print/article/173297/if-corporations-dont-pay-taxes -why-should-you/.

32. James William Coleman, *The Criminal Elite: Understanding White Collar Crime*, 6th ed. (New York: Worth, 2006), 1.

33. Piketty, *Capital*, 20–27. For discussion of reactions to Piketty's book, see Thomas B. Edsall, "Capitalism vs. Democracy," *New York Times*, January 28, 2014, www.nytimes.com/2014/01/29/opinion/capitalism-vs-democracy .html; Kathleen Geier, "In Praise of the Utopian Political Imagination," *Nation*, March 14, 2014, www.thenation.com/blog/178850/praise-utopian -political-imagination/; John Cassidy, "Forces of Divergence," *New Yorker*, March 31, 2014.

34. Piketty, *Capital*, 24–27, 298–335, 512–14, 515–39, quotations 173, 298. The OECD also emphasizes "widening wage disparities." See OECD, *Divided We Stand*, 30, 41. Studies that attribute high salaries to the rise of winner-take-all markets count munificently paid CEOs as one group among a growing number of professions in which the top talent gets the lion's share of the

rewards. This has existed for some time in the entertainment industry and professional sports, but it has now spread to other professions, including financial executives, lawyers, dentists, journalists, the fashion industry, and others. See Robert H. Frank and Philip J. Cook, *The Winner-Take-All Society: Why the Few at the Top Get So Much More Than the Rest of Us* (New York: Penguin Books, 1996)

35. Quotations from Erik Brynjolfsson and Andrew McAfee, *The Second Machine Age: Work, Progress, and Prosperity in a Time of Brilliant Technologies* (New York: W. W. Norton, 2014), 128, 144–45; Piketty, *Capital*, 304–07; Deaton, *Great Escape*, quotations 1, 7.

36. Piketty, *Capital*, 20. Appreciative reviewers include Dean Baker, "Capital in the 21st Century: Still Mired in the 19th," *Huffington Post*, March 9, 2014, www.huffingtonpost.com/dean-baker/capital-in-the-twenty-fir_b_4932184 .html; Jacob Hacker, Paul Pierson, Heather Boushey, and Branko Milanovic, "Piketty's Triumph: Three Expert Takes on *Capital in the Twenty-First Century*, French Economist Thomas Piketty's Data-Driven Magnum Opus on Inequality," *American Prospect*, March 10, 2014, http://prospect.org/article /piketty%E2%80%99s-triumph; Kathleen Geier, "Taking on the Heiristocracy," *Washington Monthly*, March/April/May 2014, www.washingtonmonthly .com/magazine/march_april_may_2014/on_political_books/taking_on_the _heiristocracy049299.php; Paul Krugman, "Why We're in a New Gilded Age," *New York Review of Books*, May 8, 2014. Commentators across the political spectrum have called Piketty's proposal to reverse inequality with a confiscatory global tax on inherited wealth unrealistic. Indeed, what chance of passage in the U.S. Congress does his call for an 80 percent tax on income over $500,000 have?

37. "Divided government and compromises will not satisfy Tea Partiers or right-wing billionaires. They want it all—the full repeal of health care reform and financial regulations accomplished during Obama's first two years; the full dismantling of regulations touching industries involved in health care, energy production, and financial services; the defunding and privatization of social entitlements for the poor and the vast American middle class; and, above all, huge cuts in the already modest taxes paid by billionaires, millionaires, and corporations. The GOP budget issued in April 2011 by Congressman Paul Ryan, chair of the Budget Committee, outlined just such a radical right-wing wish list." Theda Skocpol, *Obama and America's Political Future* (Cambridge, MA: Harvard University Press, 2012), 76.

38. Quotation from Lowrey, "Income Gap, Meet the Longevity Gap." Christopher Jencks, "a renowned professor of social policy at Harvard" who has studied the widening income gap for decades, has expressed his frustration at supporting claims about the consequences of inequality with

unassailable evidence. See Eduardo Porter, "Income Equality: A Search for Consequences," *New York Times*, March 25, 2014. But Jencks, in commenting on why the United States has a large low-wage labor market in comparison with peer countries, has declared: " 'It's the politics, stupid.' Political scientists have been churning out papers on this question for more than a decade, and while the details differ, . . . differences in income distribution seem to be traceable to differences in constitutional arrangements, electoral systems, and economic institutions." See Jencks, "Why Do So Many Jobs Pay So Badly," in Johnston, *Divided*, 71.

39. Freeland, *Plutocrats*, 243; James Surowiecki, "Moaning Moguls," *New Yorker*, July 7, 2014. Surowiecki and others attribute such outbursts to egos and to feeling disrespected: "Moguls complain about their feelings because that's all that anyone can really threaten." Probably they also want more money.

40. Liz Hamel, Jamie Firth, and Mollyann Brodie, "Kaiser Family Foundation/New York Times/CBS News Non-Employed Poll," December 11, 2014, http://kff.org/other/poll-finding/kaiser-family-foundationnew-york-times cbs-news-non-employed-poll/; "Table C: Labour Force Participation Rates by Selected Age Groups," OECD Employment Outlook 2013 [last updated July 5, 2013], www.keepeek.com/Digital-Asset-Management/oecd/employment/oecd -employment-outlook-2013/labour-force-participation-rates-by-selected -age-groups_empl_outlook-2013-table60-en#page1; quotation from Binyamin Applebaum, "The Vanishing Male Worker: How America Fell Behind," *New York Times*, December 11, 2014; Amanda Cox, "The Rise of Men Who Don't Work, and What They Do Instead," *New York Times*, December 12, 2014.

41. Several books offer such advice. Good places to start are Reich, *Beyond Outrage*, 109–38; Noah, *Great Divergence*, 179–95.

INDEX